For those who make up the
community of Kilcloon

Table of Contents

Glossary

The Medieval structure of the present day parish of Kilcloon

The Structure of the Colony:

The Colony: Was ruled by the justiciar, afterwards called the Lord Deputy or Lord Lieutenant or Viceroy, who was the king's representative in Ireland. The colony consisted of most of the east and south of Ireland.

The Liberty: Was a quasi independent unit with independent law courts, sheriff and court - ruled by a great nobleman whose representative in governing it was called a seneschal. He was the equivalent in the liberty of the justiciar in the colony. Meath, roughly coterminous with the old kingdom of Meath, was such a liberty. The first lord was Hugh de Lacy. Meath was eventually inherited by two granddaughters of de Lacy and the liberty was split between their husbands. Geoffrey de Geneville, who married Matilda de Lacy, got that part of liberty with Trim as its capital, which included all the manors of modern Kilcloon. Through failure of the male line it became a Mortimer inheritance, which in turn was inherited by the Duke of York in the fifteenth century and then by his son who became King Edward IV. Towards the end of the fifteenth century the liberty was abolished and united with the crown.

The Barony: The liberty of Meath was shared out among his lieutenants by Hugh de Lacy in large areas called baronies. Often these units approximated to the old divisions of pre Norman Meath, the Tuatha, or Gaelic petty kingdoms. There were about ten baronies in what is now County Meath.

The Manor: The baron divided his barony into manors which he granted by feudal tenure to one of his knights. In Kilcloon, Moyglare, Mulhussey, Rathregan and Ballymaglassan were eventually held from the lord of the

Liberty; Rodanstown and Balfeighan were held from the Husseys, Barons of Galtrim, the latter by knight's service.

The Parish: The parish was usually of the same size and boundaries as the manor. In Kilcloon four out of six parish churches were built beside the manorial centre and as such were probably Norman in origin.

Townsland: A unit, which in Kilcloon at least was usually occupied by a single tenant.

Free Tenants: Were made up of military tenants who owed personal service in time of war or a money contribution in lieu of it, and others who held the land in so called fee farm, paid a rent but could also hand their tenancy on to their heirs.

Farmers: Held their land on lease for a term of years for a money rent. They often owed labour services in addition to their rent.

Gavillers: Were tenants at will who were personally free, and seemed by custom to be able to hand on their holdings to their heirs.

Betaghs: Were tied to the soil, owed labour service rather than rent for their holdings. They seemed to have been descendants of the pre Norman betaghs who were tied to the land. In Kilcloon perhaps the twenty four cottagers (presumably without land) in Moyglare in the 1540 survey, were the descendants of betaghs. Those with Irish names pardoned with Walter Delahyde in 1600 were probably landless cottiers, descendants of the betaghs or the gavillers of the early Middle Ages.

Terms:

A Messauge: Was a tenancy made up of a house and land. It could be a townsland or a smaller unit.

A Curtilage: Was a house with a yard.

A Burgage Plot: Was a tenancy in a town held on a yearly rent.

The Structure of the Diocese

1. **The Bishop**

2. **Archdeacons of Kells and Meath** were the chief officials of the diocese under the bishop. The Archdeacon of Kells was rector of Nobber and the Archdeacon of Meath, rector of Kells.

3. **Arch priest, rural dean, vicar forane.** These terms were used throughout the centuries for priests with clearly defined responsibilities for a clutch of

parishes, called a deanery, in the area where they served as parish priests. They were the successors of the bishops of tuatha in the pre Norman days. The last of these bishops, the Bishop of Kells, died in 1211 and his death seemed to have freed the bishop of the diocese, Simon de Rochfort, to make new arrangements for the structures of his diocese. The duties of the arch priests were spelled out at the Trim synod of 1216. These deaneries have survived substantially intact to the present day. The arch priests are the predecessors of the vicars forane of contemporary Meath, though their responsibilities are not as sharply defined as were those of the arch priests in 1216 and the boundaries of the deaneries have been slightly modified over the years.

4. **Rectors** of parishes were appointed by the bishop, by a lay lord of the manor or by the Roman authorities. The rectors had the fixed income from the tithes and other properties of the parish.

5. **Vicars** of parishes were appointed with a fixed income by the religious orders who had the right to the parish income or by the rectors who were absent from their parishes, usually because they held other positions in the church or in the government of the kingdom.

6. **Chaplains** were ordained priests who substituted for absent rectors or vicars or were appointed by religious orders to parishes where the income was not large enough to support a vicar.

7. **Clergymen** who were ordained but were still awaiting an appointment to a parish were also called chaplains. They often appear in the records as small tenant farmers.

Terms:

Advowson: Was the right to nominate the rector, vicar or chaplains of a parish.

Impropriation: Was the assigning of the income of the parish in tithe or in property income, to a religious order, lay person or bishop.

Tithe: Was a tax of one tenth of the goods produced in a parish which were renewable every year, usually crops and the young of animals. This tax was intended to sustain the personnel and fabric of the parish church.

Chapter 1

Looking back on Kilcloon

Looking back on the history of Kilcloon is like overlooking a misty landscape that stretches away to a vast distance. At the end, great cliffs of ice loom up which scoured the land of any trace left by the old stone age people who may have been there before it, and in a slow-moving scraping of the underlying rock this ice created the rich soil that defines the land of Kilcloon today. For a time after the ice age there is nothing to be seen through the mist. Near the present, from time to time, some feature is raised above the mist and we can see it very clearly but the context in which it was set, which alone explains it, can not be seen beneath. Nearer the present more features are visible. In the landscape nearest to us, when the state began to regard the ordinary citizens, much more can be seen – census reports, surveys, rent and ownership documents survive and of course traditions handed down among the people – but the past will always have its mists that make regarding it an experience that generally evokes puzzlement and wonder, sometimes awe, but always interest. We should never forget that our predecessors were not in any essential way different from ourselves. They had the same preoccupations that we have. Their history, like our experience, is shaped by two central themes, land and religion. Land has to do with providing food, warmth and security. The way it is owned and worked and the way family and community life interact with it reveals the way we provide security for childhood, adulthood and old age. Land has to do with coping successfully with this life, and religion concerns how we can hope for fulfilment and security in the next. In our own time, life seems a bit more complicated than that, but essentially we have the same preoccupations that our ancestors had. It is an extraordinary reflection of the truth of this observation that when middle stone-age man, who had depended on the precarious supply of the hunt for survival and had been threatened with extinction every winter at least, once learned the skills of farming which provided a reasonably reliable source of food, he immediately designed for his dead impressive monuments, most of which were aligned with the rising sun. He obviously hoped to ensure, through the fertile and life-giving rays of the sun, immortality for his loved ones and eventually for himself, beyond the darkness of the grave.

If you accept that individuals can change the course of history, then it is clear that six people, all foreigners, changed in their own day the way that life was lived at Kilcloon. St. Patrick, a Roman Englishman from the mouth of the Severn river near Bristol, brought us Christianity. Hugh de Lacy, a professional soldier whose ancestors were Norman and Viking, changed the whole system of ownership, use and inheritance of land, and brought with him a new way of organising religion. Henry VIII, the English king who founded what became the Anglican Church and made himself, not as his ancestors had been, – lords of Ireland, but king in 1540, caused the religious division among our people that has haunted us since. Oliver Cromwell, an English gentleman turned soldier and politician, in the mid seventeenth century changed the pattern of ownership set up by de Lacy and laid the foundation for the Protestant ascendancy which controlled Ireland for the next two centuries.

William Gladstone, an English politician, hoped that through the disestablishment of the Protestant Church of Ireland and the transfer of land ownership to those who worked it, and granting limited self government to Ireland, he would reconcile the inhabitants of the two islands that make up the British Isles. And Eamonn de Valera, a New York born son of a Spanish father went further. He divided up the large holdings in Kilcloon which had been devoted to raising cattle, and distributed smaller holdings to people from the West, North West or South West of the country who were trying to survive on uneconomic land holdings there.

These six individuals by their vision brought about profound changes either in land ownership and use or in the faith life of the people of the parishes which make up the modern parish of Kilcloon.

This short history of the area within the present parish of Kilcloon will be divided up chronologically according to the contribution of each of these six men, and thematically in so far as that can be done with the evidence that has survived to our own day, according to land ownership, land use and the faith life of the people.

To return to the image of history as looking back through the mists of time, it is obvious that some features of the history of other areas in our county can be studied from a time when nothing survives from our own immediate locality.

When Tara Mines were preparing an artificial lake at Randalstown, near Navan, St. Anne's Well was excavated. Some flints were found around it dating from the time of mesolithic man (man the hunter) who lived there before 4500 BC. The well is near the Blackwater river and so was not required to supply water. It seems as if it was used for some other purpose, perhaps a ritual one, like that for which it was certainly used in Christian times. If this is so, then our holy wells, St. Kieran's of Ballymaglassan and St. Brigid's at Bridestream, were holy back to the time when in our parish no clue to our history survives. Again, if you wish to know how the first farmers lived in Kilcloon, the so called neolithic people, you have only to study what is known of the great tombs of the Boyne Valley and the cemetery of Loughcrew near Oldcastle. For people live there today as we do, and anyone who is interested in our way of life will find substantial clues to it in the lives of those who live in other parts of our county.

So much material has turned up on the history of Kilcloon, especially for early modern Kilcloon from 1700 to the present day, that it has been decided to divide the history of the parish into two. The first part will be concerned chiefly with Kilcloon under the Normans and their descendants up to 1700, at which date new landowners had taken over most of the land of the parish. They formed part of the so-called "Protestant Ascendancy" who owned the lands of the parish for the next 200 years. The old landowners, the so-called Old English, and the Old Irish and their adherents and those who worked the land, were excluded from any say in government, national or local in those years, and indeed from the enjoyment of normal civil and religious rights.

Ordinary people appear only very occasionally in the records before 1700. After that date they begin to appear in records like short leases of small holdings, rent rolls of landlords and eventually censuses and government reports. It is also hoped that the publication of the first part of the history of the area may encourage people alive today to share their memories, photographs and traditions which will flesh out the evidence of documents to make part two of the history of Kilcloon a living testimony to the way people lived, earned a living for their families, practised their faith, or were forced to emigrate by changing patterns in land use. The themes of land ownership, land structures, and land use which reveal how people provided food and shelter for themselves, and the themes of faith life and practice through which they coped with death and eternity, both are constant and from the beginning have shaped the local history of this area, the modern parish of Kilcloon which is made up of the six medieval parishes, Moyglare, Kilclone, Balfeighan, Rodanstown, Ballymaglassan and Rathregan. These parishes are roughly coterminous with the six manors of the same names: to study land ownership and use in the manors, and the faith structure of the parishes is merely to look at the same six areas from a different point of view. St. Paul described his home town, Tarsus, as no mean city. Looking at the long history of Kilcloon, its natives can claim also that their parish is no mean place either because it nourished their ancestors and provides a context through which the values of the past were transmitted to them and one in which they live out their lives today.

As can be imagined, an enterprise like this no matter how limited it may be, could only be completed with the help of many people. I have used the thesis of Ken Abraham on the Medieval Lordship of Meath: this thesis cries out for publication for it provides a foundation for all local studies in the county. Helen Coburn Walsh's thesis on the Protestant bishop, Hugh Brady, is comprehensive and also deserves publication. Kevin English of Kilcock shared his notes on the history of Kilcock and of the adjoining parishes of Rodanstown and Balfeighan. Bridie Murphy provided maps. Fr. Joe Dooley, John Bradley, Peter Connell and Fr. Tommy O'Connor of Maynooth made invaluable comments from their various kinds of expertise. Liam Smith and Andy Bennett of the Meath County Library put their local history archives at my disposal and I had the useful privilege of having the college library at Maynooth convenient for use. Mrs. Woods of the Russell Library put rare books at my disposal, specifically Wilkins Concilia, Vol.I; permission to reproduce the acta of the Meath synod was readily given. Justin Wallace shared with me his knowledge of the various branches of the Husseys of Galtrim, Mulhussey and Rodanstown and his copies of the Down Survey maps. The staff of the National Library made available the rent books of the Rathregan estate and some documents concerning the Wentworths of Moyglare. Mrs. Lalor-Murphy took the photographs of Sir Maurice Fitzgerald's tabletomb in Kildare cathedral, the portrait of Speaker Connolly in Castletown, Newtown cathedral in Trim and the field monuments of the parish and Eugene Larkin made it possible to photograph the earthwork at Rodanstown from the air. Ray Ward contributed the aerial photograph of Rathregan Church ruins. Oliver Hickey produced the composite map of the parish, using the maps Michael O'Donnell and his pupils at Maynooth Post-Primary School produced for an exhibition of the history of the parish in maps which they made to commemorate the Great Jubilee. The maps were on display in the three schools of the parish. The Parish Jubilee Committee has done trojan work in facilitating various activities the results of which will long remain as a reminder of the community spirit occasioned by the Jubilee itself. The committee is financing this history as one of its projects. But it could not have been published without the very generous contribution made by the Meath Leader Programme, facilitated by Christine O'Shea, its chief executive. Mrs. Joan O'Reilly typed the whole manuscript not once, but many times, and for her contribution I am very grateful. Additional typing was provided by Mrs. Máire Keane and Mrs. Margaret Clarke. Seamus McGabhann in proof-reading the work, saved it from many errors, grammatical, syntactical and historical. Mrs Julitta Clancy contributed the index. Michael Kelly of Dunboyne made available the McCleneghan papers. Thomas Mayer of Augustina College, Rock Island, Illinois provided information on Robert Luttrell. John Bruton and Des Bruton made possible the photography of bits and pieces of fifteenth century Mulhussey and the Hussey church that is there. I am grateful also to the Minneapolis Institute of Arts and to Assistant Dean A. Dankowski, who gave permission for the reproduction of Jacob Duck "Soldiers Arming themselves", to give some idea of the life of soldiers fighting in the wars of the Spanish Netherlands. I am grateful to the Castletown Foundation for permission to use the portrait of Speaker Connolly by Jervas in Castletown House. To Maynooth College for permission to use their contemporary copy of a portrait of Garret Óg Fitzgerald and to Fr. Sean Henry Adm., Mullingar for the photograph of the painting of Bishop Dease. Fr. Matthew Mollin provided English translations from medieval registers and chartularies, as did Fr. Thomas Finan. Duchas gave permission to reproduce a photograph of Newtown cathedral at Trim and Dean Townley permission to use the photograph of Sir Maurice Fitzgerald of Balfeighan and Lackagh, which appears on the cover. The design of the book is by Carton LeVert.

Note:

The spelling Kilcloon refers to the modern parish which is an area occupied by six medieval parishes. Kilclone refers to the medieval parish of that name and to the townland of Kilclone in it. Though the medieval parish was called Kilclone, it was coterminous with the Manor of Mulhussey set up as such independently of Galtrim in 1406. Rodanstown is variously referred to in the records as Raddanstown, Ballyroddan, Balrodan, Balrodane, Balroddane and Balyrothan. The name refers to the parish, the manor and the townsland. There were minor variations in personal and place names over the Norman centuries of Kilcloon.

Chapter 2

Kilcloon after St. Patrick

For nearly seven hundred years before the Normans colonised the region now occupied by the diocese of Meath there were Christians living in what is now the parish of Kilcloon, but they have left behind them on the ground and in the records very little trace of their lives or of their faith. Most evidence of their presence here is so scarce over that long period that it does not allow us to get any glimpse of people going about their every day business, their work or their prayer.

When the Normans came here the effect on the old Gaelic way of life was like that of the great glaciers of ice of ten thousand years before on the landscape; they scoured the land of most traces of life before them. Most of the place names of the townslands of the parish begin with a Norman personal name and end with "town", the English equivalent of the Latin vill or villata. Some Gaelic place names survive which indicate the one time presence of churches there. Kilclone itself is the church of the meadow; Killeaney seems to be the church of St. Fainche, sister of the more famous Enda, patron of the Aran Islands.[1] Kilrory near Balfeighan is also a church name, and indeed until Dean Cogan's time in the middle of the nineteenth century there were ruins of a church there.[2] It is never mentioned in the medieval records of churches or their income and must therefore predate the coming of the Normans. Balfeighan contains the name of St. Feighan, he of the seven wonders of Fore and of Termonfeckin outside Drogheda. Of some interest is the fact that the earl of Kildare had in his library in 1526 only two lives in Irish of Irish saints; "St. Ffeghyn is lif" and "St. Ffynyan is lif".[3] The Kildare Fitzgeralds sometime before the middle of the fifteenth century were lords of Balfeighan and there was a local tradition connecting the church of Balfeighan with St. Finian of Clonard. Apart from the names, there is a reference in the Civil Survey of 1654 to "an old chappell" at Lismahon which does not appear in any of the records of the Middle Ages:

it could well date back to pre Norman days. There are in the parish two holy wells, which in ritual use could well predate Christianity in the area. One at Bridestream is a well where the water reaches 70° Fahrenheit in winter. It is dedicated to St. Brigid and on her day, February 2nd, a huge pattern was held there up to Dean Cogan's time though the crowds were dwindling even then. The diameter of the well, he reports, as twelve feet four inches and "it is a curious fact that nearly all the females of the parish are called Brigid or Bride after the patron saint."[4] That custom has lapsed too. At Ballymaglassan there was also a holy well dedicated to St. Kieran, but it seems to have disappeared as a consequence of modern drainage. Both wells, of course, were holy in the early Christian period, and indeed may well have been centres of ritual in the centuries beforehand.

The only place in the parish which appears in the records of early Christian Ireland is Kilglyn, the wood of the glen. In the eighth century some scribe associated with Armagh collected creatively whatever traditions he could find linking various places in Ireland to St. Patrick and hence to the monastic city of Armagh; it seems that both jurisdiction and income were involved. In any case the anonymous author of the so called Tripartite Life of Patrick reports that the monastery of Cilldumhagloinn or Kilglyn (in Latin cella tumuli vituli, or the cell of the calves or foals' tomb) was founded by a St. Mogenoch who was one of four children whose mother was Patrick's sister: all were reputed to have founded monasteries and were acclaimed as saints. The author adds that their churches belong to Patrick "by consanguinity and by faith and by baptism and by doctrine; and all that they obtained of land and of churches they offered to Patrick for ever."[5] Some of the old scholars (Colgan in the seventeenth century) felt that Mogenoch was the same Mogonoch of Killecumly who was an eminent pupil of St. Finian of Clonard and in more modern times, in the nineteenth century, Lanigan guessed that he was Genoc, a Briton who followed St. Finian to Ireland, having met him in the course of his studies in Wales. The feast day of this saint is December 26th, St. Stephen's Day.[6] Giving credence to the story are two entries in the Annals of the Four Masters culled from some annals of which only scraps survived to the seventeenth century: 834 Breasal, Airchinneach, Abbot of Cilldumha and other churches died; 841 Fineachta, Abbot of Cilldumhagloinn, died. The two abbots lived not long after the Tripartite Life of St. Patrick was written and it seems as if their monastery was one of those over which Armagh claimed jurisdiction and a right to yearly tribute. It is not mentioned in the records again and there are no traces of it remaining on the ground.

It was probably defined as all other early Christian monasteries were, by a large ditch forming an enclosure in which the various buildings were made of clay and wood. There would have been a sacred area surrounding a church which acted as a cemetery. Like another cemetery uncovered in Dunboyne a few years ago, that cemetery may be uncovered some day to enable us to understand more of the life that was lived there.

Because the records of this long period of history are relatively scarce, there is no agreement among historians even on the structures through which the church provided the parochial sacraments and the Mass to the people. Presumably it was a few centuries after St. Patrick's mission before the island became universally Christian. As they say about St. Patrick: before him there were Christians in Ireland; after him the island gradually became Christian. There seems to be a growing consensus today that though there were monasteries here, some of the highest profile, like Clonard, Iona in Scotland, Durrow, and Armagh, there were also bishops, naturally, who presided over the pastoral mission to the ordinary people. There were three classes of leaders in the Irish church, the bishops, the abbots, and those called airchenneach or erenaghs of later times who controlled the property of the church and occupied this office by hereditary family right. At times the same man could occupy all three positions, bishop, abbot and airchinneach, or one or two of them. As we have seen, Breasal of Kilglyn was both airchenneach and abbot; the more shadowy Mogenogh was bishop, abbot and custodian of the monastic property, and Fineachta was just an abbot.

Though there are few written records of bishops from the kingdom of Meath, they obviously must have functioned there, and like many ordinary structures in the normal life of people they were taken for granted in their pastoral ministry, like the ordinary priests who are never mentioned either. Hence, unless they were prominent for one reason or another they never gained notice in the annals, which of course were written and preserved in monasteries.

That said, it seems from a synod held by the first Norman bishop of Meath in Trim, in 1216, only forty five years after the Normans came to Meath, that we can see something of the church organisation that existed in the pre Norman days which bishop de Rochfort was anxious to reform. His reform was both sensitive and effective.[7] As the last of the bishops died, who had evidently functioned sometime in the past at Trim, Kells, Slane, Skryne and Dunshaughlin, they were to be replaced by rural deans whose duty was to supervise the properties and the presentation of faith life in their deaneries. The last bishop of Duleek, of whom there is record, died in 1117, and the last bishop of Kells, Bishop Ua Dobhailen, died in 1211 just before bishop de Rochfort held his synod in 1216.[8]

It does seem as if the bishoprics which served the parochial life of the people were structured around the secular political divisions of large tuatha. Further it seems to have been no coincidence that the rural deaneries in many cases reflect the baronial divisions of the Norman Middle Ages, Kells, Skryne, Duleek, Ratoath – Dunshaughlin, Slane; and the rest like Deece, Dunboyne, Navan and Moyfenrath which have Trim on the border between them, reflect divisions consequent on factors which have left no trace in the records. Naturally, the divisions of Meath by Hugh de Lacy reflect the structures of government of his predecessors, shaped as they must have been by features of the landscape which of course are constant. It is no coincidence either that it was only in the 1260s that deaneries were formed in what is now Westmeath, Ballymore Lough Seudy, Ardnurcher, Mullingar and Fore, together with Duleek and Clonard. The Norman conquest of what is now Westmeath took place later and less comprehensively than it did in what is now County Meath, because the Norman heavy military technology was at a disadvantage in areas with much bogland.

Politically speaking, the kingdom of Meath was ripe for exploitation by the Normans in 1171. In the years before that date, Meath had been in a fluctuating and unsettled state, fought over by various provincial kings ambitious to control the whole island.

In the early twelfth century the major power in the island was Turlogh O'Connor of Connaught. He kept Meath weak by constant partition. In 1125 the king of Meath, Murrough O'Melaghlin, was ousted and a tripartite partition took place. O'Melaghlin was then restored and ruled Meath until captured by O'Connor's ally, Tiernan O'Rourke of Breffni, in 1143. Meath was again divided into three, ruled by Donncadh, nephew of O' Melaghlin, Tiernan O'Rourke, and Dermot McMurrough of Leinster, ally of an up and coming northern king, Murchertach Mac Lochlainn. In 1150 Donncadh O'Carroll of Louth replaced McMurrough and in 1152 Murrough O'Melaghlin and his son Maelseachlainn were restored as joint kings of Meath. Murrough died in 1153, the last king of the middle kingdom; his successors were puppets of either O'Connor of Connaught or Mac Lochlainn of Tyrone. With the support of his ally Mac Lochlainn, Diarmaid McMurrough expanded again into Meath, but with Mac Lochlainn's fall in 1166, the O'Connors of Connaught in the person of Rory O'Connor were in the ascendant again. He celebrated his marriage to the high kingship by the last official Tailteann games in 1168 and had his ally Tiernan O'Rourke persuade the Norse or Ostmen of Dublin and Wexford, together with the rest of his vassal chiefs to abandon Diarmaid McMurrough. Desperate for help, Dermot turned to foreign mercenaries with the permission of their overlord, the Angevin king of England and most of France, Henry II, and the rest, as they say, is history.

Looking at the map of the parish and the various field monuments noted on it gives some indication of the farms of pre-Norman Ireland. A number of sites formerly attributed to the pre-Norman centuries have been re-attributed to the first years of the colony. Yet enough survive to reveal an agricultural society in Kilcloon with the ring forts of strong farmers dotting the landscape, which presumably was divided up among them. The ring fort consisted of a circular ditch of about one hundred to one hundred and fifty feet in diameter within which were the earth, wood and thatch buildings for the household and its animals.(See illustration of Collistown Ringfort, p i). The houses were roughly circular and constructed with a double layer of wattles. The rough side of each layer was turned inward so that both the outside and inside walls had a smooth surface: insulating material was packed into the cavity between the two layers of wattles. The house had a diameter of more than nineteen feet with smaller outhouses having one of perhaps thirteen or fourteen feet. Beyond the circular ditch was the infield which may have had a vegetable garden attached. Though there seem to have been large fields for crops, cattle occupied a dominant place in the economy. The countryside was well wooded, with acorns of the oak trees providing food for droves of pigs.

Though warfare was endemic, with various chiefs and kings asserting themselves against one another and against the Vikings, the season for fighting was a short one, of the summer months, and ordinary people seem to have enjoyed a relatively peaceful way of life.

Footnotes

1   Ordnance Survey (1836), Moyglare parish, p5

2   COGAN, Vol. 2, p361

3   Earls of Kildare, the Marquis of Kildare, 1858, appendix 6, p320

4   COGAN, Vol. 2, p361

5   Tripartite Life of St. Patrick, p68 and 335

6   LANIGAN, Vol. 2, p233

7   WILKINS, Consilia, 1737, Vol. 1, p547

8   COGAN, Vol. 1, p36; Gwynn, The Twelfth Century Reform, p56. The Annals of Loch Cé AD 1211
     "Ua Dobhailen, bishop of Cenannus, quievit".

Chapter 3

Kilcloon after Hugh de Lacy: Land ownership and use in the six manors of Kilcloon – 1171 to 1350

An event that seemed to contemporaries just one more element in the constant struggle for power among Irish provincial kings – the bringing in of auxiliaries from abroad – signalled the beginning of a colony which in time established the rule of an English king over the whole island of Ireland.

Dermot Mac Murrough, sometime king of Leinster, attempted to recoup his fortunes by bringing in professional soldiers from the realms of the king of England and most of France, Henry II, to help him take back his kingdom. They were led by Richard le Clare, nicknamed Strongbow, from the Severn estuary, who, being of a buccaneering turn of mind, decided to exercise his military skills in Ireland. He was so successful that his overlord, Henry II, became afraid that he might use his control of Dublin and of Leinster, which he had acquired on the death of Dermot Mac Murrough, to set up an independent kingdom in Ireland. Henry decided not only that he should come to Ireland, which he did, in 1171, but also that he would establish another talented, energetic, ruthless and occasionally troublesome subject, named Hugh de Lacy, as lord of the old kingdom of Meath which stretched from the Shannon to the sea. It was through this policy that what we now know as the parish of Kilcloon quickly emerged in terms of land ownership, land use and in religious organisation and practice as a part of the Norman world, which, under the Plantagenet kings of England, included England itself, the colony in Ireland, the Welsh marches, and what is now France as far south as the Pyrenees.

The coming of Hugh de Lacy and his Normans into the kingdom of Meath brought about revolutionary changes in nearly all areas of human life. Especially in the east of his lordship which includes the present day parishes of Kilcloon, Dunboyne, Ratoath, Curragha, Ashbourne, Skryne, and most of County Dublin, most traces of an older Gaelic way of life were obliterated, and both in religion, land ownership and in land use the changes which took place were to shape life there for many centuries to come.

The revolution in religion had begun with the introduction of European norms into the Irish church at the Synods of Rathbrassil (1111) and Kells (1152) under the leadership of a few eminent reforming clerics like Ceallach, archbishop of Armagh, and St. Malachy, also archbishop for a time before he retired to Down. These changes in structure and in their financial regulation were adopted by the Irish church in Norman areas quite enthusiastically. They had also the sanction of papal approval.

The classical method of feudal conquest and settlement was effected by Hugh de Lacy. He had been granted the kingdom of Meath from the Shannon to the sea as a self-governing liberty, in effect an area with home rule, a court, law courts, sheriff and government, with its capital at Trim. He parcelled it out among his closest allies like Adam de Feipo, Hugh Tyrrell, Milo le Bret and Robert Hosse, while keeping some areas for himself like Duleek, Kells, Ratoath, in what is now County Meath, and Ballymore Loughseudy in Westmeath (Tyrrell received Newtown Fertullagh there). In fact, it appears as if, in return for grants in east Meath and around Dublin, where land was good and easily controlled by knights and their men in heavy armour, these barons, as they were called, were expected to take on areas in what is now Westmeath, where Norman military technology was not quite as successful against the natives as it was in east Meath. The modern parish of Kilcloon includes portions of the barony of Ratoath, which de Lacy kept himself, and of Deece "all the land of Deece which MacGiolla Sheachlainn held", which he granted to Hugh de Hosse (Hussey).[1] In the first are the parishes and manors of Rathregan and Ballymaglassan, and in the second the parishes and manors of Balfeighan, Rodanstown, Kilclone and Moyglare. The first barony, Ratoath, was handed over by Walter de Lacy, Hugh's heir, to his brother Hugh and, following the ups and downs of the Lacys' careers as in or out of favour with successive kings, one can trace the overlords of the two parishes involved. For most of the later Middle Ages the king himself was baron of Ratoath. Of the other four parishes in Deece, Moyglare took on a separate identity early on and was held directly from the overlord of the de Lacy inheritance. It does seem as if it had been a tuath in Gaelic times as it was treated from the beginning as separate from the rest of the barony. The other three manors had the Hussey family of Galtrim as their overlords. That family did not set up independent manors in any of these areas until at least the fifteenth century (chapters 14,15,16 and 18). De Lacy and his barons effected control over the areas they conquered by building mottes and baileys, the remains of which can still be seen all over

Meath. Strangely there are no mottes in the six parishes which nowadays make up our parish of Kilcloon. But there are ringworks in the parish which were attributed to the pre-Norman period. These, definitely in some cases (in Rodanstown and Rathregan) and probably in others, were constructed by the Normans here or adapted to their use.

De Lacy's liberty of Meath, with its capital at Trim where the largest castle in Ireland was built in the thirteenth century, and its double port established at Drogheda, was a self-governing unit owing ultimate loyalty to the crown. What is so impressive about de Lacy's career is the speed with which his liberty was feudalised and the sureness of judgement he showed in the people he depended on and in the centres he founded: Trim, and above all, Drogheda, have by their survival to the present day vindicated his strategic judgement and the few years from 1172 to 1173, and 1177 to 1186, when he was present in Ireland, give evidence of the extraordinary energy with which the conquest was accomplished. As the Annals of Loch Cé put it in 1186, Meath "from the Shannon to the sea was full of castles and foreigners".

All his barons owed fealty and military service to him as lord of the liberty. He held it from the king for the service of fifty, and later one hundred knights. His barons owed him service, generally the service of five knights; it was reckoned one knight's service was financed by twenty plough lands or carucates (each carucate was of one hundred and twenty contemporary acres). For example Moyglare was held from the lord of the liberty at half a knight's service, Galtrim at that of two knights. Of the six manors which make up modern Kilcloon, one, Moyglare was held from the lord of the liberty of Trim; three, Balfeighan, Rodenstown and Kilclone (Mulhussey) from the barons of Galtrim; Rathregan was held from the baron of Ratoath, as was Ballymaglassan. In general, and certainly in time, these military services were compounded for a cash rent. The lordship of Meath had its ups and downs as the de Lacys kept or lost royal favour. When Hugh died in 1186 his son Walter was a minor and so the lordship devolved to the crown. In adulthood, Walter got it back again but lost it when his brother Hugh, earl of Ulster, and half brother, Walter, were attainted by King John and declared traitors. Walter came back to royal favour again in the reign of Henry III when he had only two daughters, his heiresses, surviving at his death. One married John de Vernon and the other Peter de Geneve and the great inheritance was split between them. De Geneve died in 1249 and Matilda de Lacy married Geoffrey de Geneville who governed his wife's part of the inheritance with equity and judgement for over fifty years. He was a French Norman whose brother found fame as the biographer of St. Louis IX, king of France. His caput (or capital) was at Trim where a government sat with quasi-regal authority. Included in this part of the inheritance were the baronies of Ratoath and Deece, and hence all the modern parish of Kilcloon. Geoffrey de Geneville lived long. The de Lacy shortage of male heirs affected his family too. His heiress was his only grand daughter, Joan, who married in 1308 one of the great English noblemen of the day, Roger Mortimer, Earl of March. Joan's grandfather resigned the lordship to his grandson-in-law and died in 1314 a Dominican monk in Trim.

The Mortimers had their ups and downs too. Through marriage and inheritance they were owners of vast estates in England where they were earls of March, and at least in title after 1368, earls of Ulster, lords of Connaught and of course lords of Trim. Their position made them vulnerable to the changing calculations of English kings. Roger became justiciar of Ireland after his defence of his land against Edward Bruce who had invaded the country in 1315. His term as justiciar lasted from 1319 to 1321 when he fell into disfavour with Edward II and lost his wife's inheritance in Meath. A new king, Edward III, restored him in 1327. But they quarrelled. Mortimer was hanged in 1330 but his wife and grandson kept the lands and the estates in England and Ireland and the Mortimer-de Geneville inheritance at Trim.[2] And by 1350 the Mortimer family fortunes were rising again.

As well as new modes of land organisation the Normans also brought with them improved techniques in agriculture and land use. Historians agree that the late twelfth and thirteenth centuries were times of peace and prosperity in the extended Norman colony such as it was not to know subsequently. Large quantities of grain were exported and what was not to happen again until the seventeenth century, Ireland made a constant and substantial contribution to the king's treasury in London.

The survey of the manor of Moyglare made in 1540 to handle the confiscations consequent on the rebellion of Silken Thomas shows how the farms in our parish were structured, and it seems likely that these structures had operated since the beginning of the colony.[3] The very names of the townslands, Norman most of them, made up of a personal name and "town", show the way land was held from the beginning and would continue to be held until well into the eighteenth century. In only two townslands is there evidence of the family who gave it its name. In 1541 William Owen of Owenstown, husbandman, got a lease of property of "an old town called Porterstown alias Portane in the parish of Dunboyne with arable land and a wood thereto belonging for forty one years, at a rent of twelve shillings together with two watchet hens and heriots."[4] In 1547 the estate of Moyglare was leased to the Irish Chancellor, Sir Richard Rede. Among the parcels mentioned is

Porterstown, which was farmed by one James Porter of Kingiston.[5] But the rest of the names, Harris, Stafford, Brown, Grow, Parsons, Pages, Collis, Bryan, Butler, Dollan, Roden, Pierse, Padden, Ribb, Belcham, Cook, Rowan, Wayne, Warren (twenty one in all), out of the fifty seven townslands in the six parishes show that each townsland was leased out or farmed out in relatively large portions either to free tenants (those with fixity of tenure) or farmers (who paid a rent and had their rights on lease for a period of time). There were also of course the cottagers or landless labourers, or betaghs, who were needed to work it. The Normans introduced the three-field system. One large field was sown in winter grain, one in spring grain, and the other was left fallow to recover its strength. Their agriculture was centred on grain crops, though they also raised, as we can see from various charters or grants, cattle, and sheep, as well as pigs which fed on acorns in the oak woods. Looking at the 1540 survey of Moyglare and the Civil Survey of 1654 one can detect the massive concentration on grain crops characteristic of the Middle Ages in Kilcloon.

Footnotes

1   BYRNE, Irish High Kings, p88

2   This summary account of the liberty of Meath is based on Ken Abraham's Thesis, p21 ff ; Otway-Ruthven, A History of Medieval Ireland. p53,174.

3   Crown Surveys of Lands, 1540/41, with the Kildare rental begun in 1518, ed.G. MacNiochaill, p223 ff.

4   Christ Church Deeds, 1179; Fiants Edward V1, No.134.

5   Fiants, Edward VI, p134.

Chapter 4

The Buildings of Norman Kilcloon

What kind of housing did the tenants at will, the cottiers and landless labourers have in Kilcloon in the Norman centuries? We really do not know. For the vast majority of the inhabitants their accommodation must have been basic and primitive. Made out of earth and presumably thatched, these houses have gone back to the earth from which they were made. There are traces of their foundations, such as they had, in Rathregan where what was once a medieval village beside the church and manorial settlement has left clear marks on the ground on either side of a sunken way. The only excavation of basic rural housing dating from the Middle Ages took place at Caherguillamore, Co. Limerick in 1940.[1] The two houses there are, as one might expect, like similar houses excavated in England. One was 13 metres by 6; the other 10 by 5.5. Each was a peasant long house with an entrance to the west, probably single storey, a central hearth, and probably a thatched roof. The walls were stone faced with a filling of rubble and earth; the floor was the natural limestone bedrock. In Kilcloon the floors of most of these houses must have been made of hardened mud as the bedrock limestone would have been too far below the surface to be used as a floor. As late as the 1680s the floors of the two working churches of the parish were made of clay, and so the same must have been true of the houses there before that.[2] They must have been quite uncomfortable also as the smoke from the central hearth had to escape through the thatch or the front doorway. In the 1470s a levy was made on the land of the liberty of Meath and the lowest exaction was for 1 halfpenny made on houses with smoke.[3] The houses would have been dark within, affording little more than shelter and a place to sleep and not really very habitable. The constant presence of smoke must have blackened the clothes and faces of the householders and their families, just as it did until the late 1950s in similar houses in the west of Ireland and in Donegal.

Norman manorial settlement presents a peculiar puzzle in Kilcloon. This was one of the earliest areas to be settled by the Normans in Hugh de Lacy's time and yet it has no examples of the classic early Norman settlement – the steep man-made hill called a motte with its wooden tower or bretesche on the top, and a palisade around it enclosing the area of settlement called a bailey. There are many ring forts and enclosures catalogued for this area in the archaeological inventory of Co. Meath. A number are indeed ring forts and date from the early Christian period and were settlements of strong farmers, but a number clearly resemble the ring works which have only in recent years been identified with the earliest Norman settlement in Ireland. Not only that, but two of these in Kilcloon were centres of Norman settlements during the Middle Ages. One is at Rodanstown (See illustration of earthwork at Rodanstown, p i). It is the massive trivallate ring work near Rodanstown House where there is a straight and direct way from it to Rodanstown Church nearby. Unlike the classic Norman motte, this raised, artificial and flat hill is 39 metres in diameter, broad enough to accommodate a full household settlement on its brow. It is high enough to dominate the whole countryside. It was surrounded by a ditch now faintly to be traced, which enclosed an area of about 20 acres. It must be associated with the first presence of the Hussey family there. At the centre of their barony at Galtrim there is a classic motte and bailey. This Rodanstown settlement with subsequent centres at Calgath and Dollanstown, served farms of junior branches of the Hussey family and of the Boyce family until the Cromwellian Plantation 500 years after the conquest. Rodanstown, though a separate parish from Kilclone and Belfeighan, never became a separate manor as both of the others did in the fifteenth century. It remained divided into three full tenancies which were possessed by either the Husseys or the Boyces until 1654. No traces of later Norman stone buildings survive at Rodanstown, though in the 1654 survey there is mention of an old castle and a church on the site. Perhaps the reference is to this feature at Rodanstown inhabited as a wood and clay structure until the end of the Middle Ages. The other ringwork is at Rathregan which, as part of his barony of Ratoath, Hugh de Lacy gave to the Blund or White family as a manor for settlement. Again like Rodanstown it is very large – its diameter is 31 metres – and so was large enough to have accommodated in wooden buildings the lord's family, and retainers. It is beside the church. In 1654 there was at Rathregan a "stone house", later called a "castle" in 1697 which the then tenant, Richard Corbally, undertook to keep in repair. In the Ordnance Survey of 1836 it is described as the ruins of Rathregan House. As late as the end of the 19th century there was a "stone arched basement with an apartment above it" located there which has been since demolished. At the present the remains of an extensive stone house are there with brick edged windows inserted at a date after its construction. It is large enough to have been a manorial centre, perhaps constructed by the Plunketts for their chief steward after they left for Killeen in the early 15th century. (See illustration, p xi).

In the parish of Kilclone there is a rectangular enclosure at Collistown not far from the medieval church site at Kilclone, but perhaps the trivallate ring fort with a raised central area of 30 metres in diameter at Mulhussey was the predecessor of the tower house built by the Husseys in the 15th century and as such was either of Norman construction or was at least adapted by them in the earliest years of the colony.

The major early Norman settlement of Moyglare has left no trace on the ground. We know that King John, completing a circuit of his territories in Ireland, stayed on August 17th 1210 at " castellum Bret", Bret's castle, which was a convenient location at which to lodge before making an early start for Dublin the next day.[5] What the building mentioned was we do not know. Milo le Bret's son Walter, presenting property to St. John's Hospital in Dublin about 1250, mentioned the wood "extra defensum meum" which sounds like a palisade inside which were the wooden buildings necessary for an extended household – a great hall, various quarters to accommodate different manorial activities and properties.[6] When the successor to the Brets, Walter Delahyde died in 1343 his manor at Moyglare was described as "a stone tower, a hall, a chamber, a bakehouse, a granary and a dove cote roofed with straw". Though the "chamber" may indicate a separation of the lord's living quarters from those of the rest of the household, still the absolute separation entailed by the building of tower houses in the 15th century was yet to come. The specific mention of the tower as made of stone seems to indicate that the rest of the buildings were made of wood and clay and hence no trace of them survives on the ground.[7] It is tempting to relate the "stone tower" of 1344 with the stone gateway with living quarters which has survived to the present day (see illustration, p i) but what remains on the landscape seems to have been built in the 15th or 16th century style and hence was probably a replacement of the "stone tower" of the 1340s. For the record, the Delahyde demesne complex in Dunshaughlin is described as "a messauge in which was a hall, a stable, a byre and a tower thatched with straw".[8] It did not have the same status as the complex at Moyglare. In a survey of 1540 the demesne farm of Moyglare had a castle or stone house, a yard, a garden and various other "necessary buildings".[9] Perhaps a Tudor style mansion or stone house was built at Moyglare in the early 16th century when the Delahydes were then both influential and affluent and by 1601 there was " a widow's house" or dower house at Moyglare.[10] Apart from the gate house the whole complex of the Moyglare building has disappeared, replaced in the 1780s by the Georgian mansion which is now a hotel. When the wars of the Confederation of Kilkenny broke out, Moyglare was burned as it was owned then by an English officer, Sir George Wentworth. It is described as a "mansion" and in the Civil Survey of 1654, when it had been rebuilt and refurbished after the fire of 1643, it is described as "a large stone house, a mill, a pigeon house and farm houses", whereas the small tower house now to be seen at nearby Moygaddy is described as a castle. In 1709 it is described as "a manor house".[11] Though there are only two so-called tower houses to be seen, albeit in ruins in the parish of Kilcloon, there were many more built in the late Middle Ages. Tower houses marked the final ascent of affluent tenants or manor lords into privacy. The extended household, which as a unit characterised the early Norman settlers who seem to have lived together in the bailey or outer yard of the central complex of a manor, was finally separated from the lord's family. However, it is often claimed that these towers were not intended for defence; of the two surviving in Kilcloon only one, at Mulhussey, has a wall with a so-called batter or deviation from the vertical to deflect stone or metal cannonballs. Still, it is hard to claim that the plethora of tower houses mentioned in the records has nothing to do with the shrinking of the area of peace to what became known as the Mahery or Pale at the end of the 15th century. The ten-pound subsidy to encourage the building of castles in Louth was extended to Meath in 1429. It seems to have covered one-tenth of the cost of the building and was discontinued on grounds of cost in 1449.[12]

By then it seems as if most free tenants in our area lived in what seem to have been tower houses. In 1642 a list of places where cavalry and foot could be quartered "bordering on Bermingham's country", on the border between West Kildare, Offaly and Meath was submitted for consideration to the Council in Dublin. Mulhussey was a town and had a strong castle "able to receive 200 foot"; Dollanstown was a vaulted castle able to receive 100, Calgath a vaulted castle fit to receive 50 foot, Balfeighan a town and castle fit to receive 100 men. Significantly Rodanstown isn't mentioned; it presumably was still a complex of buildings made of earth and wood. Other castles were at neighbouring Garadice, Gallo, Agherpallas and Lynch's Knock in Summerhill. The Civil Survey of 1654 describes these places mentioned as castles and in addition Rodanstown had "an old castle"; the castle at Balfeighan had become decayed and at Kilglin there was a "stone house". Outside, but close to the parish of Kilcloon, Garreris had a castle, Arrotstown, Kilmore parish, had one also, as had Clonlyon, and in Moynalvey was a stone house, together with an old castle. Culmullen had a stone house as had Galtrim. In the other parishes which make up Kilcloon, Ballymaglassan and Rathregan, there was "a ruinate old castle" at Blackhall and at Rathregan "a stone house", called in

1697 a "castle" which the then tenant, Richard Corbally, undertook to keep in repair.[14] As late as the end of the 19th century there was a stone arched basement there with an apartment over it. It was demolished eventually in the late nineteenth century. It sounds remarkably like the castle described in 1642 as fit for military use and like the tower houses which survive in ruin on the ground. In short, the whole countryside seems to have been peppered with stone houses or castles which at the very least could be adapted quickly for military use. It is hard not to associate this building with the increasing lawlessness in the areas near Dublin in the 15th century and the consequent legislation in 1477, 1488 and 1494/95 for the great ditch which went from Dublin "as the avenlyfy ronneth to Clane in the Magherie, and also Mayane (Maynooth) and so the waters of Rye by Kilcocke also Ballyfeghane and so to the parish of Laracor" and thence by Bellewstown near Trim and Athboy to the Hill of Lloyd and thence to the sea at Dundalk. It was principally intended, one presumes, to make it difficult for the King's Irish enemies or the gaelicised Normans to drive west cattle seized in predatory raids. Stone towers or castles were an obvious complement to it.[15]

With the exception of three glebe houses, two parochial houses, a police barracks and Bridestream House built in the 18th century, all the houses dating from before 1850 in Kilcloon are on the sites of what are known to have been the houses of prominent free tenants or centres of manorial lordships dating back to the Norman conquest. In Balfeighan there are the ruins of an 18th century house near the church and graveyard which was inhabited up to 40 years ago. In Rodanstown there are the 18th century houses of Rodanstown itself, Dollanstown and Calgath. In Moyglare there is Moyglare Manor, Moygaddy House and Newtown House in Newtown Moyaghey which was a farmhouse in the Civil Survey of 1654. Kilgraigue House was the home of the Foster family since the conquest perhaps, and Killeaney House was the home of the steward of Moyglare in the time of the Wentworths.[16] Neither of these is mentioned in the Civil Survey an indication that they were not tower houses and were not made of stone. Kilclone/Mulhussey has the ruins of an 18th century house expanding the original tower house of the Husseys. Blackhall House and Ballymaglassan House had pre-Cromwellian castles, as had Staffordstown House and Dollysgrove. In Rathregan there was the castle of Rathregan itself. At the Manor of Parsonstown there are no medieval remains and in a comprehensive lease of 1580 of Parsonstown Manor no house is mentioned. Perhaps like that of the Fosters, the house did not appear in the records as it was not made of stone, though there was a "farme" house there in 1654 "with houses of office and two cottages".[17]

The 18th century houses which can be identified in Kilcloon today point to a remarkable continuity of settlement going back to Norman times and perhaps in one or two instances beyond that to settlement in Early Christian Ireland. The Civil Survey of 1654 records what must have been fairly substantial single farm houses in Kilclone, Newtownmoyaghey, Brownrath, Growtown, Polebane, Staffordtown, Wyanstown (4 "farme" houses), Woodland, Creymore, Parsonstown and "1 thatch hous" in Belshamstown, and thus indicates the structures of land holding which had persisted from the Norman settlement of the area with one leaseholder or tenant holding a townsland. No clear records predate that survey except one of 1540 when houses, apart from the manor settlement at Moyglare, are not mentioned. Though there are no buildings given in the Down Survey map of Ratoath barony for Rathregan, buildings are shown for Ballymaglassan. There is a substantial castle marked at Blackhall Big and another at Blackhall Little. What look like tower houses are marked for Staffordstown, Brownrath, Blackhall Big, Waynestown and Growtown. There is a church at Ballymaglassan, two cabins or farmhouses in Growtown, Polebane and Staffordstown and one at Blackhall Little. (See illustration of map of Deece and map of Ratoath, p iii-iv). In the Down Survey map of Deece (1657) it seems that buildings were only sporadically inserted. George Booth's stone house in Kilglyn is there but neither Balfeighan tower house or church appear. In Rodanstown there is only Calgath. There is no manor house or church marked in Moyglare, though there is a small building at Kilgraigue, and six houses shown indicate some kind of village not far from the bridge over the Rye water at Kilcock. In recent times traces of occupation have turned up on the left side of Knocknatulla road leading to Balfeighan. In Mulhussey (Kilclone) there is no church marked at Kilclone, but the tower house and small chapel at Mulhussey are shown. In other words the Down Survey was concerned with indicating land ownership only. The buildings in the parishes appear occasionally and perhaps then by accident. In the 1654 survey "cabbins" are mentioned and cottages, but since the main purpose of the survey was to make clear the religion of the landowner, the extent of his holdings and the use made of the land, the mention of cabins or cottages does not seem to have been anything more than sporadic. Only in Rathregan, Mulhussey and perhaps in Dollanstown is there any mention of a village and as we have seen that the quite substantial village of Rathregan is clearly visible on the ground. (See illustration of Sunken way at Rathregan, p xi). The rectangular enclosure 19 metres by 17 in Portane is not mentioned in the Civil Survey (neither is the townsland itself as it was treated as part of Rathregan). Portane appears for the first time as a discrete townsland in the first Fingal rentroll to survive, from 1702, but the shape and dimensions of the enclosure make it likely to have been used at least as far back as the Middle Ages, if not constructed then.[18]

At Blackhall, a trivallate ring fort destroyed in the recent past was marked on the Ordnance Survey of 1836 as the site of a castle. The central area had dimensions of 50 metres by 57 and it seems likely that, with wooden buildings upon it, it was the predecessor of the "ruinate old castle" mentioned in the Civil Survey of 1654.

At Kilgraigue there is a circular area 58m in diameter, which becomes visible at times because of the seasonal changes in vegetation. It is near the relatively modern Kilgraigue House, which, in turn, is on the site of the Foster family home, a location of habitation perhaps from the conquest, and certainly from 1415 when the Fosters were tenants of the lord of Moyglare.[19]

At Ballymaglassan there is an artificially constructed circular area with a diameter of 50m, also defined by vegetation changes. This townsland was the centre of the manor of Ballymaglassan throughout the Middle Ages.

The houses of the ordinary people do not appear on the records for another two centuries though it is most likely that the fourth class houses that appear in 19th century census returns must have had continuity in style at least with the "cabbins" and "cottages" of the Civil Survey of 1654, and with the houses of the twenty four cottagers who lived on the Moyglare demesne in 1540.[3]

Footnotes

1   Archaeology of Medieval Ireland, T.B. Barry, p73

2   Bishop Dopping's Visitation Book, ed. Ellison, Riocht Na Midhe, Vol.V, No. 2,1972. p4, 5.

3   Statutes of Ireland, Edward 1V, ed. Berry, p291

4   Mac Clenaghan Papers, p3, 48.

5   C.D.I. Vol.1, No.360, 361.

6   Register of Hospital of John the Baptist, No.377.

7   Abraham quoting P.R.O.c.135/75/3.

8   Abraham quoting P.R.O. c.135/75/3.

9   Crown Surveys, 1540 to 41, ed. Mac Niochaill, p223

10   Calendar of Patent Rolls, Philip and Mary 1, (1553/4) p71; Patent and Close Rolls Elizabeth (1600) p567.

11   Civil Survey, Vol. 5, Meath, ed. Simington, p53; Journals of the House of Lords, 19th December 1709, p23.

12   Calendar of Archbishop Alen's Register (1172 to 1534) ed. McNeill, RSAI, 1950, p23; UJA, 1st series, Vol. 2 (1854), p42, 43; Richey, Lectures on the History of Ireland down to 1534, Dublin 15,1869, p212; State Papers Henry VIII (1530/52) Vol. 2, 504, 505.

13   History of Affairs in Ireland, Gilbert, Vol. 1, p49.

14   Fingal Papers, N.L.I.(not catalogued)

15   c.f. 12.

16   Wentworth Papers N.L.I., dd. 10560 ff.

17   Civil Survey, Vol. 5, Meath, ed. Simington, p87; MacCleneghan Papers, p351

18   The Fingal Papers. N.L.I.

19   Christ Church Deeds 866.

Chapter 5

The Manor of Moyglare – 1171 to 1350

Hugh Tyrell – Lord of Moyglare

Not untypical of the Norman knights who came to Ireland in the last years of the twelfth century was Hugh Tyrell. His career illustrates the cosmopolitan origin of the Norman lords who came to Ireland and the size of the kingdom ruled by Henry II. It stretched from Hadrian's Wall on the frontier with Scotland to the Pyrenees and the borders of Muslim Spain. Born about 1130, the second son of the Lord of Poix in Picardy, he hitched his wagon to a neighbour's star whose family originated in Lassey in Normandy and so was called Hugh de Lacy; he was not disappointed. By 1160 he held two knight's fees in de Lacy country in Herefordshire where de Lacy had served the Angevin king, Henry II, defending in an unruly and restless fashion the Welsh marches or borderlands between England and Wales. Hugh eventually held property from de Lacy in Worcestershire, together with two manors in more peaceful territories, Kingsworthy near Winchester and Tyrell Avon in the New Forest. A relation of Richard de Clare, otherwise known as Strongbow, Tyrell was tempted by the Irish adventure and was one of the ten knights under the leadership of Raymond le Gros, the fat one, who landed at Baginbun in Wexford in 1169. For that disobedient act the king, Henry II, confiscated Tyrell's two lucrative and peaceful manors in Hampshire, Avon Tyrell and Kingsworth. But when his mentor Hugh de Lacy came to Ireland with his king in 1171 Tyrell got his Hampshire estates back and was in high favour again. De Lacy was set up as a counter balance to Strongbow, by now king of Leinster, and given to conquer for the king the fissiparous kingdom of Meath with the service of fifty knights. In the great division that took place Tyrell got three knights' fees in Castleknock, which included what is now the Phoenix Park, Mulhuddart, Clonsilla, Chapelizod, Kilsallaghan and Cloghran. His grant from de Lacy was dated 1173 and by 1177 it was confirmed by Henry II when he held it directly from the king. By 1173 Tyrell's first wife, Isabel of Vignacourt, whom he had married in 1171, had died and he married another Norman French lady, Marie Desenarpont. His interest in France had revived when his brother Walter died without issue in 1171 leaving Hugh the sixth lord of Poix. He now had interests in all three of the Angevin lands, France, England and Ireland.

There was also a practical and active religious dimension to Tyrell. It was a family tradition. His grandfather Walter had gone on the first crusade in 1096, and was present when Jerusalem was taken in 1099 with vast bloodshed and massacre. By 1100 he was back in England, the hunting companion of the son of William the Conqueror, William II called Rufus, and was evidently responsible for his death in the New Forest through a misdirected arrow. He naturally fled to France but was soon reconciled with the new king, Henry I, and he founded two religious establishments in England, the second in 1131, sometime after the birth of his grandson Hugh. In 1131, also he went to the Holy Land, this time as a simple pilgrim and he died there. His son, called the Chevalier, went on the second crusade in 1146.[1]

In the same tradition, Hugh in Ireland favoured the priory of St John of Jerusalem, run by a military order formed in the Holy Land at the first crusade to provide medical and hospital services to crusaders. The first Irish house of this order was founded by Strongbow on the site of an early Christian monastery at Kilmainham.[2] This did not prevent Tyrell with Philip of Worcester (the justiciar or king's representative in Ireland) attacking Armagh in 1185 and plundering its monastery, though unlike Philip who brought as his spoil the Bacal Iosa, the reputed crozier of St. Patrick, permanently to Dublin, Tyrell returned his spoil. The story is that the two horses drawing the cart that contained a great cooking pot stolen from Armagh were burned to death in a mysterious fire. Remembering the maledictions hurled at the noble bandits by the good monks of Armagh, Hugh thought it prudent to return the plundered loot. Even the bishop of Louth, then present, said of the same Hugh in the hearing of many of his army: "that man this year will certainly meet with a grievous misfortune. Never was it known that the tears and curses of so many good men were spent in vain." Perhaps this event or the alliance with Worcester caused a break with Hugh de Lacy, his former benefactor, which said Giraldus Cambrensis, the chronicler of the Norman invasion and its aftermath, "plunged nearly the whole kingdom into confusion".[3] From subsequent documentation over rights in the liberty of Meath it seems that after Hugh de Hosee was granted the barony of Deece he handed back to de Lacy the manor of Moyglare, who gave it to Hugh Tyrell who granted it to Milo le

Bret before de Lacy died in 1186.[4] A few years later Tyrell, by then nearly sixty years old, went on the third crusade to rescue Jerusalem from Saladin who had taken it in 1187. Tyrell was at the siege of Acre in 1191 with Tyrells from Poix and the king of France together with Richard Coeur de Lion. He had settled his affairs in 1191 leaving some more land to the priory at Kilmainham, his Castleknock estates to his elder son by his second marriage, Lyons in Kildare to James, his second son and Avon Tyrell in Hampshire to his brother Roger. Moyglare went to the heir of Castleknock. Aged nearly seventy, Hugh returned from this crusade to France.

He died in 1199 and was buried in the abbey of St Peter at Selincourt, one of the religious houses founded by his grandfather. He lived long for his time and reflected that buccaneering spirit associated with second and subsequent sons in feudal Angevin territories, which in religious matters expressed itself in involvement in the crusades. His lordship of Moyglare remained in the family with the Brets as their vassals, until at least the end of the thirteenth century.[5]

The le Brets of Moyglare

Milo le Bret, the senior member of his family, seems to have been a knight in the household of Hugh de Lacy in Herefordshire and was one of the chief followers of Hugh when he came to Ireland with his lord, Henry II, in 1171. Le Bret, with the other chief lords of de Lacy's household, had obviously a key role to play in Henry II's plans to set up a liberty of Meath as a check to the ambitions of Strongbow, by then ruler of Leinster. Le Bret's first lordship was that of Rathfarnham; another le Bret lived in Santry; Adam de Feipo was lord of Santry, and Hugh Tyrrell was lord of Castleknock. It is as if these and other lordships were intended as a sort of cordon sanitaire set about Dublin to act as its outer defences.

In that extraordinary outburst of energy which characterised the early years of the Norman conquest, in the east, south and north of Ireland, le Brets held manors in Tipperary, Limerick and Cork together with Moyglare in Meath. Milo and his brothers Ralph, Adam and William appear in the records all over the south and south west of the country, setting up lordships, swapping them for others, retreating from ones which stretched their resources unduly (like Ely O'Carroll) and endowing monasteries and hospitals.[1]

As we have seen, Hugh Tyrrell handed over the manor of Moyglare, after a brief period of occupation, to Milo le Bret, though he remained the direct feudal overlord, holding the manor from the lord of the liberty of Meath. Milo le Bret was then lord of the manor of Moyglare and also responsible for the parish of Moyglare which served the le Bret family, the extended family, the free tenants, and the farmers and cottiers who lived and worked there. Milo le Bret granted to the Augustinian monastery of St Thomas in Dublin full responsibility for the parish which involved the right to receive the tithes and clerical income from the manor and parish and to appoint its serving priests.[2] He was more generous to St Mary's Cistercian abbey in Dublin. His first ecclesiastical grant to that abbey was in 1185, a small farm called Drumsaron outside the city of Dublin. About 1200, Milo, with the voluntary permission of Roger the chaplain, granted the income from the church of Donaghmore along with sixty acres of land with tithes of Tolagh Lif, Baligorman, Disseldevein, Culcurri, and that land which William le Poer "owed to me of Belet". In 1540 the abbey still had the rights to the church of Donaghmore near Ratoth so presumably the other place names are of neighbouring areas or parishes.[3]

Another charter, undated, granted property near St John's hospital in Kilmainham to the white monks and in 1210 (for his soul, that of his wife Matilda and of Hugh Tyrrell) he gave to the same monastery free right to timber, both green and dry, from his wood at Moyglare and to do all that enjoying this privilege entailed. He also added the right to put pigs to graze (presumably on acorns in the oak wood) in the same place. Milo's son, Walter confirmed the grant about 1226.

But the main beneficiary of the le Bret charity was the hospital of St John the Baptist outside the new gate at Kilmainham. It had been founded by a layman and his wife before 1188, on their property outside the city walls, on the north side of the road leading to Kilmainham. It was both a hospital and a religious house for men and women. The founder's name was Ailred the Palmer, an Ostman, and citizen of the Norse kingdom of Dublin before the Anglo-Normans seized it in 1170. The hospital was endowed by Henry II with the village of Palmerston, near Chapelizod, and by one Roger Camerarius with the village, or "vill", of Palmerstown in Fingal. It was destroyed by Edward Bruce in 1317 when he camped in the suburbs of Dublin. By 1334, it was rebuilt and catered for 155 poor sick persons.

A tribute, not only to the generosity of its benefactors, but also to the needs addressed by the hospital (its brethren lived under the Augustinian rule) is contained implicitly in the extents of monastic possessions drawn up in 1540 over three hundred years after its foundation. The hospital still served its useful purpose; among the debris disposed of then was fifty beds: "these have no value beyond their use for the sick", and a lot of its income still came from Bret endowments in Dublin about Palmerston, which became part of Milo le Bret's estate, and from many parishes and large tracts of land given by him and his extended family in Tipperary, Limerick and Carlow.[5]

The fortuitous survival of the register of St John's hospital, the register of St Thomas's abbey and the chartularies of St Mary's Cistercian abbey reveals the generosity of the family in succeeding generations: other monasteries which may likewise have been endowed have left few records behind them. By chance, a record survives of a grant by Geoffrey le Bret, Milo's great grandson, of the ecclesiastical income from the parish of "Dounnemonet" or Donemona, near Nenagh, County Tipperary, about 1300 to Holy Cross abbey in the same county.[6]

It seems as if Milo le Bret's brothers came to Ireland with him or followed him soon afterwards. Ralph was certainly his brother, and presumably Adam and William were also his brothers. None of them seem to have figured in the high politics of their day: their chief and only interest seems to have been the acquiring of property which they did with notable success all over Ireland.

Their surnames survive in place names in the midlands, in Tipperary and in the west. They also were generous, especially to the hospital of St. John, as an extended family and in succeeding generations during the thirteenth and early fourteenth centuries. In the charters sealing the grants le Brets witnessed le Bret endowments. In the years from 1198 to 1210, the first generation le Bret endowments were most abundant. Milo confirmed the grant of Henry II of Palmerston to St. John's in 1198. His endowment was witnessed by Adam, William and Ralph le Bret, by Hugh Tyrrell, and by Leonisius de Bromiard, who was lord of many manors in the baronies of Deece and Ratoath about Moyglare. About the year 1200 le Bret grantors and witnesses appear in no less than twenty-seven charters of endowments. Milo granted timber from his woods at Moyglare and other things necessary for a house, pasture for pigs and for cattle from the same place. Alex de Stokes presented Clonbrogan, County Tipperary, to St. John's, with the permission and confirmation of his lord, Milo le Bret. Adam le Bret presented the income of ten parishes to the hospital and his brother Ralph gave a burgage plot in Limerick, the tithes of Rathdrum, County Tipperary, with the church of Coleman in the same county, one tenth of the military dues of a knight "which I have from my lord, Milo le Bret", and with his permission, in Cooleagh County Tipperary. William le Bret, about the same time, presented the income from Clogher and Kilcooly, County Tipperary to the hospital, as well as twenty six acres of Kilcullen also in Tipperary, and the tithes of many places associated with Clogher "for the sustenance of the sick who lie there" in the hospital of St. John. In 1217 Milo granted to St. John's twenty shillings from a holding called Karrecclivan, near or in Rathfarnham, together with all the tithes of bread and ale and meat and water parsnips and fish, of his house at Rathfarnham and a messauge (a house with land) one Gilbert held of him near the river, together with the right to graze six cattle with his own in the common pasture. His son, Walter, confirmed this grant about 1250 of both the tithes from Rathfarnham and the twenty shillings from land in Kimmage, which seems to be that called Karrecclivan in his father's grant. About 1250, Walter gave four shillings to St. John's which were his dues or rent from Peter the Miller for four acres in Rathfarnham, along with one tenth of the apple harvest in Rathfarnham and the right to timber in the form of branches or charcoal in Moyglare "extra defensum meum" – outside my defences or palisade at Moyglare. Walter's son, Milo, in 1279 presented a messauge at Moyglare and yard in the "villa (of Moyglare) which chaplain Horonan (O'Ronain) formerly held" to the hospital. The lot was described as between the messauges of Roger Corr and Roger Haliday and commanded a yearly rent of twelve pence.[7]

The picture of land tenure presented here – three houses and land and their tenants – emphasises the way the manor had been organised quickly after the first grants at the end of the previous century. It certainly fits the picture of Moyglare reflected in the survey made in 1540 and also shows the local clergyman, a chaplain with a Gaelic name (unique in the annals of Moyglare for many years to come) and not the vicar of Moyglare, living in a fairly comfortably sized holding which was held, not as a free tenancy but, on a lower level, as a farm.

Geoffrey le Bret, the next lord of Rathfarnham and Moyglare, lived from about 1250 to 1320. He was active in businesses beyond his lordship. He was for twenty years one of those responsible for the defences of the marches, "conserver of the king's peace of all the valley of Dublin", and was summoned to fight for Edward I in France in 1297, and also against the Scots in 1302 and again in defence of the realm in 1309, 1314, 1315, 1316 in the days of Edward Bruce.[8]

His son Milo, and grandson John, were, in turn, sheriffs of Cork, and Milo fought in the king's wars in Flanders. The le Bret connection with the south was still sustained. Towards the end of the thirteenth century, in 1278, Geoffrey got an allowance for his custody of the castle of Roscrea and acquired Carrick on Suir from the Cockerell family. And in 1299 he exchanged it with the king for Rathcon. Carrick was then granted to the Butler family, one of whom, Edmund, became earl of Carrick and justiciar of Ireland.[9] In 1318, Geoffrey confirmed his concession of Clonbrogan in Tipperary to St John's, and in 1319 that of Rathfarnham.[10] A major contribution to his status was made by his wife, who with her two sisters were the heiresses to the daughter of David Fitzgerald, Baron of Naas, and his wife Matilda, daughter of Hugh de Lacy, Earl of Ulster, son of the first lord of the liberty of Meath. Fitzgerald, being the head of the senior branch of the family, had extensive properties in Wales, held there since before the Fitzgeralds arrived in Ireland; they also had substantial properties in Kildare.[11] Geoffrey died about 1319 or 1320 and his son Milo confirmed all his grants to St. John's hospital in the same year. Sometime between Geoffrey's death and that of Sir Walter Delahyde in 1343, the manor of Moyglare changed hands, probably by purchase, and the connection between Moyglare and the Tyrrell and the le Bret families was finally broken.[12] A new family, the Delahydes, acquired the lordship of Moyglare and they were to retain it for the next three centuries.[5]

Footnotes

Hugh Tyrell – Lord of Moyglare

1   Alma Brook/Tyrell gave this account of the Tyrell family in Irish Family History, Vol.2, 1986. Her article is based on a history of the family by J.H. Tyrell "A General History of the Tyrells" 1904. A more sober account is contained in two articles by Eric St. John Brooks in the J.R.S.A.I, 1933, 1946. Though there was a relationship between the Tyrells of Castleknock and the Walter Tyrell who was responsible for the death of William Rufus, King of England, Brooks claims that it was not one of direct descent but rather one of kinship; both were members of the same extended family. Brooks claims Hugh Tyrell was probably the son of one Rocelyn Tyrell, a knight of de Lacy, in Herefordshire who held two manors there.

2   Dalton "A History of County Dublin" reprinted in 1976, p303. Henry II in 1177 "enfeoffed Hugh Tyrell in the land of Kilmahallock, with the appurtenances, together with the moiety of the river Liffey, as far as the water course near the gallows". (Ware's Antiquities, c.27). Hugh Tyrell bestowed the same said lands on the prior of the hospital, and "with the concurrence of his brother, Roger, further granted to the same prior, Chapelizod, Kilmainham free from all secular services and burdens, with all liberties and free customs in wood, meadows, pastures etc." Richard, Hugh's son, confirmed his father's donation by a subsequent deed, c.f. The song of Dermot and the earl "Castleknock, in the first place, he (de Lacy) gave to Hugh Tyrell, whom he loved so much." p229, line 3138. De Lacy made Tyrell his constable at Trim.

"Then Hugh de Lacy
Fortified a house at Trim and threw a trench around it,
And then enclosed it with a stockade.
Within the house he then placed
Brave knights of great worth; then he entrusted the castle
To the warder ship of Hugh Tyrell;
To the harbour he went in order to cross
The high seas to England." Ibid. line 3222 ff.

3   CAMBRENSIS, Giraldus "Topography of Ireland" translation John J.O'Meara, Dundalgan Press p72

4   C.D.I. 1285 to 1292 (1292) No.1075, p471.

5   Cal. Jus. Rolls, 1295 to 1303, p246.

The le Brets of Moyglare

1   Eric St John Brooks, Knights' Fees in Wexford, Carlow and Kilkenny passim.

2   Register of the Abbey of St. Thomas, Dublin. ed.Gilbert. p24; the grant was confirmed by cardinal John di Salerno in 1202, ibid, p24. An interesting comment is made implicitly in two letters referring to the same grant in the Register of St. Thomas's (XVIII and XIX). The parish is described in the first as Meinclare, Meincaddy etc." In the second as Magelare, Magedde and Teachmarcan. The stah and teach both mean a house, the first in Norse and the second in Gaelic. The "stah" seems to hint at a Viking presence at Moyglare in the previous centuries; Teachmarcan is not identifiable today.

3   Chartularies of St. Mary's Abbey, Dublin, ed.Gilbert, p125 to 127; Extents of Monastic Possessions, 1540 to 1541, ed. White, p30, 253

4   Register of the Hospital of St. John the Baptist, Dublin, ed. Eric St. John Brooks passim.

5   C.P.R. 1330-4, p552; Extents of Monastic Possessions, p55 ff.

6   GWYNN & GLEESON, History of the Diocese of Killaloe, p289; C.D.I. Vol.3, No.149

7   Register of St.John the Baptist passim

8   C.D.I. 1285 to 1292, p73; C.D.I. 1293 to 1301, 124, 396 and 404

9   C.D.I. 1293 to 1301, p96; C.D.I. 1252 to 1284, p228, 518, 534, 260 and 257

10 Register of the Hospital of St. John the Baptist, p200, 231

11 Calendar of the Gormanston Register, ed.Mills & McEnery, xiii, p3; C.D.I. 1293 to 1301, 482; St. John Brooks, Knight's Fees, p149 and 151

12 Calendar of Inquisitions, 1343, No.533; Calendar of Patent Rolls, Edward III, 1345 to 1348, p42.

Chapter 6

The Husseys of Galtrim and the Manors of Kilclone, Balfeighan and Rodanstown – 1171 to 1350

As we have seen the Barony of Deece, a discrete unit controlled by the O'Melaghlin before 1153 and inhabited at some time by the Deisi, an Irish tribe, was handed over by Hugh de Lacy to Hugh de Hosee (alias afterwards Hussey), who proceeded to parcel his barony into manors, the primary units of lordship in Co. Meath.[1] Normally the responsibility of providing for the spiritual care of the tenants fell to the lord of the manor, who owned what was called the advowson, or right to present to the bishop a candidate to be parish priest or rector there. As we have seen, Moyglare in the 12th century was hived off as a separate manor under the lord of the Liberty of Meath. The Husseys of Galtrim seem to have allowed eleven of their manors to have manorial status with themselves as overlords. The lords of these manors gave responsibility for the religious life of eight of them to the Augustinian Abbey of St. Thomas in Dublin, two to the Augustinians of Llanthony in Wales, to whom Hugh de Lacy had given much income from his estates in Meath, and one to the monastery of St. Peter in Trim; the other two, Scurloughstown and Agher, seem to have remained in the possession of the lords of those manors. In the south of the barony, the Husseys kept three of the six parishes of Kilcloon, Kilclone, Balfeighan and Rodanstown, in their own hands, together with Drumlargan and Gallo, as chaplaincies to swell the income of their rectory of Galtrim. It seems as if, in parallel with this, the Husseys did not allow these manors to develop independently, but kept them as free tenancies or as farms which they could repossess and control in succeeding generations. Both Balfeighan and Kilclone were hived off as discrete manors only in the first half of the 15th century and Rodanstown, divided into three holdings at Calgath, Dollanstown and Rodanstown, only gained manorial status for each of its tenancies, perhaps as late as the end of the 16th century.

The Husseys of Galtrim married heiresses and expanded their inheritance, as the Plunketts were to do after them. At one stage in the early 1300s the Fleming baron of Slane and John Hussey married two daughters of the de Geneville lord of the liberty of Trim and acquired between them the manor of Culmullen.[3] The Husseys also married a Petit heiress in the early 1400s and acquired the manor of Rathkenny.[4]

In fact, apart from a certain prominence in local government in the late 14th century when the baron was knighted in 1359, appointed a Justice of the Peace in 1361, and in 1382, and was summoned to Parliament in 1359, 1375, 1380 and 1394 (he was Supervisor of Judges in 1382 as well), the Husseys concentrated on their estates and their marriages all through the Middle Ages.[5] Perhaps their experience in supporting the rebel de Lacys against King John and the difficulties they experienced in being restored to royal favour proved a cautionary tale for succeeding generations.[6] They did not receive summones, as the le Brets and the le Blunds did, to serve Edward I in France and in Scotland in the early 1300s, and the records only tell of one occasion when a serious disagreement with the Lord Deputy landed the baron of Galtrim in the jail of Dublin Castle (1448-1449). In practice, when the Husseys set up Mulhussey or Kilclone as a separate manor to be held directly under the lord of Trim, to provide a perpetual inheritance for the family of Nicholas Hussey, second son of the baron, and handed over Balfeighan as a tenancy to the earls of Kildare, the connection between these manors and the Husseys of Galtrim was broken. There were still feudal applications due until the 16th century from the two junior houses of the Husseys and the Boyces of Calgath in the parish of Rodanstown. There, one free tenancy was held by a junior member of the Hussey family and two others by the Boyces of Calgath and Dollanstown. Very little has survived in the records of those who were major tenants, small landholders or farmers in these three parishes before 1350, though there is mention of the Husseys of Rodanstown and Boyces of Calgath and Dollanstown in some law cases of the thirteenth century.[7]

Footnotes

1   Ware quotes from Hugh de Lacy's Charter through a transcript thereof, c.f. Orpen Ireland under the Normans, Vol 2, p85.

2   c.f. Holding on: The Husseys of Galtrim, Justin Wallace, Maynooth College, p6, ff.

3   Ibid. p9.

4   Ibid. p9.

5   ABRAHAM, Ken, Appendix 4,5,6.

6   c.f. Orpen 1, p255, 16th July 1210, Carrickfergus was taken by King John; among the people taken was Hubert Hose of Galtrim.   Archbishop Alen's register, p308.

7   Cal. Jus. Rolls 1295-1305, p195; Cal. Jus. Rolls 1305-1307, p490

Chapter 7

The Manor of Rathregan – 1171 to 1350

Very little survives in the records about Norman Rathregan. It was one of the smallest of the manors which make up modern Kilcloon and is in the barony of Ratoath. Ratoath was kept by Hugh de Lacy as a personal fiefdom when the structure of his liberty was laid down and he granted Rathregan to the le Blund family, variously known in succeeding centuries as Blount, White and Albus (the Latin word for White). Presumably the name derived from the nickname of an eponymous ancestor. Though de Lacy handed over the parishes of his barony either to the Augustinians of St Thomas in Dublin or to the monks of Llanthony in Wales, in contrast, Rathregan was handed over some time after 1206, by the Blounts, to the Augustinian canons to whom the bishop of the diocese, Simon de Rochfort, had entrusted his cathedral at Newtown, near Trim.[1] Technically, these monks had an obligation to appoint a vicar to Rathregan, but at least once, when the taxation lists appeared about 1300,[2] it was lamented that there was not sufficient income from Rathregan for a vicar. Presumably a chaplain at a negotiable salary was appointed instead.

All that survives physically of the Blounts at Rathregan is the great earthwork just behind the ruin of a later church. (See illustration of earthwork at Rathregan, p viii). It is large enough to have served the le Blund extended household of family, retainers and servants. Le Blunds figure in the surviving records from the thirteenth and fourteenth centuries but the Rathregan branch of the family do not until John le Blund appears at the end of the thirteenth century. In 1299, he got a judgement against a Thomas de Ledwych for thirty nine pounds two and fourpence in the de Geneville court of the liberty at Trim.[3] It was a substantial sum of money in medieval Ireland as evidenced by the goods and chattels seized by the sheriff of Meath to pay for it. There were twenty crannocs of wheat in a stack (valued at twenty pence the crannoc), twenty crannocs of oats (at sixteen pence the crannoc), sixty acres of wheat sown at two shillings an acre and sixty acres of oats sown at twenty pence an acre. In an echo of modern customs in matters involving land and law, the sheriff could find no buyers. The incident underlines the comparative wealth of John at Rathregan. He had inherited from his father, Walter, lands in Carbury in Kildare, but that land, part of the marchlands near O'Connor country in Offaly was not productive of much income. Ownership could only be asserted fitfully. It was sold to the Birminghams, some of whom were at times at the centre of Anglo Norman government in Dublin (Sir John Birmingham was justiciar 1321 – 1323) and others were indistinguishable in conduct and in their control of land from their Gaelic neighbours.[4]

In 1297 John le Blund was involved in a law case where one Michael de Cravel alleged that with a number of de la Feldes, John le Blund had assaulted him one night at Paynestown, County Meath. A few days later de Cravel got permission to withdraw the charge on paying a fine of one mark (thirteen shillings and fourpence), half of which was to be paid by one of the de la Feldes. At this distance and from such limited information it is hard to see what was behind the incident beyond local rivalries which had to be resolved outside the court, for no further records have survived.[5]

John was one of those summoned to parliament in 1311[6] and like his neighbour, le Bret, was expected to play his part in the defense of the realm in 1315 and in 1317 when the threat of Edward Bruce hung over the island. He played a minor role in local government. With many more in 1316 – 1317 he investigated with Edmund le Bottiler, the justiciar, the involvement of two de Lacy brothers, Walter and Hugh, in the recent invasion of Ireland by the Scotsman Edward Bruce.[7] In 1317, the new justiciar, Roger Mortimer, investigated by inquisition "John Blund, alias White" of Rathregan, concerning two hundred marks missing from the official accounts; to what effect does not appear in the records.[8]

In 1359 Hugh le Whyt, a knight of Rathregan, sold his manor of Donmurhill and Balymurlerhan in Kildare, with the advowson of the church of Donmurhill, to Walter de Birmingham, the lord of Carbury. The lawyer involved in this deal was Richard Plunkett of Beaulieu near Drogheda, the second son of John Plunkett, who was the first Plunkett to move from law to lordship.[9]

Evidently one result of the business was the selling of the manor of Rathregan to the Plunketts who kept it for the next six centuries. There were still Whyts in Rathregan and in the area adjoining for centuries afterwards. In 1428 one William Wytte of Rodanstown granted to another William Wytte of the same parish a messuage and land in Ballymaglassan: among the witnesses was Jon Wytte of "Raregan".[10] The messauge evidently went to the hospital of St. John at Kilmainham as the document appears in its register. There were Blounts in Rathregan until recently but whether of the le Blund stock, who were lords of the manor before the Plunketts, is not known.

Footnotes

1   Mention of a vicar about 1300 (C.D.I. 1293 to 1301, p260) is the first albeit indirect reference to the monastic ownership of the parish appointment and income. Presumably the handing over took place early in the thirteenth century after the building of the cathedral at Newtown had begun.

2   C.D.I. 1303 – 1307, p263.

3   Calendar Justiciary Rolls of Ireland, 1295 to 1303, p226, 249.

4   Guide to English financial records for Irish history, Analecta X, p19.

5   Calendar of Justiciary Rolls Ireland, 1295 to 1303, p274 and 280.

6   Abraham Appendix 4, p491.

7   Chartularies of St. Mary's Abbey, Vol.2, p407

8   Patent Rolls, 31 Edward 1, quoted by McCleneghan, p350.

9   Gormanston Register, p139, 140.

10   Register of the Hospital of St.John the Baptist, Dublin, p375 (No.584).

Chapter 8

The Manor of Ballymaglassan – 1171 to 1350

Ballymaglassan is a manor in Ratoath, a barony which Hugh de Lacy reserved for himself. This manor, with many others in Deece and in Ratoath had Leonisius de Bromiard, a major client of Hugh de Lacy, as its first lord. His grant before 1194 of advowsons of parishes to the abbey of St Thomas in Dublin, indicates that he was one of the most prominent sub tenants of the lordship of Meath. His manors included Kilmore, Rathgormley, Derpatrick, Knockmark, Culmullen, Kiltale, Dunshaughlin, Killeglin, Grennoch, Donamore, Ratoath and of course Ballymaglassan.[1] But Ballymaglassan never became a manorial centre. The land of the parish was owned up to the nineteenth century by various lords whose manorial centres were elsewhere. The records are silent about it from the 1194 grant of the parish to the Augustinian monks until, in 1289, a quarrel about land ownership led to a court case involving Nicholas Bacun, sheriff of Meath, and various members of the de Crues family over a carucate, or one hundred and twenty acres (about 350-400 statute acres) of land in Ballymaglassan.[2] As in all law cases the bare bones of the report fall far short of the full proceedings which alone can reveal the issues involved. It seems as if the father of Nicholas Bacun, sheriff of Meath, held the disputed property and was deprived of it by the overlord of Ballymaglassan, Hugh de Lacy, who gave possession of it to Milo de Crues. Crues seemed to have had more influence in England than in Ireland. A grant of free warren (for rabbits) in his demesne lands in Ballymaglassan, given in England, was witnessed by the king's brother, the earl of Cornwall, the bishop of Exeter and the king's chancellor, the bishop of Bath and Wells.[3] The wording implies that the whole manor was possessed by Crues and only a relatively small part of it was involved in the Bacun action. The business was complicated by another action for possession of the carucate of land, taken by Robert Fitzrichard Crues, who was obviously a relation of Milo. Robert did not show up at the time of the court case. Whether this was by accident or design, we do not know, and Milo got possession. The case taken by Nicholas Bacun came up in 1288 with Milo and Robert on the same side and Nicholas failed to appear. The case came up again in 1291, and this time Nicholas was present but Milo did not appear: it turned out afterwards that he could not have attended, as he was in prison at the time of the trial, consigned there by Nicholas de Clare, treasurer of Ireland and archdeacon of Dublin.

In the ensuing appeal Nicholas Bacun did not appear, Milo de Crues had died, and his case was pleaded by one William de Vessy, guardian of Thomas, Milo's son and heir. In 1291 the case came up again and through a technicality Bacun was given possession.[4] The whole case indicates that the de Crues or Cruice family had substantial holdings in Ballymaglassan in the late fourteenth century, that in a very litigious society, technicalities were used by those au fait with the law, like the sheriff of Meath, Nicholas Bacun, to win their cases, and that non appearance at court, then as now, was used by litigants to achieve their purposes. After this series of law cases, Ballymaglassan disappears from the records until the early years of the reign of Edward IV (1473).

Footnotes

1   Register of the Abbey of St.Thomas, Dublin, ed.Gilbert, p242.

2   C.D.I. 1293 to 1301, p374, C.D.I. 1285 to 1292, p265.

3   C.D.I. 1285 to 1292, (1285) p82.

4   C.D.I. 1285 to 1292, p45.

5   C.D.I. 1285 to 1292, p373.

6   C.D.I. 1285 to 1292, p423.

Chapter 9

Kilcloon after Hugh de Lacy: Religion in the six parishes of Kilcloon – 1171 to 1350

Just as the Normans instigated revolutions in land ownership, land settlement and land use, so they brought about a revolution in the organisation of religious life and, though we can only guess at this, in the faith life of the people. Just as Europe came into Ireland first in architecture (at Cormac's chapel in Cashel) and in religious structures like the territorial diocese, and eventually the parish, so those who brought European norms and the organisation of society in feudal ways, the Normans, allied themselves with the Irish who were implementing these reforms in church life. Ireland had been divided up into dioceses at the synods of Rathbrassil (1111) and Kells (1152). The Irishman Eugenius who became bishop of Clonard in 1174, just after the Normans came systematically into Meath, was an enthusiastic champion of new arrangements which were to bind the church to the new lordship and its masters quickly. Parishes were set up in each manor and both priests and churches were financed by a tax called the tithe on all the produce of the land. As Bishop Eugene put it: under penalty of soul, one tenth of grain, cattle, lambs, goats, pigs, wool, flax, ale and hay, all goods renewable in a year (should be given to the church) as "in the holy church throughout the world".[1] In pre Norman days the structures of the church seem to have been financed primarily by income from church property controlled by its hereditary custodians called airceannach or erenaghs. Now that it was to be financed principally by the tithe, it seemed prudent to encourage land owners to hand over to various monasteries responsibility for both church income and church staffing. Otherwise they might be tempted to divert parish income and appoint clergymen on less than proper criteria. That was indeed to happen in the 1540s, when after the Reformation monastic rights and properties were laicised again. The bishop enthusiastically encouraged the lords of the manors to hand over the care of souls in their manorial parishes to various orders of monks, like the Augustinian canons of St Thomas in Dublin and the Victorine canons of St Peter's who took care of the cathedral in Trim (all six parishes in Kilcloon were eventually impropriated or controlled by one or other of these monasteries). That put the appointment of parish clergy firmly in the hands of Norman monks, and perhaps their religious training also. There is evidence that the monks of St. Thomas in Dublin provided for the support and education of twenty five young clerics who lived in the abbey as long as they wished to pursue their studies there. In England, such young clerks were taught plain song and psalter as well as grammar. Perhaps from them came some of the vicars of Moyglare and the chaplains of Ballymaglassan.[2] This arrangement meant that, for the future, the Norman abbots would be in control of the nomination of the parish clergy and so ensure that they were Norman, or at least were conditioned by Norman ethos in service and in law.

In fact, through the whole Middle Ages up to 1500 only one cleric with a Gaelic name, "Chaplain O'Ronain", surfaces in the records of the six parishes of Kilcloon; he was a witness to a deed of Milo le Bret in 1280.[3] There was another inducement to handing over a responsibility for the parishes to an abbey like that of St Thomas: it was a royal foundation set up by the king's representative in Dublin, Fitz Audelen in 1177, and so attracted the attention of nobles who wished to curry royal favour. Perhaps the bishop's encouragement (and that of his successor Simon de Rochfort (1194 – 1224)) reflected his judgement that he could control the monks by canon law a lot easier than he could control the volatile Anglo Norman lords. Above all, de Rochfort encouraged his barons and knights to hand over the parishes to monastic control to ensure that Norman thought processes on church organisation, which were the European norm, could find structural expression in his diocese. In all, fifty nine parishes in Meath, Dublin, Kildare, Wexford and Kilkenny were impropriate, as they called it, to St. Thomas's in Dublin.[4] This great number made it impossible for the abbey to staff all its parishes with its own monks, and in any case since Pope Urban III's time (1185 – 1187) monks were forbidden to serve parishes where they could not return to their abbeys or granges each night.[5] "In ecclesia ubi monachi habitant, populi per monachum non regatur." Such was the policy of the first two bishops of Meath in Norman times, the Irishman Eugene, and Simon de Rochfort who moved the centre of his diocese from Clonard to Trim. De Rochfort died in 1224 and the next two bishops ruled briefly, one for two years and one for three. Then in 1230, a Dublin canon of St. Patrick's, Richard de Angulo (de la Corner or Nangle), was elected bishop by the clergy of Meath. Quite obviously he was chosen to focus on a particular grievance – the down side of the grants of parishes to monasteries like that of St. Thomas. By then, most of the income from the parishes went to the monasteries and the income of those who served in the parishes in general was very small. Besides, the bishop had very limited control over the fabric and personnel of the churches. Richard de la Corner was still only bishop elect when he wrote to the pope, Gregory IX, to appoint a commission to examine and judge the claims of the bishop to the patronage and income of the parishes of Skryne and Tara, and others then in the possession of the abbot and convent of St. Mary, the Cistercian abbey in Dublin, and of the prior and brothers of the hospital of Jerusalem in Ireland.[6] In time he challenged, not only some of the other major abbeys who had been granted the patronage of many parishes in the diocese, but also some of the lay lords who had kept the patronage of their own parishes in their own hands.

The question, of course, transcended that of control by parochial clergy of the income from their parishes; it effectively concerned the power of the bishop over the structures through which the sacraments, the Mass and the rituals of religious life were made available to the people in their parishes. The monasteries had been in effective control of both patronage and income of many parishes since they had been granted them forty or fifty years previously and the challenge to those rights was made by the bishop before two commissions set up by the pope, Gregory IX, (1227-1241) which sat in Drogheda. The first concerned control of the income from the parishes of Skryne and Tara presented to St Mary's, Dublin, by Adam de Feipo, the baron of Skryne, when his brother joined the Cistercian order there. It also concerned other parishes presented to the same abbey, roughly at the same time, by the knights who were de Feipo's vassals. The bishop pleaded the immemorial rights of his predecessors, and the illegality of the monks serving the parishes or appointing those who did. Only the bishop should present and appoint vicars to these parishes, and convert the fruits of the parishes over and above the income due to the vicar, to the bishop's own use as bishop of the diocese. Besides, he claimed that the power of controlling parishes was specifically against the ordinances of the Cistercian order. The monks argued peaceful possession of their privileges for fifty years, an indult from the pope to present to parishes and enjoy the income thereof. They also produced muniments which contained confirmation of these rights by de la Corner's predecessors. The monks won the case, but in compensation they were to pay twenty pounds of silver to the bishop in two tranches, one on the feast of St. Peter in Chains and the other on that of the Purification of the Blessed Virgin Mary. Moreover the bishop was entitled to a butt of wine if the monks were tardy in their payment.[7]

None of this related to the parishes of Kilcloon, but the next challenge did, for it concerned those parishes controlled by the Augustinian abbey of St. Thomas in Dublin, among them Moyglare and Ballymaglassan. Again, the bishop claimed the rights of patronage and control over the income ceded by the lay lords in the first years of the conquest fifty years previously. The abbot and convent, he claimed, took the fruits of the parishes they controlled out of the diocese and province, to the detriment of the common good of the diocese of Meath. Besides, he said, the monasteries were forbidden by canon law from personally serving in those parishes and from appointing vicars there by ordinary authority.

The abbot and convent replied that the right to present to these parishes and to enjoy the income of the parishes had been given by the lay lords, and this had been confirmed, not only by the bishop of the diocese but also by his holiness, the pope, himself. The benefices, moreover, had been enjoyed peacefully for the preceding fifty years. To the bishop's point about extracting the fruits of the parishes for spending in Dublin, they claimed that it had never been specified that the income had to be spent in Meath. It was perfectly legal that, necessary expenditure being deducted, these incomes could be spent on the provision of hospitality in Dublin and on the sustenance of the brethren there. Besides, and this perhaps was one of the nubs of the altercation, the abbot and his convent were not compelled to create vicarages and appoint vicars to them; they could appoint mere chaplains, especially in cases where there was no income adequate for a vicar in a particular parish. This commission settled the income of the vicarages impropriate to St. Thomas's. In the list of parishes which had vicars, the vicar of Moyglare was to have an income of seven marks (four pounds thirteen and fourpence) (Ratoath had fifteen marks, Laraghcor had thirteen, Knockmark ten, Dunshaughlin ten, Trevett one hundred shillings, Kilmore ten marks, Culmullen six, Sydden ten and Donaghmore, near Babesbridge, Navan, had ten). A reflection of the stability of monetary value and of the significance of the decisions of this commission is the fact that almost three hundred years later, the rent paid by the then lay inheritor of the patronage of Moyglare was exactly seven marks or four pounds thirteen and fourpence, and indeed it was to be the rent paid to the crown for the next century after that.[9] The tithes of Dunshaughlin, too, were leased in 1540 for six pounds, thirteen and fourpence, the same sum (ten marks) which had been the vicar's agreed income in 1235. There was no list of approved salaries for chaplains.

An agreement was brokered by the papal delegates. The abbey and monks were to present vicars or chaplains to the parishes to be instituted by the bishop. The bishop was to have an ongoing responsibility for supervising the parochial clergy.

The vicars were to be responsible for ordinary expenditure in the parish church (one presumes that meant vestments, sacred vessels and all things necessary for saying Mass, conferring the sacraments and burying the dead). The abbot and convent were responsible with the vicar for extraordinary expenditure according to the proportion of parish income each enjoyed. As far as chaplains were concerned, both ordinary and extraordinary expenditure was to be the responsibility of the abbey in Dublin. A convention emerged eventually that the vicar and monastery were responsible for the chancel or sanctuary area of the church and the parishioners for the nave or body area. In practice, it was the lord of the manor who had the real responsibility for the nave or body of the church. The abbot and convent were responsible for ecclesiastical tax, which was not to be noticeably out of kilter with that payable at the time of the settlement of differences.

Strangely to our customs there was much emphasis on the obligation of the abbey to provide hospitality in Dublin and of the vicars to provide hospitality in their parishes. Those vicarages which were of some prominence, were usually easily accessible from the king's highway and so provided the service nowadays provided by hotels or inns. The chaplaincies were excused this obligation; though some of them could afford to do so, and others were near the granges of the abbey (abbey farms, as at Trevett) which had the burdens of providing hospitality, others were both "poor and far from the public roads and the confluence of people". The high proportion of monastic income needed to provide necessary hospitality in Dublin (perhaps among the demands on the monastic income was the providing of bed, board and lodgings to the twenty five young clerks above mentioned) was accepted as sufficient to justify the abbey having the higher proportion of parish income in those parishes served by chaplains. The salaries of the chaplains, though not spelt out in cash terms, were to be those decided already in a provincial council held at Drogheda in the time of Donatus O Fidabra, Archbishop of Armagh 1227 to 1237. Presumably this was the norm against which could be measured the discharge of the monastic responsibilities to the curates of the parishes, when both the local bishop through his rural deans, and the archbishop of Armagh, in his inspection every three years of the dioceses in his province, examined the fabric and structures and personnel of the parishes.

The decrees of the delegates were acceptable to both sides. Silence was imposed in the matter and if either of the parties, bishop or abbot, or their successors, were to challenge any of the decrees the offending party was subject to a fine of a thousand pounds of silver.

To compensate the diocese and bishop for the parish income which left the diocese for the abbey in Dublin, the patronage of the parishes of Nobber, Kilpatrick, Knock, "Dissert" and Dunmoe were to be transferred to the bishop. In fact Nobber, a parish with a high income, became attached to one of the two archdeacons who were, after the bishop, the principal officers in the government of the diocese. The agreements between the bishop and the two Dublin monasteries are the only two surviving from the Middle Ages. They are contained in two sets of foundation documents carefully preserved in St Mary's and in St Thomas's (and as we have seen used to good effect in disputes with the bishop).[10] They have been published in the last hundred years. There must have been other documents of agreement between the bishop and the other religious orders with head houses inside and outside the diocese. Judging by the extent of monastic properties drawn up in 1540 consequent on confiscations, the same kind of solution must have been effected in those cases also.

In Kilcloon parish, apart from Moyglare and Ballymaglassan, Rathregan was impropriate to the Victorine or Augustine canons of Newtown, in Trim, who served the diocesan cathedral there; Kilclone itself, Rodanstown and Balfeighan were still controlled by the Hussey, barons of Galtrim. Bishop de la Corner, as we shall see, was more successful in challenging the rights of the Husseys to appoint the rectors of Galtrim and the chaplaincies attached to it, of Kilclone, Rodanstown, Balfeighan, Gallo and Drumlargan, than he was in the case of the parishes of his diocese impropriate to the different monasteries.

The two decisions at Drogheda made by the papal commission formed part of a debate ongoing in the universal church, surfacing in discussions at general councils, and in the decrees of successive popes. It concerned the control of the parochial structures in the diocese and was central to the faith life in the parishes. What control were the monasteries to have over the appointment of parochial secular priests and over the income of parishes? In Meath, over half of the parishes were in monastic control for most of the Middle Ages and it was only at the Council of Trent (1547-1554) that all responsibility for the faith life of the people, making available to them of the Mass and the sacraments, was concentrated in the hands of the local bishop. Strangely, as we can see, the transfer by the state of the control the monks had enjoyed over parochial appointments, to lay people, in the reign of Henry VIII, was one of the main reasons why Ireland did not become Protestant and it was the complete control over parish appointments, over the faith life of the parishes placed in the hands of the Catholic bishop by the Council of Trent that ensured that Ireland became a Catholic island in a northern and Protestant sea.

As far as faith practice was concerned, little evidence survives to enable us at this distance to make judgements if indeed they are ever possible. But church legislation of the Middle Ages concerned the enforcement of the payment of tithes, the provision of Mass and the sacraments, the ritual and liturgy involved, the enforcing of the decrees of Canon Law on marriage and on clerical life. In Kilcloon there were holy wells at Bridestream in Rodanstown parish and at Ballymaglassan which attracted vast crowds until the beginning of the nineteenth century on the feast days of St. Brigid at the former and of St. Kieran at the latter. Easter confession and even weekday Mass-going seems normal from one incident that has come down to us in an account of a court case (chapter 20). In the beginning of Norman Kilcloon there were grants of rights to Dublin monasteries who provided social services and who ran hospitals and there were grants of property to sustain the fabric of the two cathedrals in Dublin. The archbishops of Armagh took very seriously their triennial visitation to Meath which they made usually through commissioners. Some of their registers have survived which show that their concern was with the fabric of the churches, the life of the clergy, the adequacy of their income, and the presence of public sin in areas like marriage, clerical concubinage and the alienation of church property. Incidentally, these registers tell of Easter communion and duty, the expected norms governing marriage and married life and the organisation of worship and ritual in parish churches. No Meath episcopal register of the yearly visitation of the bishop has survived but they surely concerned the same preoccupations as the archiepiscopal registers of Armagh. From the synod of 1216 this obligation of visitation was placed primarily on the rural deans.[11] The dean of Ratoath/ Dunshaughlin supervised Ballymaglassan and Rathregan, the dean of Skryne, the other four parishes. In reading the account of the visitation of Archbishop Sweetman of Armagh in 1377[12]. there are indications that receiving holy communion at Easter was a normal practice and that in many parishes there was, in the public life of the church, nothing untoward to report. The churches were looked on as sacred places and in them malefactors could claim sanctuary. As the initial Norman successes began to suffer from some strain, there was a growth of lawlessness even in Kilcloon. Court cases of murders and robberies appear in the records as much as they do today but there was no public questioning of the Christian faith. There was corruption at times in its structures but its claim and responsibility to guide all through life to eternity was taken for granted, especially in a society where life, even for the rich, was short, and often ended suddenly, and that of the poor was focused much of the time on survival from one day to the next.

As far as the churches are concerned in which people worshipped, received the sacraments, heard the word of God preached, or sought sanctuary when for one misdemeanour or another they were pursued by the law, little enough remains on the ground. Of the six parishes in Kilcloon, the medieval church has been completely replaced in three parishes by modern or relatively modern Protestant churches; in the others, only bits and pieces have survived, mostly from the later Middle Ages. The earlier churches mentioned in the records have left at best their ground plans in the form of stumps of side walls. Every one of them is surrounded by a cemetery. Once a church was built, people wanted their dead buried as near the church as possible (inside if they had the muscle to insist on it) so that the relations and friends every week on their way to Mass would remember them and pray for them in the presence of God. Ironically, nowadays these churches are gone and only the abandoned graveyards, seldom visited, remain.

The Synod of 1216

In 1216 Simon de Rochfort, first Norman Bishop of Meath, held a synod in his cathedral in Trim, which was then being built. Its ruins even today are impressive. Fittingly, de Rochfort's effigy is inserted in one of the walls. It was the largest cathedral in medieval Ireland and was staffed by the Victorine canons of St. Augustine from their monastery of Sts. Peter and Paul in Trim. (See illustration of Simon de Rochfort in Trim Cathedral, p v). The decrees of the Synod have survived and they established how the diocese of Meath was to be organised until relatively modern times.

Evidently in pre-Norman times there were quite a few bishops in what is now the diocese of Meath. In the early Christian church there were monasteries, bishoprics and hereditary ecclesiastical families who controlled church property. This synod (see illustration of its cathedral, p v) set up new structures in what is now County Meath, which fifty years afterwards were extended to the western half of the diocese. The synod was the final act in a process by which the bishopric of Meath became coterminous with the liberty of Meath, an indication of that close relationship between church and state characteristic of the Norman colony. Not without significance was the moving of the centre of the diocese from the Early Christian monastery of Clonard to the caput of the new liberty, Trim. In future the bishoprics of Trim, Slane, Kells, Skyrne and Dunshaughlin were to be suppressed as their bishops died, and they were to be replaced by rural deaneries headed by an arch-priest who would not only live there but also have a care and responsibility for both priests and their parishioners. Not unreasonably the arch-priest had to be a priest first. When he died or was deposed the bishop alone had the right to replace him.

Each year he had to visit each parish in his deanery and regard the condition of the parish churches. The dean was to exhort the parishioners to repair the fabric if that were needed. They were to ensure that the houses of pastors and chaplains were properly roofed. They were to regard corrupt habits in the parishes, and, if these were not rooted out, the problem was to be referred to a synod of bishop and clergy.

A fair indication of the furnishings of the church was an admonition to the deans to ensure that books, vases, vestments, and other ornaments were to be properly kept. Strangely there is no mention of chalices. They were to see to it that canonical penances imposed by the bishop or by his officials on delinquents be duly proclaimed with fitting solemnity in the churches of the deanery. On admission to office the archpriests were to take an oath to discharge their responsibilities faithfully. These were to include presenting to the bishop or his officials, the names and surnames of every individual within the deanery who, with good reason, was charged or suspected of some infamy which was to be corrected or punished by episcopal authority.

The deaneries were to meet the clergy of their deaneries every three weeks, personally or through their messengers, or in an extraordinary gathering if some matter of grave consequence judged as such by the bishop, was to be communicated. The deans were to take special care that lay people did not have undue influence on or intrude into the benefices or parishes. The diocesan provincial decrees were to be constantly explained to the priests in each deanery "lest they sin through ignorance". It was the responsibility of the priests to explain those decrees which concerned them to the ordinary people.

The archpriests or deans were prohibited from involving themselves in the making of wills, dealing with matrimonial cases, or cases of simony and of criminal cases involving the clergy for which deprivation of the benefice was the penalty. The rural deans were prohibited too from exercising unfair exactions on their subjects, either personally, or by using others to do so. Finally, if the deans were negligent, remiss or disobedient, and this was obvious from the testament of worthy witnesses, then they were to be suspended until they mended their ways.

These decrees were intended to complement the triennial visitation of the archbishop of Armagh and to ensure that both the rights and responsibilities of the clergy in providing for the pastoral care of their parishioners were properly observed.

The last bishop of Kells to appear on the records died in 1211 and it was no coincidence that the rural deaneries which in one form or another have survived to the present day, in many cases roughly reflect not only the boundaries of the Norman baronies but also the boundaries of the tuatha which formed petty kingdoms in pre-Norman days. The deaneries indicate that continuity beneath the colonisation and church reform, which was a characteristic of all medieval history. For the record four of our parishes were in the deanery of Skyrne – Kilclone, Balfeighan, Rodanstown and Moyglare. The other two, Rathregan and Ballymaglassan, were in the deanery of Ratoath/ Dunshaughlin. The modern parish of Kilcloon is in the deanery of Skyrne and there is in each deanery a vicar forane, the modern equivalent of the arch priest who replaced the bishops in pre-Norman Meath. Reflecting the gradual extension of Norman presence in the west of the diocese, Ardnurcher, Mullingar, Ballymore Loughseudy and Fore became rural deaneries about 1265. Duleek and Clonard became rural deaneries at the same time.

Footnotes

Kilcloon after Hugh de Lacy:
Religion in the six parishes of Kilcloon – 1171 to 1350

1   Register of the Abbey of St.Thomas, p259.

2   Anglo Irish Church Life, 14th and 15th centuries, A. Gwynn in A History of Irish Catholicism, Vol.2, p30, 31.

3   Register of St.Thomas, No.259.

4   Extents of Irish Monastic Possessions, 1540 to 1541, ed.White, p25 ff, Register of St.Thomas, passim

5   The Poor Vicars Plea (1704), Thomas Ryves, p42, ff.

6   Chartularies of St.Mary's Abbey, Dublin, ed.Gilbert, p165.

7   Ibid, p165.

8   Register of St. Thomas, p243, ff.

9   Ibid, p243, 244; Extents of Monastic Possessions, p36; Calendar of Inquisitions, Elizabeth 1627, 5343, 6132.

10 Register of St.Thomas, p243 and 246.

11 WILKINS, Concilia, Vol.1, p547.

12 A Calendar of the Register of Archbishop Sweetman, ed.Lawlor, p219 ff., (Proc.R.I.A., XXIXC(1911)).

The Synod of 1216

1   WILKINS, Concilia, Vol 1, p547. The surviving synodal decrees of Irish medieval dioceses seemed to be copies of decrees drawn up in England for English dioceses. The Meath synodal decrees are the exception and hence reflect more than any other, conditions in the diocese itself.

Chapter 10

The Church in Moyglare –
1171 to 1350

When Hugh de Lacy was granted the liberty of Meath by Henry II, he obviously began its construction in the areas nearest Dublin where the land suited the military technology of his barons, knights and men. He granted Hugh de Hosee what became known as the barony of Deece and that included the manor of Moyglare and the right of appointment (advowson) to the church there. De Hosee for reasons unknown gave Moyglare back to de Lacy who granted it to "my intrinsic friend" Hugh Tyrrell.[1] They fell out, as we have seen, about 1184, and some time later Tyrrell granted the manor to Milo le Bret, his neighbour at Rathfarnham.[2] It was Milo le Bret, in Bishop Eugene's time, who handed over the church of Moyglare to the abbey of St Thomas in Dublin. It had been founded by the justiciar or king's representative in Dublin, Fitz Audelen, in 1177. The monastery was subject to the rules of the canons regular of St Augustine of Arroasie, in northern France, which had been introduced to Ireland by St. Malachy. The grant – and in it is the first mention of a church building at Moyglare – was confirmed in 1202 by John Cardinal di Salerno, papal legate in Ireland.[3] There were at least twenty churches in Meath handed over to the monastery of St. Thomas, including that at Ballimaglassan. As we have seen they were staffed by secular priests. These were presented to the bishop of the diocese as fit in knowledge and character for ordination, and began their priestly life as chaplains. Then they had to wait for an appointment as vicar or priest in charge of the small parishes, made by the abbot of the monastery in Dublin. That there was a constant presence of chaplains here is indicated by surviving evidence. There is evidence also of absenteeism of vicars. In 1309 the provost of the chapter of Limerick was directed by the curia in Rome to accede to the request of Master John de Lascapon for a canonry of Limerick with reservations of a prebend for one John de Farrendon, "not withstanding he has a canonry and prebend of Clonfert and the vicarage of Mancle (Moyglare) in the diocese of Meath". As a condition of permission to remain an absentee, de Farrendon had an obligation to provide for the pastoral needs of Moyglare by appointing a chaplain to it. Such absenteeism often indicated a priest or cleric who, in making a career for himself in the papal service in Rome, at court in England or in church governance in Ireland, needed an income to sustain his position .[4]

The name of four vicars of Moyglare have come down to us. Richard Felde witnessed a deed in 1379, John of Farrendon was vicar in 1309, one Henry in 1332 and William White in 1380.[5] Again if a rector or vicar needed a substitute, he had to commend a chaplain and present him to the abbot of St. Thomas's in Dublin for approval.

There were many chaplains living in small farms about Moyglare who evidently did not have official or permanent appointments to parishes. This we know from the fortuitous survival of the deeds of a small piece of property, (about 60 statute acres), in Bryanstown and Rodanstown presented in 1488 by one Francis Estrete, sergeant at law, to the canons of Christ Church to finance perpetually a yearly Mass of the Holy Ghost for his soul and the souls of his family. By the earliest deed (1280) one John de Bruyn granted the property to his son Thomas; Sir Geoffrey Brett was lord of Moyglare and the deed was witnessed by Sir W (no name given) vicar of Moyglare, Richard the Forester, (was he the ancestor of the Fosters who held Kilgraigue in 1415?), Walter Fitz Andrew and John the clerk. The conquest of a century before had laid down structures through which land was held, which were now deep rooted and normal, feudal and Norman – no Gaelic surname appears in these deeds.

In 1280, Reginald de Bruyn, clerk, granted to Thomas de Bruyn a field called Aedcnuk in the tenement of Moyglare (in fact in Bryanstown) and among the witnesses to the deed were Walter de Bruyn, Walter Fitz Andrew and Hugh the clerk. By 1398 Thomas, son of William Boys (Boyce) released to Nicholas Sex (or Seys), chaplain, and John Sex, a messuage, curtilage (yard) arable land, wood and pasture in Bryanstown to take effect after his death; while he lived the yearly rent was a rose and the feudal services due to the lord of the manor. By 1401 it was a Thomas Hore who granted it to William Hore and Robert Walsh, Richard Rede, Robert Stakepool, William Cornewalsh and Richard Ectore, all chaplains. In 1415 Richard Foster of Kilgraigue, John Hussey of Balrodden, Richard and Maurice Seys of Maynooth witnessed the transfer by John Seys of Balrodden of his properties in Bryanstown in the lordship of Moyglare and in Balrodden in the lordship of Galtrim to Thomas Spark and Nicholas Nugent, chaplains.

In 1439, a messuage "with a dovecote lately built thereon" in Balrodden, and a messuage, thirty acres of land, an acre of wood and three acres of meadow in Bryanstown were granted by James Marschall of Clane, chaplain, to John – son of Thomas Seys of Dublin. Marschall had been given the property by Nicholas Seys, a chaplain. The same properties were granted by Matilda, alias Moldyn Arthure, daughter of Janet Seys, sister and heiress of John Seys, late of Dublin, clerk, in 1485 to Francis Estrete, sergeant at law.

In the same year, her son, John Welsh, handed over to Estrete premises in Dublin granted him by Martin Brune – chaplain. In 1488 Estrete handed over Bryanstown and Balrodden properties in trust for the canons of Christ Church to two clerics in Dublin, Master John Warying, rector of Mulhuddart and Sir Thomas Laundy of Dublin, chaplain, together with properties in Crumlin and in Midnighastoun near Colpe, south of Drogheda. The property was leased out to Lawrence Delahyde in 1587 and seems to have been disposed of before 1654.[6] The profusion of chaplains in every generation seems to point to a clerical way of life, a little like that of many Greek Orthodox parish clergy of today. A small income from the church being insufficient to sustain a reasonable living on its own, the clerics were indeed, like their successors of the penal days, small or middle sized farmers with property which seemed to fall into the hands of clerics in succeeding generations.

Of course the tithes – or one tenth of the produce of the lands – went to the abbey of St. Thomas in Dublin; it is reckoned that in general one third of the parish income went to the local clergyman. The standard income of the chaplains was three marks (two pounds ten shillings) per year, the wages of an unskilled labourer in thirteenth century England. It was the responsibility of the archbishop of the northern province to visitate the dioceses in his province every three years, either in person or through his officials, and it was his obligation to ensure that the Mass and sacraments were available to the parishioners of each parish. The bishop had rural deans who, in their yearly visitation, had the same duty; – to examine the fabric of the churches and ensure that those who served as vicars in parishes attached to monasteries were properly paid. We know that there was a church in Moyglare by 1202, but little is known about it. Perhaps it began as a small rectangular building with a thatched roof, and then because of his wealth the local lord built a stone rectangular building like those seen all over Meath, with a double bell cote "and a few rooms at the west end to accommodate the priest of the parish". The chancel or altar area was separate from the nave, but whether the separation could be identified externally at Moyglare we do not know. Unfortunately for the record the church was completely replaced by a nineteenth century Protestant church before Dean Cogan in his history of the diocese of Meath could record its measurements. No medieval tombstones survive on the ground though no doubt there are Delahyde tombs still under the surface.

Just as speculation on the size or decoration of the church of Moyglare must be based on the ruins of churches surviving on the Meath landscape, which must have been its models, so must speculation on the faith life and practices of the people be based upon what we know of the broad context in Meath at this time. Very little evidence survives to allow us perceive the nature and the quality of the way the people of Moyglare lived their faith in the early Middle Ages.

Footnotes

1   C.D.I. 1285 to 1292, No.1075 (p470)

2   C.D.I. 1285 to 1292, p470.

3   Register of the Abbey of St.Thomas. p224.

4   Calendar of Papal Letters, Clement V, 1309.

5   Christ Church Deeds, 739. In the lease of 61 years to Laurance Delahyde a fine of two fat beeves is mentioned "towards the reparation of the steeple" of Christ Church. The yearly rent was 20 shillings Irish and the extent was 28 acres, probably about 60 statute acres.

6   Christ Church Deeds, 744, 762, 790, 929, 930, 933, 949, 350, 348, 100; The First Chapter Book of Christ Church Cathedral, Dublin, 1574 to 1634, ed.Gillespie, p44.

Chapter 11

The Church of Galtrim and its chaplaincies at Kilclone, Balfeighan and Rodanstown – 1171 to 1350

Just as the Husseys, barons of Galtrim, successfully kept what normally would have been discrete manors in their barony, to ensure long term control over them, so they also successfully kept what should have been the separate parishes of Kilclone, Balfeighan and Rodanstown, together with Gallo and Drumlargan, as chaplaincies to swell the income of their rectory of Galtrim. The rectory of Galtrim in consequence became the source of tension between the Husseys, the bishop, and eventually the Augustinian monks of the cathedral at Trim. In the taxation survey of the early thirteen hundreds Galtrim had an income of forty pounds thirteen and fourpence which made it, after Kells, where the archdeacon was next to the bishop in position and had an income of eighty pounds, the second richest parish in the diocese. Its only rival in the income stakes was Trim, which had an income of forty pounds nine shillings and two pence. Moyglare, as we have seen, had a good income of ten pounds, Ballymaglassan one of six pounds thirteen and four pence and that of Rathregan, which was nearer the diocesan average than any of the others mentioned, was three pounds six and eightpence.[1]

As we have seen, there were a number of related reasons why the Norman lords gave responsibility for the religious life of their manors to the various religious orders, principally the Augustinian canons and the Cistercians of St Mary's Abbey in Dublin. The down side of the arrangement was of course the diluting of the bishop's control over those who staffed the parishes of his diocese, though the visitation of the archbishop and of the rural deans of the diocese went some way to ensuring the integrity of the incumbents and the payment to them by the monasteries of a reasonable income. The problem with the three parishes in the barony of Deece, Kilclone, Rodanstown and Balfeighan, was that they were chaplaincies not controlled by a monastery but controlled by the Husseys who were barons of Galtrim. They were in a more fluid state than the other parishes in Kilcloon as regards income: private arrangement, especially as there was an over-supply of priests looking for appointments, could not have favoured the chaplains appointed.

We have seen that Bishop Richard de la Corner in the beginning of his episcopate tried to assert control over those parishes which had been granted to the various abbeys by the Norman lords fifty years before. He had relied on a papal commission to do so, but the result only confirmed the privileges of the abbeys involved. The bishop relied on less legal instruments in his differences with Walter Hussey over control of the parish of Galtrim and its chaplaincies. Evidently Walter had committed some serious crime in a church context for which he was excommunicated. The bishop proposed to lift the excommunication if Walter would hand over to him the right to appoint to Galtrim. Negotiations, as they say, were ongoing, but before they could be completed to everyone's satisfaction, Walter was killed at a place called Fynerath. It was then that the bishop moved somewhat over the frontiers of legality. He refused to allow Walter to be buried on church grounds until Lucy, his wife, handed over the keys of her husband's deed chest. There Bishop de la Corner found Walter's seal and used it to confirm a document he drew up transferring the avowson of Galtrim to the bishop of Meath and his successors. The then rector, one Philip le Norman, was expelled and the bishop appointed a very talented and ambitious young man, William de la Corner, his own son, to the vacant parish. Naturally there was a hue and cry locally but the bishop was a determined man and his decision prevailed.[2] So things rested as William de la Corner went on from strength to strength in his career in the church both in Ireland and in England. A canon in the chapter of St Patrick's in Dublin, he got permission to hold extra benefices in 1256 besides Galtrim and Athboy, which had an income of thirty eight pounds. Obviously his talents were recognised in England where he became rector of Skipworth, Yorkshire, in 1257, a canon of Salisbury in 1264, a canon and prebend of Exeter in 1267 and was one of the two candidates for the vacant archbishopric of Dublin in 1271. The chapter of St. Patrick's elected him but the chapter of Christ Church chose Figmund Le Bruin, then chancellor of Ireland. The pope put Le Bruin aside because of irregularities in holding benefices, De La Corner withdrew his nomination; the pope selected someone else. William's career was crowned by appointment as Bishop of Salisbury in 1288 where he died in 1291. His strength was in law and in public life. He had been a papal chaplain since 1256, legal advisor to Christ Church Cathedral Priory at Canterbury and gave service at the curia of Archbishop Pecham there in 1280.

He went on royal mission in 1269, 1271 and 1289 and was a procurator at the papal curia. He is buried in the nave of Salisbury Cathedral "between the morning altar and the altar of the Holy Spirit". A contemporary supplied his epitaph "magnae authoritatis virum tunc regni consiliorum", a man of great authority in the councils of the kingdom.[3]

When appointed to Salisbury in 1288 he had to relinquish some of his benefices – including Galtrim. It was then that Hugh Hosee, Walter's nephew and heir, took the opportunity to recall Bishop Richard's illegalities of many years before and claim his right to nominate the next rector of Galtrim. The bishop, Thomas St. Leger, asserted the claims of the bishop and the case was heard in Trim where the de Genevilles ruled half of the old de Lacy inheritance as a quasi independent fiefdom. Hugh Hosee produced in court "free and lawful men of the venue of Galtrim" before de Geneville's sheriff and won his case to nominate to the parish, and got damages of fifty marks (thirty three pounds six and eightpence) which was not far from the yearly income of the rectory. The rectory of Galtrim then went back to the Hussey family but sometime before Bishop St Leger died in 1320 he had replaced Hussey as impropriator of the parish.[4]

Unfortunately, the wealth of the rectory attracted people like William de la Corner who needed the major income from a number of parishes to sustain their high-flying careers in Ireland, England or in Rome. The canon law stated that in certain circumstances the appointments to parishes devolved on Rome where an institution called the Datary dealt with the numerous and conflicting claims on parishes emanating from all over the church. Among the reasons for the devolution of appointments to Rome was election to high office in the church and pluralism without dispensation. Often facts at Rome didn't quite tally with those at home, and there was much material for lawyers to work on. Galtrim provides examples of many problems caused by its wealth and the attention of lawyers. One William de Clare, after the Council of Lyon (1274) obtained the church of Braffeston in the diocese of York, Beanover in the diocese of Cork, and a canonry and prebend in the church at Arbrekan (Ardbraccan, the residence of the medieval bishops of Meath) to which, it was claimed, the parish of Galtrim was annexed.[5]

Obviously it was not thus annexed, and in any case, the good lawyer, William de la Corner would not have taken kindly to William de Clare's claim. However, soon after de la Corner's elevation to Salisbury in 1288, the bishop of Bath, who was also the king's chancellor, got a dispensation for William de Clare to become the rector of the parish of Galtrim.[6] By one of the coincidences of history the mechanism for collecting de Clare's income from Galtrim has survived. William's brother, Nicholas, treasurer of Ireland and archdeacon of Swords proved to be short in moneys due to the crown, and William, who had substituted for his brother when he was in England, was observed removing some parchment membranes from the treasury and was investigated. In 1292 one Edmund de Burford produced in Trim the fruits of the church of Galtrim for de Clare, thirteen pounds six and eightpence. In 1293/94 master Geoffrey de Bath produced the fruits of Galtrim at Trim. For the Hilary term they were eleven pounds six and eightpence. The total of goods came in value to thirty-one pounds six and eightpence. At Easter 1295 Edmund de Burford and Geoffrey de Bath produced thirteen pounds six and eightpence at Trim, which was the caput or capital of the de Geneville lordship of Meath. More details given include a sum of forty shillings from Hugh Hussey, baron of Galtrim and four pounds four shillings from William, the vicar of Knockmark. Evidently, de Clare held also the benefice of Kells, County Kilkenny, for which he received five pounds six and eightpence. The total income came to sixty-four pounds thirteen and fourpence, a very considerable sum in medieval Ireland.[7]

Just as our knowledge about the relationship between the abbey of St. Thomas and the parishes of Moyglare and Ballymaglassan comes from law cases, so also does our knowledge of the fortunes of the rectory of Galtrim and its chaplaincies. This is both an advantage and a disadvantage. On the one hand, bitter lawsuits allow the myths of uncertainty about the medieval past to roll back and reveal living human beings about their interesting but usually nefarious business. On the other hand, no society can be judged by the law suits that its members bring against one another. From the whole fourteenth century nothing survives about faith life in Galtrim. Perhaps one could sum up its history as the archiepiscopal visitators summed up the state of affairs in Ballymaglassan in 1377. Nihil sciunt nisi bonum: (they knew nothing but what is good about it).

Little enough of the medieval parish churches of the chaplaincies of Galtrim remain. In Kilclone, some walls can be seen, showing it to have been twenty one metres long, making the nave only a metre or so short of that of Rathregan. No features survive to indicate when the church, whose ruins are there now, was built and there is no reference to the church or to its chaplains all through the Middle Ages. Kilclone was never the centre of a manor, and where a church is beside the residence of the lord as it is in Moyglare, Balfeighan and Rodanstown, one can make a case for dating the origins of the church to the Norman conquest and the subinfeudation of the area. Kilclone was held by the Husseys of Galtrim as one of the manors of the barony and they held it directly from the de Lacy and de Geneville and Mortimer lords of the liberty of Meath. Only in 1406 did the baron of Galtrim set up one of his younger sons, Nicholas, as lord of the manor, to hold it directly from the lord of the liberty. He built the manor house at Mulhussey, four miles from the parish church. These faint hints, taken with the place name, the church of the meadow, seemed to point to a pre-Norman ecclesiastical site where the graveyard now is. From 1406 the centre of the manor of Kilclone was at Mulhussey, and obviously to convenience the lord of the manor and his family, a small church was built there (it is only 8.54 metres long) to serve the family, and a small graveyard was constructed to bury them. Both are fifteenth century in origin and coincide with the beginning of the separation of the manor from that of Galtrim. A number of stones in the fifteenth century style have survived. (See illustration of stones from Mulhussey with ogee arches in the 15th century style, p vii).

The church of Balfeighan is about two-thirds the length of the church of Kilclone, and has a chancel or altar area separate from the nave. Fragments of the chancel arch remain and there is an ogee arched window, both features of High Gothic fifteenth century buildings in Meath. (See illustration of fragments from Balfeighan Church with 15th century featues, p viii). The Husseys had leased the manor to the earls of Kildare and in the mid fifteenth century, Thomas, the seventh earl, gave it to his second son, Thomas, together with the manor of Lackagh, in County Kildare. This branch of the Kildare family held Balfeighan until the plantation of Cromwell. It seems reasonable to connect what must have been a substantial and costly rebuilding of the church to the Kildare presence in the manor, and specifically to the establishment of the manor for the junior branch of the family. The proximity of the church to the centre of the manor seems to point to a Norman origin of the first church there, built, no doubt, soon after the Norman conquest, by a family now unknown, who were then substantial tenants of the Husseys of Galtrim .

Not far from Balfeighan church is Kilrory. Now it is only a mound topping a graveyard. There was a church there fifteen and a half metres long, and Dean Cogan reports a local tradition of its once having been a monastery.[8] But it does not appear in any medieval documents and presumably it had no income from the parish. It is too near what was the parish church of the chaplain to have been a family church for the lords of the manor. The indications are that there was a pre-Norman church on the site. Its Gaelic name – Kilrory, Cill Ruaire – seems to support that claim.

Rodanstown is a small parish. The medieval church was replaced by a Protestant one, perhaps by the owner and builder of Rodanstown House, the Speaker Connolly, in the early eighteenth century and so even the size of the old church can only be guessed at. (See illustration of Rodanstown Church, p viii). There still exists a substantial vault beneath the church which perhaps is medieval in origin. The name of only one priest serving there in the whole of the Middle Ages has survived in the records. Peter, clerk of Balrodden, had land east of an acre of land worth twelve pence a year, which Symon, son of Gordon, granted about 1240 to the hospital of St. John the Baptist in Dublin.[9] Evidently Peter was one of the many chaplains in the area who worked their own tenancies as well. The tenancy in Rodanstown, with that of Bryanstown in nearby Moyglare, given over by Francis Lestrete in 1485 to Christ Church in Dublin, shows in the relevant deeds the presence of many chaplains, unbeneficed clergy in fact, as tenant farmers all through the Middle Ages in both Moyglare and in Rodanstown.[10]

Galtrim and its chaplaincies disappear from the records for the whole of the fourteenth century but at its end however it figures in a flurry of benefice collecting in the Roman curia, an activity associated with the presence there of a remarkable cleric of the diocese of Kildare called John Swayne.

Footnotes

1   C.D.I. 1293 to 1301, p259.

2   C.D.I. 1285 to 1292, p233, ff.

3   The career of William de la Corner is summarised in Pontificia Hibernica, Sheehy, p259; Fasti Ecclesiae Sansberiensis, W.H.Jones, p198; Calendar of Papal Registers, Papal Letters, Vol.1, p333, 418, 457

4   C.D.I. 1285 to 1292, p234; Chancery Miscellanea, 1289, 17, Edward I, Analecta VIII, p263; Rot. Pat. et Claus, Hib.Calend, p221, No.III (10). Plea Rolls, vol III, 19, Edw.1 (1290 – 91) Master Wm Barbador (Officialis of Meath), Master Austin of Notingham and Master Henry Serle, acting in the place of Thomas, Bishop of Meath, who is abroad, refuse to admit a cleric presented by Hugh Hussey to Galtrim. They produced a document dated Dublin, Saturday after the feast of St. Luke, a.r. 17, Oct 1289 whereby Hugh Husse remits to Bishop Thomas and his successors all rights and claim which the parson of Galtrim had.

5   Calendar of Papal Registers, Papal Letters, Vol I, Nicholas IV, (1292), p550.

6   C.D.I. 1285 to 1292, p296. William de Clare in 1289-90 was locum tenens of the treasurer, his brother Nicholas, who was in England. Evidently some irregularities in the treasury funds took place and the brothers concealed them. In an interchange between William and certain merchants of the society of Ricardi of Lucca in Italy, who were claiming the right to levy new customs by royal decree, William showed himself powerful, forceful and determined in opposition; the affair seemes complicated and perhaps William was desperate! Ibid. p598.

7   C.D.I. 1293 to 1301, p197.

8   COGAN, Vol.2, p361, 40, 61, 90, 136, 197.

9   Register of the Hospital of St.John the Baptist, Dublin, No.248.

10   Christ Church Deeds, Nos. 100, 350, 348, 744, 762, 790, 929, 930, 933 and 949.

Chapter 12

The Churches of Rathregan and Ballymaglassan – 1171 to 1350

Rathregan manor fell to the Blount family at the conquest and it was one of the manors in Hugh de Lacy's own barony of Ratoath. Blount handed the responsibility for the appointment of the parish priest and the income of the parish to the Victorine canons of Trim who were responsible for the cathedral of the diocese there. The handing over was confirmed on 2 July, 1330 when Hugh, son of John Blount of Rathregan handed over to the monks of Trim a pond in Rathregan and the advowson of the parish. One Peter de Kermerthym on the same day handed over two parts of all corn and two parts of tythes of hay to the same monks.[1] Obviously there was a need for parochial income to support the cathedral at Trim for which the monks were responsible and among the parishes impropriated to St Peter's in Trim was the parish of Rathregan. It seems that the abbey appointed not vicars but chaplains there. In the tax returns of about 1300 the income from the parish was about five marks, or four pounds per year. The vicarage is stated as worth nothing "because it does not suffice for burdens".[2] Nothing survives of the early church in Rathregan as it was replaced in the fifteenth century by a church of which the ruins still remain.

Ballymaglassan is by far the largest civil parish in the area, but little enough of its secular or religious history has survived in the records. One of the first Normans who controlled it was a knight of de Lacy, Leonisius de Bromiard. He held manors in the barony of Deece – Kilmore, Rathgormley, Dirpatrick, Knockmark, Culmullen and Kiltale – and in the barony of Ratoath – Dunshaughlin, Killeglin, Greenock, Dunamore and Ratoath. Sometime before the death of Bishop Eugene in 1194, and after the death of Hugh de Lacy in 1186, he handed the responsibility for the faith life of all these parishes to the abbey of St Thomas, together with that of Ballymaglassan and a number of other parishes whose names have so changed since as to elude identification. He also granted to St. Thomas's the right of common pasture in these parishes. Ballymaglassan was never a vicarage, but rather a chaplaincy, a position precarious in income, in status, and perhaps in stability.[3] The grant was confirmed by the lord of the liberty of Meath, the heir of Hugh de Lacy, Walter de Lacy, early in the episcopate of Simon de Rochfort.[4] As we have seen the efforts of Bishop de la Corner to assert episcopal control over appointments and income in these parishes in 1235 were in vain. The name of only one chaplain of Ballymaglassan has come down to us from the Middle Ages, "Thomas the clerk of Ballymaglassan", who with William Le Bret of Staffordstown, Philip de Arbothan and John Presthop was an arbitrator in a law case involving locals and local land in 1289.[5] In the taxation lists for the diocese, drawn up early in the fourteenth century, the income of Ballymaglassan was ten marks, or six pounds thirteen and fourpence, which bears reasonable comparison with that of Moyglare, ten pounds, in the same list, and was twice the income of Rathregan.[6]

The only clue to the quality of faith life in Ballymaglassan in the Middle Ages is provided by one reference in the register of Archbishop Sweetman of Armagh, who by his commissioners visitated Ballymaglassan in 1377.[7] The laconic comment of the archbishop's men in Ballymaglassan was "nihil sciunt nisi bonum", they knew or found nothing but good there. This very favourable comment, of course, refers to the public face of faith practice and to the fabric of the church. In the same visitation it was used of nearby Rathbeggan. But it was not just a casual comment: the registers are full of more colourful and indeed damning comments.

In nearby Grennock, the visitor claimed, no doubt with pardonable exaggeration, that the local chaplain, Sir William Magenich, did not know how to read, sing, perform offices, baptise or teach his parishioners (it seems he was illiterate at least in Latin). He was deprived and the chapel shut, but he sent a boy in through the chancel window to open the door, and kept it open for three days. And in what he did not do, of course, we can see something of the rituals that were performed in a parish like nearby Ballymaglassan by the chaplain. Obviously he was judged at least adequate in teaching what we would call the catechism to his parishioners. He seems to have had a reasonable expertise in the teaching of the church, as he read the offices (performed offices). This may refer to the monastic custom of saying the "Office" which was eventually incumbent on all the clerics of the church. It is clear that singing was part of the liturgy of the Mass – and other acts of worship. Was the music used that which we now know as Gregorian or plain chant and did that custom spread from the monasteries which controlled the appointments and by implication the training of the secular priests in their parishes? We can at this distance only guess, but the negative evidence from Grennock does throw some shadowy light on the positive side of faith life in the parish of Ballymaglassan in the Middle Ages.

All traces of the medieval church of Ballymaglassan have disappeared because a Protestant church has been built on the medieval site. Of course the cemetery which began with the church is still in use and, no doubt, there are grave stones of the Middle Ages still lurking under the surface. One can only surmise that the church was like those others in the locality, of which ground plans in the form of wall fragments still survive. Ballymaglassan was not a major manorial centre all through the Middle Ages, though minor centres at Blackhall, Ballymaglassan itself and Staffordstown appear in the documents. There was a holy well dedicated to St Kieran near the church; perhaps its presence so near the church hints that a church may have been there before the Norman conquest.

Footnotes

2   History of the Diocese of Meath, ed. Curran, vol III, p1128.

3   C.D.I. 1293-1301, p260.

3   Register of the Abbey of St. Thomas, p242.

4   C.D.I. 1285-1292, The orginal grant was witnessed in the presence of Simon, bishop of Meath, between 1194 and 1204.

5   C.D.I. 1285-1292, p821.

6   C.D.I. 1293-1301, p260.

7   Calendar of the Register of Archbishop Sweetman, ed. Lawlor, R.I.A. XXIX c (1911), p263.

Chapter 13

Norman Meath – 1350 to 1655

Just as the first century and a half of Norman Meath had been a time of rapid conquest, consolidation and substantial prosperity such as Ireland was not to know again, so in the next century the colony was under pressure from a revitalised Gaelic civilisation. There was the invasion of Edward Bruce in 1315, followed by a plague, a cattle murrain and finally, in 1348, the Black Death. The colony from then on was in a relative decline. It was never again to provide a revenue to the king's treasury in London until, in the 1630s, briefly and unfortunately for him, Thomas Wentworth, Earl of Strafford, introduced his so called Rule of Thorough. Kilcloon after 1350 was vulnerable to pressure from the Gaelicised Normans of Westmeath and Offaly who had become "more Irish than the Irish themselves", and from the Gaelic tribes of the same area.[1] In Kilcloon too new families became lords of the manors which make up the modern parish: the Delahydes of Moyglare, the Husseys of Mulhussey, the Fitzgeralds of Lackagh and Balfeighan, the Plunketts of Rathregan, and in Ballymaglassan, the Rochfords of Kilbride and the Wesleys of Dangan. It was a time when castles or tower houses were built for defence. And in the late fifteenth century a great ditch which enclosed the so-called English Pale was built to protect the colony about Dublin, North Kildare and East Meath.[2] All the manors of Kilcloon were within it.

It was also a time of prosperity. Tower houses were expensive to build, as also were stone churches. Churches were expensively decorated in the High Gothic style as were monasteries. Bective and the Augustinian abbey at Navan are examples. So are the churches of Killeen, Dunsany, Rathmore and Loughcrew, all built by the Plunketts. In our own parish there are fragments of windows and a chancel arch at Balfeighan, decorated in the High Gothic style, and High Gothic windows at Mulhussey. Rathregan, the largest church in the parish of Kilcloon, was probably a Plunkett church also though, perhaps because the Plunketts did not live there, no stonework survives to compare in quality with that in Killeen and Dunsany. There are no traces of church rebuilding in the other parishes of Kilcloon in the fifteenth century as Protestant churches have been built on their foundations at Rodanstown, Moyglare and Ballymaglassan.

By 1350 the Mortimer family fortunes were again in the ascendant. Roger Mortimer II's son, Edmund, married in 1368 the daughter of the Duke of Clarence, son of the king, Edward III, who through her mother was the heir of the de Burgos, lords of Connaught and earls of Ulster. Edmund's son was lord lieutenant of Ireland in 1392. He came with Richard II to Ireland in 1394-95 and was killed in a skirmish at Carlow in 1398. His son, Edmund, died of the plague at Trim in 1425, and the de Geneville Mortimer portion of Hugh de Lacy's great liberty was inherited by the Duke of York, uncle of the king and lord lieutenant of Ireland. After 1447, his power base in Ireland was, naturally, at Trim where he proved to be a generous benefactor and in return he won the loyalty of the nobles of his liberty to the house of York. He invaded England in 1460, and was killed at the Battle of Wakefield, though in the following year his party, the followers of the white rose of York, won the battle of Towton and his son became king of England as Edward IV. Edward inherited, of course, the de Geneville and Mortimer liberty.

The liberty was suppressed in 1460 but restored soon afterwards. The lords of Meath found the independence of the liberty convenient. The government and the earls of Kildare did not as it formed a power centre away from Dublin and Kildare. It was suppressed again in 1472, restored by the king in 1473, abolished again, restored in 1478 and finally abolished in 1479. But from the Norman conquest onwards, the barons of Ratoath and Deece, and many of their sub-tenants, looked to Trim as their caput and to the de Genevilles and Mortimers as their feudal overlords, who provided justice through their courts and sheriffs and a focus for their loyalties.[3]

The second half of the fifteenth century saw the rise to constant and effective power over the colony and its Council at Dublin of the house of Kildare in the persons of Thomas, the seventh earl (1456 – 1478), Garret Mór the eighth (1478 – 1513) and Garret Óg the ninth earl (1513 – 1534). With each of them, as we shall see, were associated in various ways families who held land in the six manors which form present day Kilcloon. Among them were the Delahydes of Moyglare, the Fitzgeralds of Balfeighan, the Boyces of Calgath, the Husseys of Mulhussey, and the Rochfords of Kilbride, who held a substantial part of Ballymaglassan. This period came to an end with the rebellion of Silken Thomas, who was briefly the tenth earl of Kildare after his father, Garret Óg, died in the Tower of London in 1534.

In spite of the confiscations, which followed the death of Silken Thomas and the fall of his house, the sixteenth century was a time of relative prosperity also. The Husseys of Mulhussey got a new prominence in the locality, but it can be said with truth that the rebellion of 1534 set off in religious and political affairs a century of uncertainty and dissatisfaction which ended in the O'Neill wars (1596 – 1603), the plantation of Ulster, (1607), the harsh rule of the ruthless lord lieutenant, Thomas Wentworth, earl of Strafford (1634 – 1640) and the rebellion of 1641. This rebellion was the last hurrah of Norman Ireland when both races, Old English or Anglo Norman and Gaelic Irish came together, briefly, to rule the country before falling before the army of the parliament of England under the lord protector, Oliver Cromwell.

Footnotes

1   Cf. Ken Abraham's Thesis p21ff; Otway Ruthven, A History of Medieval Ireland, p277 ff.

2   Cal. Archbishop Alen's Register, ed.Charles McNeill (RSAI) p250, 251; U.J.A. first series, Vol 2, (1854), p42, 43; Lectures on the History of Ireland down to 1534, Richey, Dublin, p212.

3   ABRAHAM, Ken, p21, ff.

Chapter 14

The Manor of Moyglare – 1350 to 1638

The Delahydes 1350 to 1534

In any society which does not enjoy the advantage of a permanent bureaucracy, clientship shapes public relationships. As a man rose in political affairs, he gathered around him talented people who rose with him. The feudal system by which Norman Ireland was governed was one in which clientship was the cement that bound society together. The king required talented servants, but there was always a tension between talent and threat, hence the very varied fortunes of great magnates in Ireland like Strongbow, de Lacys, and de Burghs. They were alternatively high in royal favour, fugitives from royal vengeance and, in time, high again in favour. So it was with their clients, up today and out tomorrow.

Against that background can be set the fortunes of the Delahydes of Moyglare. The permanent problem of what to do with talented younger sons of landowners complicated family life. Often the death of siblings solved the problem, but if it did not do so, those whose talents were obvious in administrative or military matters had to carve out a career as crusaders, as adventurers in territory to be won by the sword, or as administrators for those who made the conquests, or in the church.

One of the great noblemen in the England of King John and in the early minority years of his son Henry III, was William Marshal, "the great Marshal" as he was called. Effectively regent of England for the young Henry III and unwaveringly loyal to the throne, William had been rewarded with the hand of Isabella de Clare, only surviving daughter and heiress of Strongbow and of his lordship of Leinster in Ireland. William died in 1219 and in 1221 his son Richard came to Ireland to reorganise and expand his inheritance of Leinster. The Marshals came from the area around Bedfordshire in England and naturally recruited a loyal and talented staff from the younger sons of their larger tenants. Among them was Roger Delahyde from the manor of La Hyde near Luton.

The family can be traced back in Bedfordshire to the Norman conquest of England. Of the four sons of John Delahyde, the eldest, Gilbert, settled in Stodham, Bedfordshire; his son, Roger, was a client of the great Marshal.

A charter from the earl exists, protecting him and his friends for their support of the king. The third son of John, another John, was abbot of St. Albans. His brother, Fulk of Luton, died in 1225 and was father of Alan Delahyde, seneschal or chief official of the vast English and Welsh estates of William Marshal, Earl of Pembroke.[1] The Roger who came to Ireland was more than likely a brother, a cousin or close relation.

Roger was in Ireland by 1223 when he witnessed the charter of St. John's priory in Kilkenny. He was "gone to Ireland" in the service of the Earl Marshal in 1228 and was a burgher of Dublin in the same year. In 1229 he was Earl Marshal's seneschal or chief administrator in Leinster, and again in 1231 – 1232. He acquired lands in Wexford where he had a law suit with the bishop of Ferns over burgage plots in New Ross, had land in Sliabh Margy in Laois where he constituted (presumably for his master) Dunamace as a town.[2] Some time after his arrival in Ireland he married an heiress to the manor of Ballymadun, situated between Garristown in County Dublin and Ratoath in County Meath, which became the seat of the family.[3] The manor in north County Dublin made him relatively safe from the fluctuating fortunes of his masters.

In 1231 William Marshal died suddenly and was succeeded by his brother, Robert. Robert had his differences with the king, Henry III, now an adult and careful of noblemen who were powerful and ruled in places like Leinster, where his control over them was minimal. In an act of treachery Robert was assassinated at the Curragh in 1234, an act which contemporaries held in particular horror. In internecine quarrels ordinary people died like flies and were expendable; the leaders lived to thrive on another day when they could usefully be restored to favour. Roger Delahyde had supported his lord against the king and received pardon, with many others, for his stance, on paying a substantial fine in 1234. He held property near Arklow too, adjacent to that held by another client of the Earl Marshal, de Wellesley; the families of both were to relate in a complex way to one another over the next four centuries. Roger was dead before 1245 and was succeeded by his son John, who augmented his Ballymadun estate by inheriting the substantial dower lands of his wife's uncle and by buying out tenancies on it.[4]

His wife died in 1243 and he married a daughter of Valerian de Wesley (the name Valerian was to appear in successive generations of Wesleys who owned Dangan near Summerhill and for many years substantial portions of the manor of Ballymaglassan).[5] John died in 1281, to be succeeded by his son Roger.

His was a rich inheritance; the receipts of Ballymadun for the five years, 1276 – 1281 came to the very handsome sum of a hundred and seventy three pounds, one shilling and eight pence.[6]

The Delahydes disappeared from the records in Wicklow and in Wexford. Evidently the connection with the Marshals having ended, (Roger Marshal's great patrimony was divided between his five sisters) the Delahydes concentrated on interests about Dublin. Sometime after 1300, it seems they purchased the manor of Moyglare from Sir Geoffrey le Bret of Rathfarnham or from his son Milo or grandson, John, because Sir Walter Delahyde owned it at his death in 1343.

The family went from strength to strength and acquired property in Dunshaughlin and in the border barony of Carbury in Kildare, which acted as a barrier to the Irish O'Connors and O'Mores of Offaly and Laois. There was a commercial and legal side to the family also. A branch settled in Drogheda and became in time one of the leading merchant families there. Another set up a branch in Lough Shinney, north of Dublin, and in Punchestown. The Moyglare family produced scholars and eminent lawyers in many generations.[7] For three centuries the Delahydes formed a network of extended families, witnessing one another's wills, intermarrying members of the broader family, with cousins marrying cousins, and ensuring by long entailed wills that no matter what disaster sudden death might bring to the families, the family itself would survive, with its influence and wealth intact.

One can chart the rise to prominence of the family in its first appointments to local government. Walter Delahyde was sheriff of Meath in 1342.[8] James Delahyde, his son, was knighted in 1374 by Lionel, Duke of Clarence. He was sheriff of Limerick, escheator of Ireland, seneschal (or chief administrative officer) of the liberty of Meath of which the lord was Edmund Mortimer.[9]

The escheator in the thirteenth and fourteenth centuries held an office of key importance as he was responsible for, among other things, the revenues of vacant dioceses and vacant abbeys until a new bishop or abbot was appointed. Being seneschal was of course no sinecure; in 1374 James Delahyde could not attend the king's Council in Carlow because of the wars in Meath.[10] He was killed in that same year and at once the Council instructed Delahyde's successor as seneschal of the liberty to seize his properties, with the exception of Moyglare, to settle debts due from his time as sheriff in Limerick, seneschal in Meath and escheator of all Ireland.[11]

His wife appealed to the Council, then sitting at Naas, and spelled out what had been seized, four bullocks, six heifers, twenty hogs and some acres of corn. She had six children, now orphans, unprovided for and the goods were returned.[12] The incident does reveal the precarious nature of even the most influential of positions and how easily they could be lost.

The manor of Carbury in the north west of Kildare was located in marchlands. Its owner in the early fourteenth century was Richard de Birmingham who became Irish justiciar. His daughter married Robert de Preston, soon to be lord of Gormanston, and an efficient lawyer. Through the deaths of Birmingham's sons, Preston's wife became briefly heiress to Carbury, for a day or two after her brother's death, before succumbing herself to the then prevalent plague. Her inheritance of Carbury fell to her husband, to the great discontent of various of the Birminghams who resisted their new lord's pursuit of his inheritance. Robert Preston was unsuccessful in asserting his rights and as a solution to his difficulties in a property quite far from his base at Gormanston, he evidentally came to an arrangement with John Delahyde, sheriff of Meath, who could more effectively assert ownership in north Kildare.[13] Preston swapped Carbury for Ballymadun which was not far from his base at Gormanston and near Dublin. The result was a shifting of focus by the Delahydes from north Dublin to the Meath and Kildare border and specifically to the manor of Moyglare. And the family of Moyglare was well placed to take full advantage of the rise to substantial power in royal government in the fifteenth century of the successive heads of the Fitzgerald family, the earls of Kildare, who lived at nearby Maynooth.

The family only really attained prominence towards the end of the fifteenth- century when the head of the family, Sir Walter Delahyde, became one of the close advisors of the earl of Kildare, Garret Mór, who in effect was ruler of Ireland from 1478 to 1513, and of his son, Garret Óg, who succeeded him. Sir Walter married a daughter of Ronald Fitz Eustace of Portlester, near Athboy, who was also a member of the Kildare clique. Fitz Eustace was treasurer of Ireland from the accession of Edward IV in 1460 and , sometimes combining this office with that of chancellor, was Garret Mór's right hand man in the Irish Council. Still another member of the Kildare clique was the earl's brother, Thomas, who had received the manors of Balfeighan and Lackagh from his father, Thomas, the seventh earl (chapter 16). Another daughter of Fitz Eustace, Alison, married Garret Mór and died in 1496 when her husband endured one of his brief sojourns in the tower of London. It is said she died of a broken heart and of shock at the temporary reversal of the family fortunes. And she was lamented by the Irish poets of her time as she was a patron of their work. After 1478, when Garret Mór became justiciar, Walter Delahyde became collector of customs at a salary of sixty-six shillings and eight pence: his position was confirmed in the reign of Richard III. He was appointed after 1478 as constable of the castle of Wicklow at a salary of twenty marks per year.[14] In 1482, on important business concerning Irish affairs at the royal council at Westminster, he and Thomas Cusack got expenses of thirteen pounds six and eightpence.[15] Another member of the Kildare clique was James Estrete who was the king's sergeant at law and got the manor of Ratoath for his pains, and granted to Christ Church in Dublin properties in Balrodden and Bryanstown. The deed of gift was witnessed by Garret Mór, the lord deputy, Sir Ronald Fitz Eustace and by Sir Walter Delahyde.[16] With Garret Óg, Walter Delahyde was the executor of Garret Mór's will when he died in 1513.[17] When Garret Óg (see illustration of Garret Óg, p x) was taken in a skirmish by the O'Connors in 1528, Sir Walter with Wesley of Dangan was the emissary who negotiated his release.[18] In 1528 he is styled chief steward of the earl of Kildare[19] and presumably as one of the ongoing rewards for service, loyalty and influence, he, together with Richard Delahyde of the Ward, and Alamo Usher and Thomas Stens of Dublin was given the lucrative office of collector of "petty customs and cocket" in the ports of Dublin, Drogheda and Dundalk for a payment of three hundred and seven pounds to the exchequer; all customs above that figure, of course, were the property of the assignees.[20]

The association with the house of Kildare brought the Delahydes much advantage in terms of political influence and wealth, but that association turned to disadvantage when in 1534 as a consequence of the rebellion of Silken Thomas, eldest son of Garret Óg, grand nephew of Lady Jenet Delahyde and foster son of Sir Walter, the properties of the earldom and of the Delahydes were confiscated by the crown.

The Delahydes and the Rebellion of Silken Thomas

Just as the Delahydes of Moyglare had risen high in influence and power through their connection with the house of Kildare, so also did they fall through the same connection. As we have seen, the two houses were close in blood and in politics. Sir Walter Delahyde's wife was the sister of Garret Mór's first wife and Garret Óg had entrusted to his aunt, his eldest son Thomas, nicknamed Silken, to be fostered. Many explanations have been given by historians in recent years to explain the seemingly irrational and impetuous reaction of Silken Thomas, deputising for his father as lord deputy in Dublin, to rumours of his father's execution in London. It was said that it was his foster brother, James Delahyde, who gave him the letter containing the false report. Some historians mention the interests of the emperor Charles V in Ireland: his aunt Catherine had just been repudiated as Henry's queen. Another element mentioned is a plan, however misguided, by Garret Óg himself to show how essential was the rule of the house of Kildare in Ireland. But certainly contemporaries of consequence had no doubt of a substantial Delahyde involvement. The Master of Rolls in Dublin wrote to Thomas Cromwell, the up and coming power at the court of King Henry:

> "we have in warde in the castell of Dublyn Dam Jenet Eustace, Sir Walter Delahyde's wif, which was the earl of Kildare's aunt, and most of servants with him and by all probable conjecture, she was the chief counsailour and stirrer of this inordinate rebellion. She is the traitoress foster moder; and by the Delahids, her two sonnes, James and John, Thomas Eustace, which is her nephew, the same was begone, and hitherto is meynteyneol and upholden; and the tyme that this army scomfited the traitour, and had him in chase, for his socour he fled, with himself and a boy, to her, unto Delahids castell of Balyna and there was rescued".[1]

In January 1535 there was a letter to the government from William Lynch of the Knock, who reported that the rebellion was begun by Justice Delahyde and Jenet Eustace (Lady Delahyde). He heard this from Walter Hosey or Hussey of Mulhussey, then dead, who had been a friend of Fitzgerald with whom he made an arrangement for the safety of his lands. Dame Jenet had provided for the furnishings and victualling of Maynooth castle.[2]

James Delahyde was called "principall counsailor" to Silken Thomas. He was with him when the archbishop of Dublin, John Alen, fleeing for his life to England, was taken and imprisoned in the castle of "Tartayne" (Artane) within the county of Dublin and Thomas caused him

> "to be drawn out of his bed and brought before him. And the same archbishop kneeling in his shirt and barfooted and barheaded before him, asked of him mercy, immediately without any restpite, most shamefully and trayterously murdered and killed out of hand".[3]

Despite the story put abroad by Thomas afterwards that it was a mistake, (he claimed that he said "beir uaim an bodach" (take the churl away) and his henchmen took him literally and killed the archbishop) the result was excommunication. In the contemporary magnificent prose;

> "the said Thomas accompanied with John Fitzgerald, Edward Rorkes, and Dyversse other Evyll disposed persons, most shamfullie tyrannyusly and cruellie murdered and put to death the said archbishop; for which abhomynable, detestable and dampnable acte, according to the prescriptses and ordinances of holy church, we publishe and declare Thomas Fitzgerald, John Fitzgerald, Olyver Fitzgerald, James Delahyde, Edward Rorkes, John Telyng, Nicholas Wafer and all other, which gave commandment, counsaille, favour, helps, ayde, assistance, comforte, or

consent id to the same, or after thaete commytted, ded ratifie, accept, approve, or wilfullie defende it, or socor, or receyve any such saide personnes to be excommunicate, accurseol (sic) and anathemagate. And to all the extent all cristen people may the rath take knowledge thereof, and avoide and esehue daunger of the same we invocate and call in vengeance aquaint the said Thomas and every of the persones aforesaid, the celestiall place of Heven, with all the multitude of angels, that they be accursed before them and in their sight, as spirittes condempned; on the devil to stand and be in all their doings, on ther right hand, and all their acts should be synfull, and not acceptable before God. "[4]

In time, Maynooth castle fell (but not before the governor, James Boyce from Calgath, had the contents scattered and stored away). Actually it fell because of treachery: Silken Thomas had entrusted it to another foster brother, Christopher Parese of Agher, who betrayed it for cash to the lord deputy, Sir William Skeffington. He got his cash but lost his head:

"Why, Parese, "quoth the (lord) deputie", "coudst thou finde in thine heart to betray his castell that hath bein so good lord unto thee?" "My lord," said Parese, "had I wist you would have dealte so straitly with me your lordship should not have woune this fort with as little bloud shed as you dyd." At this a "gentleman of worship" called Boyce said in Irish "antragh,which is as much in english as "too late", whereof grewe the Irish proverb to thys day in that language used," too late quoth Boyce".[5]

The fall of Maynooth castle broke the back of the rebellion and Thomas decided to look for help from abroad soon afterwards. An agent of the London government in Lisbon reported in July 1535:

"My lorde, for to sertify your lordshippe of the nwis that is here, the fourteenth day of June, ther come to cadix (Cadiz) for imbaxador a man of erlonde, hois name is Sir Jamys Delahyde and has brought letters to the emperor from Thomas Fegarit, wher in his petision is that the emperor will give hym aid with men and ordinse".[6]

Accompanying James Delahyde was Parson Welsh of Ballymore Loughseudy and one Henry Power. But when they finally got to meet Charles V he informed them that they were too late: Thomas Fitzgerald and all his uncles had been executed at Tyburn. At home Sir Walter Delahyde, knight, and his wife

"the ladie Gennet Eustace were apprehended and brought as prisoners by master Brabson, vice treasurer, from their towne of Moyclare to the castell of Dublin, bycause theyr sonne and heyre James Delahyde was the only bruer of all this rebellion, who as the gouernour suspected was set on by his parents, and mainly by his mother.

*The knight and his wife, lying in duresse for the space of twelve
Monethes, were at severall tymes examined and, not withstanding all
presumptions and surmises that could bee gathered, they were in the
ende founde guiltlesse of their sonne his folly. But the Ladie was had in
examination apart, and entyced by fayre meanes to charge hir husbande
with hir sonne hys rebellion, who being not woonne thereto with al the
meanes that coulde be wrought, was menaced to be put to death, or to
be rackt, and so with extremitie to be compelled, whereas with
gentlenesse she coulde not be allured to acknowledge these apparent
treasons, that neyther hir husbande nor she coulde without great show
of impudencie denie.*

*The gentlewoman, with these continuall stormes heartbroken,
deceassed in the castell: from thence hir bodie was removed to the grey
Friers with the Deputy his commaundement and it should not be interred
until his pleasure were further knowne, adding withall, that the carkasse
of one who was the mother of so arrant an Arch traytor ought rather to
be cast out on a Dunghill to be carion for Ravens and Dogs to knaw
upon, than to be layd in any Christian grave. The corps lying foure or five
dayes in this place, at the request of the ladie Jennet Golding, wife to Sir
John White Knight, the governour licensed that it should be buried".*[7]

The mopping up operations at home had been long and tedious and Silken
Thomas could rely on a network of allies carefully constructed by his father
and grandfather among Old English and Gaelic Irish alike. The government
in Dublin negotiated and Thomas accepted its terms. For one thing the lord
deputy Leonard Gray who had succeeded the recently deceased
Skeffington was the brother of his stepmother. Thomas had a promise that
he should be pardoned

*"upon his repayre into Englande. And to the ende that no trecherie might
have bene misdeemed of eyther side, they both receyved the Sacriment
openly in the campe, as an infallible seale of the covenance and
conditions of eyther past agreed."*[8]

Before news of Thomas's incarceration in the tower of London could get to
Ireland, Thomas's uncles were rounded up – even those who had opposed
him. And with a completely amoral disregard for honour, for fair play or
justice all the uncles were executed at Tyburn together with the nephew.
Obviously the extermination of the house of Kildare was decided on, but
as so often happens in these matters, one Fitzgerald got away – Gerald,
nephew of Sir Leonard Gray and half brother of Silken Thomas. After many
adventures in Ireland where the old network of the Kildare allies proved
crucial, Gerald with his tutor, Thomas Leverous, found his way to Italy and
to the household of Cardinal Reginald Pole, cousin of Henry VIII and focus

for all those who opposed the religious changes Henry VIII was introducing in England.[9]

Meanwhile, still an outlaw, James Delahyde moved to Scotland – Henry Power had been pardoned but prudently remained in Lisbon and James Delahyde had to die in exile.[10]

As so often had happened in the past, those disgraced in one reign were rehabilitated in another and in the reign of Edward VI, soon after his father Henry VIII died, the first steps in the restoration of Gerald, earl of Kildare to favour and to property began.[11] It was completed in the reign of Queen Elizabeth when, with so many others like him, he conformed, nominally at least, to the Established Church and received back all the properties of his ancestors.

Walter Delahyde occupied the Moyglare estate until his death. The Carbury estate went to an English soldier and adventurer, Sir Henry Cowley or Cawley, whose descendants held onto them until in 1728 they became Wellesleys and moved to Dangan in Summerhill.[12] The Dunshaughlin property was restored to John Delahyde, Sir Walter's second son, who claimed successfully that he had been forced, for safety, to appear to be involved in the Kildare rebellion.[13] But the Delahydes never did figure on the national stage again: their energies went into recovering their manors of Moyglare, Carbury and Dunshaughlin, on the terms on which they had held them before.

The Survey of 1540

Among the most comprehensive and interesting sources of information on land use and ownership are the surveys required by the state when it confiscates the land of defeated rebels. The survey of 1540 arising from the rebellion of Silken Thomas was no exception.[1] It covers the extensive estates of the earls of Kildare which were forfeit to the crown and the estates of Sir Walter Delahyde of Moyglare. In the modern parish of Kilcloon the Kildare estates included the villata or manor of Ballymaglassan, held by William Wesley of Dangan, for which he paid two marks or twenty five shillings a year. He held a fee tenancy; that involved ownership, in effect, for which a smaller rent (similar to a ground rent today) was paid to the titular owner. Newtownmoyaghey, a Kildare property held of the manor of Moyglare, had one hundred and sixty acres arable, eighteen acres of meadow, three "quarters" of pasture and six acres of wood and underwood. Five tenants – Peter Boyce, Patrick O'Melone, John McGrayde and two others paid eight pounds per annum, provided ten days ploughing, and ten of turf cutting. They were available for five days work in autumn and presented five hens and four hawks annually, altogether worth nine shillings and four pence. There were five cottages where the tenants were available for five days work in autumn and presented five hens. The five days work and the five hens were together worth twenty pence. Evidently the latter were labourers on the lands of the tenants mentioned above. The total income from Newtownmoyaghey was eight pounds, eleven shillings. James Boyce received these rents and for them paid sixty shillings to the king's commissioners. This James Boyce had been constable of Maynooth castle during the rebellion and a receiver of rent for the Kildare estates at least in Laois. The acreage of Newtownmoyaghey was given as one hundred and eighty four acres plus three "quarters" of pasture. Some of this property was in the manor of Moyglare and some in the manor of Rodanstown. The sixteenth century acre was far larger, not only than the modern acre, but also than the plantation acre which was used as a measure in the Cromwellian plantation in the sixteen fifties. Newtownmoyaghey is given as containing two hundred and eighty seven plantation acres in 1654 and six hundred and five statute acres in 1854. In 1540 most of the land was under the plough: one hundred and eighty acres arable, eighteen meadow, three "quarters" of pasture and six acres of wood. In 1654, one hundred and sixty six acres were arable, with sixty in meadow and one hundred acres in pasture. In other words, in little over a century, in this holding at least there had been a substantial shift in land use towards a pastoral economy.

The estate of Walter Delahyde was also forfeit. It was composed of three distinct parcels. The estates in Carbury, County Kildare, which contained the castle of Ballyna, had been acquired in the fourteenth century. After this confiscation they were given to an ambitious New English soldier named Henry Colley or Cowley, whose family, despite a grant of reversion of the estates to the Delahydes in 1587, managed to hold it until one of them succeeded a cousin, Garret Wesley, to the Wesley estates in Meath at Dangan and Ballymaglassan on condition that he took the Wesley name. His descendants became in one line marquises of Wellesley and in another the dukes of Wellington. The other tranche of Delahyde lands was the manor of Dunshaughlin and its various attachments. It too was confiscated but came back in time to Sir Walter's second son John, whose descendant lost it when he was convicted of murdering his wife in 1603. The remaining tranche of property was of course the manor of Moyglare itself. The demesne farm had a castle or stone house, a yard, a garden and various other "necessary buildings". There were five woods there, le Curraughe, le Lough Wood, Henriston Wood, Black Curragh and Bolyon; together they made up an estimated twelve acres. There were one hundred and eighty acres arable and seven in meadow. There were four messauges (houses with a garden), together making up eighty one acres arable and pasture. These had twenty-four cottages. There was a water mill and one hundred and twenty acres in moorland, giving an income of twenty three pence "with various customs and suit of court from certain lands", in Bryanstown. The total land in contemporary measure was three hundred and ninety nine acres. That became four hundred and eighty seven acres in 1654, and nine hundred and fourteen statute acres in 1854. Apart from the moorland the vast bulk of the land in the demesne was under the plough, worked, one presumes, mostly by the families of the twenty-four cottagers. Delahyde owned two messauges, seventy acres arable and pasture, a wood called Bryanstown wood and five cottages in part of Bryanstown; from the rest he got a chief rent with customary duties or services of four shillings and two pence. This piece of land in Bryanstown was probably that presented by Francis Estrete, sergeant at law, to the church of the Holy Trinity, (Christ's Church) in Dublin in 1488.[2] The tenant had effectively become an owner, subject only to a fixed and small rent. There were ninety one acres in Bryanstown in 1654 and three hundred and twenty six acres in the Griffith valuation of 1854.

Delahyde also had some land in Porterstown – fifty acres arable – and some five messauges with (certain lands) from which he got a chief rent. In Killeaney, he had two messauges, eighty one acres arable, three cottages and three acres "land"; it was reckoned as two hundred and twelve acres in 1654 and three hundred and fifty seven acres in the Griffith valuation. He held one messauge with seventy four acres in Affolis, and a chief rent from fifteen acres there, one messauge and seventy three acres arable in Barrackstown, four messauges and fifty six acres in Kynnyne (Kimmins?), thirteen acres in Henriston (Harristown?), nine acres in Stephenstown (the name has long since disappeared), thirty five acres arable and seven in meadow in Moygaddy and one pound of pepper from certain lands in Moygaddy. This latter was probably the nominal rent for the fourteen acres which the vicars choral of St. Patrick's in Dublin had acquired in the years before the Reformation. It was leased by Andrew Forde, a Protestant, in 1654 and went back to the Moyglare manor in 1664 when the lease was taken over by Sir George Wentworth.[3] A chief rent was paid by a tenant, often someone who had lands elsewhere, who could dispose as he pleased of the land which carried with it the chief rent. There was a ten-shilling chief rent from land in Kilgraigue (the tenant was a Foster whose family had been there at least since 1415 when Richard Foster of Kilgraigue witnessed a document[4] and George Foster owned the townsland in 1654). There was a fourteen-pence chief rent from Butlerstown, two and six chief rent from Valestol (?), twelve shillings and eight pence from Owenstown (the tenant was Owens, who had land in Portane (Dunboyne barony), three shillings chief rent from Little Moygaddy, fourteen pence chief rent from Killeaney and seven shillings chief rent from Bally (magillan?). Old Graigue and Timlins do not appear in the survey and perhaps Valiston and Stephenstown, otherwise unknown in modern times, refer to them. The picture of the manor of Moyglare emerges clearly. The demesne itself was worked by four tenants and twenty four cottagers. The other townslands were occupied by substantial tenants (Bryanstown, Killeaney) who had cottagers to do work on their farms. Barrockstown had one messauge of seventy three acres held by a substantial farmer; there were four messauges with fifty six acres in Kynnyne (Kimmins ?).

There were thirteen acres in Henristown, nine in Stephenstown, thirty five acres arable and seven in meadow in Moygaddy. For the rest, the chief rent, relatively small in Kilgraigue, Butlerstown, Valeston?, Owenstown, Little Moygaddy, Killeaney and Ballymagillin, shows how some tenants had become over the years small landowners there. Where use of lands is indicated it is either arable, the vast bulk of it, or meadow. It was characteristic of the organisation of the manor that the same families held tenancies there over very long periods. The earl of Kildare held Newtownmoyaghey in 1540 and also in 1641. Rochford of Kilbride held land in Butlerstown in 1540 and in 1641. Holywood of Artane held land in Affolis in 1540 and 1641. Owen held land in Owenstown, Talbot of Dardiston held Little Moygaddy and Killeaney in the same years. Porter of Kingiston held land in 1540 in Porterstown, and in 1641 Walter Porter of Newtown held land in this manor also. Fosters held Kilgraigue from 1415 to 1641 and perhaps from the early thirteenth century.[5] The twenty four cottagers in Moyglare demesne perhaps indicate the survival of the betaghs of the early Norman period, labourers tied to the land and of Old Irish origin. Perhaps they appeared in the next generation but one, when many from the manor with Old Irish names were pardoned with Walter Delahyde, a younger son of the manor, for involvement on the side of the Old Irish in the wars of Hugh O'Neill in the late 1590s.

Only in such a shadowy fashion do those who till the soil appear in the records. All indications are that at all levels in the manor of Moyglare, the same families owned it, held tenancies of various kinds in it and worked it at least during the late Middle Ages.

The Delahydes – 1534 to 1638

The fortunes of the Delahydes never quite recovered from the disaster of the Kildare rebellion. Though Sir Walter was never attainted, his three sons were, James, John and Edward the parson of Kilberry. James went to Spain to obtain imperial help from Charles V, the Holy Roman Emperor who was also Charles 1 of Spain. When he and Parson Walsh of Loughseudy met Charles they were informed that their master, Silken Thomas, with all his uncles, was dead at Tyburn. Of the Fitzgerald family, only his half brother Gerald survived: he had been spirited away and eventually got to Rome. James's companion, Henry Power, was pardoned through the good offices of the emperor, Charles, but James, the heir of the Delahydes, was to die still a traitor in Scotland. John had surrendered in the south and successfully pleaded that he had given help to Silken Thomas for fear of his life. Edward, the priest, died in 1535.[1] Lady Delahyde had meantime died in Dublin castle. The Delahyde estates were taken into the king's hands and disposed of in three lots, Moyglare, the Kildare estate centred on Ballyna castle and Carbury, and Dunshaughlin. Sir Walter still had some property in Moygaddy and that which had come to his wife through her family, the Eustaces of Portlester near Athboy. Moyglare was leased in 1538 by the crown to Sir Richard Rede, Lord Chancellor, and in the reign of Edward V1, Keeper of the Privy Seal.[2] The lease was to take effect after Sir Walter's death. Rede seems to have been content to draw an income from the estate which he probably leased back to Sir Walter. Within the next few years Sir Walter was dead and his grandson, Lawrence, the eldest son of James, still attainted, was the head of the family. On November 27th 1560 Lawrence got the estate of Moyglare back from the crown, as the twenty one-year lease of Sir Richard Rede had expired.[3] He seemed to have been tainted by opposition to the cess, a tax opposed by the Old English of the Pale and by association with the earl of Kildare who was an object of government suspicion in the 1570s. In 1578 he was pardoned, together with Edmund Shiel of Moyglare and James Shiel of Russell Court County Kildare "chirurgeons".[4] The road back was difficult. Evidently the crown leased Moyglare back to Lawrence. In 1585 Sir Henry Wallop sent a packet of letters to London by Lawrence Delahyde whom he recommends "as one of the best housekeepers for hospitality and entertainment in the Pale".[5] It was sent in January and the letters expressed thanks for his friendly advertisement. The visit to London was successful. The queen granted a reduction in the rent of such lands of the inheritance of his father as would be worth fifty pounds English.

Lawrence did not live to see the final success of his efforts to re-establish his family. On the 17th September 1586 Richard, his son, got the reversion of the Dunshaughlin estate for forty years from 1587 which had been leased in 1578 and before that by a lease of 1569 to John Plunkett; he got various other reversions of leases in Kildare as well.[6] His mother, Joanna, in 1576, got back the lands of Kildare which had been leased to Henry Colley or Cowley, at a rent of twenty seven pounds three and sixpence. They included the castle and manor of Castle Carbury, the lands of Carbury, Cloncoyne, Kilmore, Carshewen, Dyrregant, Ballihagen, Kylballogibbe, Recoghan, Renoghan Halt, Clonough, Kinnamury, Ballymarky. Touragigh, parcel of the manor of Ballyna, County Kildare, possessed of Walter Walsh, attainted, was also granted to her at a rent of twenty seven pounds three and sixpence reserved in the grant to Cowley in tail male by fielty and free socage forever.[7]

The final grant came in 1588. Joanna got Moyglare,"all the lands of Bryanstown, Gillinstown (Ballymagillin) Tonlegyge, Harristown, Killeaney, Ashwolle (Affolis) the new town of Moyagh, Porterstown, Leynaghton, Ballegortaghe, the Kimmins, the Barrocks, the new town of Rath Germlegilgreye, Baldongel, (Owenstown), Myche Moygaddy". She also got "Little Moygaddy, called the Bannocks, in the tenure of John Rochford, Little Moygaddy in the tenure of Thomas Talbot of Daweston, Butlerstown and Gallo which belonged to the same manor".[8] The fine was thirty pounds English. The return or regrants of former properties were not as generous or valuable as they first appear in the documents, as ownership in varying degrees gradually took place only when the former leases fell in. For example, the Kildare lands were returned to the Delahydes in 1578 but in December 1601, Joanna Delahyde of Moyglare, widow of Lawrence, whose son and heir, Richard, had died some time before that, was bound with her brother James Hussey for five hundred pounds to the queen. She had to guarantee that Walter Delahyde, Richard's brother, who had been freed from Dublin castle and was left in "the widow's house at Moyglare", did not depart without licence from Dublin and would come if summoned within twenty days before the Lord Deputy and Council. They further had to guarantee that he would "be of good and dutiful behavior towards her majesty's true subjects, especially towards Ann Colley, her children, tenants, servants and her majesty's ward of Castle Carbury and that he (would) not procure or advise any act or thing which may be to their hurt or prejudice".[9] In other words, though Lord Dunsany got the wardship of Luke, who was Richard's heir, Walter was custodian of the family fortunes and was forbidden from trying to push the Colleys out of the Kildare lands Joanna Delahyde had been granted in 1586. In time, the Delahydes sold their rights in these Kildare lands, which eventually reverted to the Colleys.[10] The Dunshaughlin lands went to John Delahyde.

Hugh O'Neill, earl of Tyrone, after a complex relationship with queen and government, rose in a rebellion in 1595 which threatened the survival of English rule in Ireland. Not unreasonably, Richard Delahyde was very careful when the rebellion broke out and kept a studied neutrality. The same cannot be said of his brother Walter, who fought for O' Neill for four years before 1600. In 1599 a report to London complained that "both those counties of east and west Meath are infested by those Irish sects viz. O'Mulloy..." "the Delahydes with the Connors and enemies to the patentees of such lands as they heretofore lost by rebellion; they are with Walter Yongerle in rebellion."[11] More precisely, in the same year, when there was a certain panic in Dublin that the recently agreed cessation of hostilities with Hugh O'Neill might well be in danger, proof was proffered that "there lieth in a camp within a mile of Maynooth, which is but ten miles from Dublin, three hundred of the base Geraldines and Delahydes, now in this time of cessation and take up beeves from subjects daily, saying they will (offer) Tyrone's bill for payment, which is a great scorn to any honest mind to hear the like".[12] In 1600 "bastard Geraldines (two base brothers of the late earl) were still in rebellion, of whom one has a pension of three shillings per day from her majesty, with whom is associated one of the Delahydes and Lynagh O'Donnell and certain of the Eustaces, of kindred to the late Viscount Baltinglass."[13] These activities show the dark underside of the web of Anglo Irish families who were politically loyal to the government, though increasingly alienated because of its political and religious policies: people like the Delahydes who had been judged subversive on at least two occasions since 1534 made common cause, not only with their cousins, the Eustaces, who had risen out under Viscount Baltinglass in 1582, but also with the O'Connors of Offaly, the illegitimate children of the Anglo Irish lords and younger sons of the same families. These obviously were attracted to the leadership of O'Neill by his rebellion which would give them some chance of regaining a stake in the land of their ancestors which otherwise had eluded them. When Walter surrendered he was first on the list of at least fifty with addresses in Moyglare and the surrounding townslands who were pardoned with him. One presumes they were associates of the Delahydes mentioned in the report of 1599.

Among the list of those pardoned were farmers, yeomen and soldiers; they lived in Moyglare, Dollanstown, Killeaney, Kilgraigue (two Fosters among them), and Moygaddy.[14] They obviously fought with Walter in the rebellion and probably went off with him to the Spanish Netherlands when he went to join the regiment of O'Neill. In the year 1602 more people from the parish were pardoned, Turloch O'Boyle of Kilclone, Patrick O'Boyle, Brian O'Boyle and Richard Malley of Moyglare. They surrendered in Offaly with about twenty five of the O'Connors.[15] They probably formed part of the "Delahydes with the Connors, enemies to the patentees of such lands as they heretofore lost by rebellion". The O'Connors were trying to reverse the plantations of their lands, which had taken place forty years before. When these engagements failed, their leaders like Walter Delahyde and his brother George took them to the Spanish Netherlands for the military career they had trained for in Ireland. It was no accident either that they found their place in the regiment of the O'Neills set up formally in Flanders in 1605. One somewhat romantic incident happened in Moyglare in 1607. The young Brigid Fitzgerald, daughter of the Earl of Kildare, got a letter from her new husband, Red Hugh O'Donnell, while walking in the gardens of Moyglare. It told her of the flight of the earls, her husband and Hugh O'Neill, who were leaving Ireland forever to go into exile abroad. She never met him again and was still receiving a royal pension in 1661, fifty four years later.[16]

At home in Moyglare, Luke Delahyde, son of Richard, who had died about 1600, was heir to the estate. Being a minor, he was given as ward to Lord Dunsany. In adulthood he never seems to have been able to do more than hang on to his properties. They were in lease to a number of New English noble tenants and when that lease was up in 1627 he mortgaged the estates for ninety-nine years.[17]

In the 1630's there is evidence of New English moving in to lease or buy property in the parish, and the Moyglare estate was encumbered with a loan of four hundred pounds from the Dowager Countess of Kildare.[18] In the late 1630s, Luke finally sold his properties; when the Lord Deputy, Thomas Wentworth, was looking around for an estate to provide a revenue of five hundred pounds a year for his younger brother George, he got his fixer, Sir George Ratcliffe, to purchase Moyglare for nine thousand pounds. It appears that Luke Delahyde remained on at Moyglare, perhaps as a leaseholder.

Certainly he was transplanted to Connaught in 1655, where the seven hundred and seventy seven acres he got there corresponds to roughly one third of the Moyglare estate.[19] One third of an estate was granted in Connaught to those papists who had not shown constant affection to parliament, though they had not been involved in the confederate wars. Luke is not found in the Books of Survey and Distribution of 1672 which reflect a fairly final picture of the land settlements. Though he does appear in decrees of innocence of the early 1660s, he may have sold his entitlements in Connaught and returned to Moyglare. In any case – and he must have been a very old man by then – he last appears in the Dopping Visitation of 1682 as patron of the parish of Moyglare.[20]

The association of the Delahydes with Moyglare was broken soon afterwards; at least the name does not appear in the records subsequently. And it does seem that as leases held by Catholics on the Moyglare estate fell in they were given to Protestants. As we will see, the Delahydes in successive generations were soldiers in the Irish regiments of the Spanish armies, which fought prinicpally in the Netherlands. A Colonel Michael Delahyde distinguished himself in the wars in Ireland of King James and King William. He seems to have been killed in 1690, but whether he was of the house of Moyglare is not known.[21] At any rate, by the end of the seventeenth century, a family which had owned the manor of Moyglare for over three hundred years was replaced by new occupants and owners with different heritages, different values and a different religion: first the Wentworths, who were originally from Yorkshire and settled eventually in Kent after Sir. George Wentworth's death, held it until 1736, when the Arabins, Huguenots from France, bought it and held it until the mid nineteenth century. And so they were to dominate Moyglare and Kilcloon for the next century and a half.

The Wild Geese from Moyglare[1] – 1600 to 1650

Together with quite a number of his contemporaries in the O'Neill wars, Walter Delahyde had a bleak future before him in Ireland. With a number of other Old English younger sons, like Thomas Preston, later to find fame as the Old English rival to Owen Roe O'Neill during the wars of the Confederation of Kilkenny, William Darcy of County Meath and Magnus Geraldine as he was called, of the family of Kildare, Walter Delahyde made his way to the Spanish Netherlands, then ruled as a semi-autonomous principality for the Spanish king by his uncle and aunt – the Archduke Albert and the Archduchess Isabella. Since the northern and Protestant provinces which now make up Holland or the kingdom of the Netherlands, had revolted against Spanish rule in 1568, there had been a state of sporadic war between the Catholic south and what were increasingly called the United Provinces of the north. In 1586, Sir Thomas Stanley had brought with him from Munster the human leftovers from the Desmond rebellion. He brought them with encouragement from London to fight for the Dutch, but they soon changed sides and fought for the Spanish in Flanders. Soon this Irish group became a regiment, or tercio, as it was called in Spanish, of Irish troops doubly welcome because of the very high death rate caused by contemporary methods of war. The pike and the halberd ensured the high death rate, and increasingly the highlands of Castille, traditional suppliers of men to the Spanish army, were not capable of answering the royal demands for more and more troops. Flanders, in a way, was a home from home for the Irish too. Spain was Hugh O'Neill's natural ally; a Spanish expedition had come to Kinsale in 1601. And the Spanish Netherlands was a place where many of the Old English of the Pale sent their children for education. Seminaries for Counter Reformation priests had been set up in Douai (founded by a Meath man Christopher Cusack in 1591), and at Lille and Tournai and Antwerp. The Franciscans now founded their house of studies in Louvain where the disjointed remains of the Gaelic literary tradition were compounded into the Annals of the Four Masters. The chaplains to each of the companies of the Irish regiment, twelve in number before 1609, were taken from among the Irish clerics who were for one reason or another resident in the Spanish Netherlands.

After Sir Thomas Stanley's death the organisation of such Irish soldiers as there were in Flanders was haphazard; in any case the O'Neill wars in Ireland made soldiering at home more attractive. But in the years after 1600 when Hugh O'Neill's star was waning in Ireland, the presence of his second son Henry, first in Spain where he had been sent by his father as a hostage before the Spanish expedition of 1601, and then, after October 1605, in Flanders, provided a focus for the raising of an Irish regiment there especially since the English king James had signalled his lack of opposition to such a development in 1605. A truce had been arranged between England and Spain in 1604. After the defeat of O'Neill and his surrender in 1603, there was an increasing supply of Irish soldiers of fortune in the Spanish Netherlands, among whom were Walter Delahyde and his brother George. One presumes that Walter brought with him a large number of those who had been pardoned with him in 1600, children of tenants of large holdings in Moyglare like Gerrot and Richard Foster of Kilgraigue, John Delahyde of Killeaney, farmer, and those from smaller holdings like the O'Boyles of Kilclone and Malie of Moyglare, Burnett of Moyglare and many more.[2]

As was inevitable after the wars and with the peace about to settle between Great Britain and the empire of Spain, both sides had a common interest in disposing of the flotsam and jetsam of soldiery floating around Ireland. The English wished to get rid of a constant worry and source of unrest and the Spanish archduke wanted soldiers for his armies in the Netherlands. By 1605 Captain Walter Delahyde was given permission to act as a recruiting agent of the king of Spain to round up soldiers in Ireland. "Captain Delahyde, Maurice Geraldine and William Darcy (were) permitted to get as many to go abroad with them as possible". Not without significance was the fact that those that got licences to recruit in Ireland from the London government were all of Old English background. All through the next two decades, as a minor thread in its foreign policy, the London government tried to exploit the differences between the two traditions, Old English and Old Irish, of those who served in the armies of the archduke and archduchess in the Spanish Netherlands.

An interesting letter survives from the governor of the Tower of London on the conditions awaiting the recruits in London on their way to the

Netherlands. There were, he wrote to Cecil,[4] the king's chief minister, "one hundred Irishmen outside the Spanish ambassador's lodgings". The constable of East Smithfield brought five or six "that speak English". "I learnt Captain Delahyde, Irishman, took up two hundred of them in Munster, Connaught and Leinster by warrant as he told them from the king to levy such as were willing to serve. They embarked at Waterford, landed at Penrin in Cornwall and came to the city. Their captain gave them only two shillings per man and for want of money they have sold their swords and some apparel to defray their charges. They often repair to the ambassador's lodgings because Delahyde lodges there". One hundred and twenty were sent over by Captain Darcy who had not yet come over himself. "They have so often presented themselves on the north side of Tower Hill beyond the postern before that tower where the titulary Desmond (the Geraldine pretender to the earldom of Desmond) was lodged, in such numbers and with such demonstrations of affection to him that I had him removed to a prison in Cold Harbour, where he can neither be seen nor see any of them, which he exceedingly stomachs". The soldiers and their camp followers the governor called "mere rogues and lewd people; they lived by stealth, pilfering and shifting, who dispensed themselves abroad in the daytime and lodged there in the night". He went on to say that at the end of a new lane called Hogs Lane, towards fields leading to Ratcliff, a cluster of base tenements termed Knockfergus were peopled with Irish of a very base sort, who lived only by begging. In the entire households, he claimed, there was not "stuff" worth more than forty pounds.

There is a nice contrast in the governor's letter between their loyalty to their old chief, the titular (or sugan) earl, as he was called, and indeed to Delahyde himself, and the squalor and misery attending on their stay in London. Few evidently could speak English; one wonders what happened when they reached the Spanish Netherlands and indeed how many made it there at all.

Walter was back in Ireland recruiting in 1606 with Lord Gormanston, Cusack and Darcy, and reports in government circles in London indicated that these Palesmen wished to leave their service in the Spanish Netherlands and come home.

Before his departure from the Low Countries (he was suspected of being a spy by Henry O'Neill), one "Trawe" had "made insinuations" with "one of the captains of the Irish regiment, called Delahyde who being disconsolate with his usage here (in the Low Countries) is willing to leave the place and to employ himself in the breaking of the regiment".[5] If the offer really was made, it was not taken up by the English government. It was safer to have Irish men like Delahyde, however ambivalent in their loyalties, outside

Ireland fighting foreign wars than to have them at home where they could be a source of disaffection and unrest. Other spies evidently at work in the previous year, perhaps with more accuracy informed the Protestant archbishop of Dublin, then the king's chief minister, that the people from the Pale with Henry O'Neill – Delahyde, Cusack, Lord Gormanston, William Darcy – all wished to return "if they hear of some stir in Ireland to come and succumb them".[6]

In 1608 Walter figured with some distinction at the siege of Rhemberg and was rewarded for his work, but in 1609 because of a scarcity of Irish soldiers whether because recruitment was more difficult with relative peace at home or because the appetites of war had become more voracious, the companies in the tercio or regiment were cut from twelve to six; among this company the captains surviving were Walter Delahyde and Don Eugenio O'Neill (in Ireland afterwards known as Owen Roe), who on the death of Henry O'Neill became in effect colonel of the Irish tercio because the titular colonel, John O'Neill, Henry's half brother, was still a very young child. Walter was given a pension of forty crowns a month by the archduchess, the joint viceroy, and she arranged that he be "about our person where he will enjoy the grant in future."[7]

Letters survive from 1613 to William Turnbull, the English agent or charge d'affaires in Brussels, from a number of Old English sources in the environment of Brussels, giving news of local opinion and local reaction to fluid relationships between France, Spain, the United Provinces and England. One letter from Turnbull to Robert Cecil, the chief minister in London, is a memorial "contaying instructions for captaine Walter Delahyde of such points concerning the business he knoweth of as hee is to treat with the king's majeste".

It contained instructions for Delahyde's journey to London for an interview with the king to uncover to him a plot discovered in the Low Countries; "to give his majeste a taste of the business you may aquaint him that the substance of the plot (as you are informed) is to betraye and retayne parte of his kingdom to the Spanyard; and then, to assayle his sacred person and the person of the hopeful prince and heir apparent." Measures were to be taken "for the safety of your brother Captain George Delahyde".[8] How seriously such information was and is to be taken is problematic. In the event, nothing happened and Walter settled down as a respected agent of the archduke and to remain the competent soldier he always seemed to have been. But the point remained and it was to surface in 1625 when it was decided to promise Old English soldiers in Flanders the "same rank in the king's service abroad and this will bring back those whose lands are in the occupation of others". Those who had deliberately joined Spain in hopes of returning with armed malice must be delicately treated. Captain Preston, Delahyde and Fitzgerald principally to be respected and their example will be helpful for others – " the mere Irish are hard to win."[9] A constant thread in government policy was to keep contact with the Old English in Flanders and use the good will thereby created to keep the rift between them and "the mere Irish" as wide as possible. Not insigificant was the fact that the licence to recruit for Flanders army was given by the government in London only to Old English people like Delahyde, Preston and Fitzgerald. No Old Irish names appear on surviving lists. Captain George, Walter's brother, was never among the recruiters. His career had not as high a profile as had that of Walter, though he got a pension of twenty crowns in 1612 from Philip II in consideration of his contribution to the army and because "he abandoned forfeited estates in Ireland." In 1620 George offered to raise a company of two hundred at his own expense. The offer was accepted but George died in 1622.[10]

In 1622 Walter was back in Ireland, not entirely to the delight of the viceroy in Dublin, Lord Faulkland, "Captain Delahyde has lately drawn three hundred men to the parts thereabouts near Dublin pretending to do as Captain Fitzgerald had done, but no shipping was at yet in readiness, so he laid the soldiers upon the country who became a burden to the people; but they would do their best to hasten them away with all speed, as they did the former."[11]

Walter was back in 1623 when he recruited a hundred above the expected two hundred men. By 1631 Walter was a captain in the garrison of Ostend. (See illustration of 'Soldiers Arming Themselves' by Jacob Duck, 1600 – 1667. Soldiers in the Dutch Wars about 1630, p xiii). And in 1634 one George Hope was recruiting in Ireland for Walter Delahyde. Owen Roe had ceased being acting colonel of the tercio in 1628 when John, Earl of Tyrone, came of age. But Tyrone soon moved to Spain and Don Eugenio became a full colonel. In 1633, Walter's son Stephen, was in his father's company and he became its captain in 1636, presumably when Walter had retired. Walter was called back to the colours in 1640 when he went to Arras to assist Owen Roe in his classic defence of the city. It was Owen Roe's actions at Arras which confirmed him as one of the leading military commanders of his day. Walter got forty crowns a month pension as a former captain having served forty years in the king's service, "the first four of which were served in the wars in Ireland". The ensign of Captain Stephen was sent to recruit in Ireland in 1641 when negotiations were taking place to transfer the Irish Catholic army recruited by the Irish viceroy, Strafford, to the services of the king of Spain. None of the Delahydes seem to have returned to Ireland for the confederate wars. By then (1638) Moyglare had been sold to the Earl of Strafford. Walter still enjoyed his pension, and lived with

Stephen, his son, who was later killed at the recovery of the Fort of Mardoch in 1646. Walter returned to the garrison of Hal where the pension continued "in consideration of his great age and of his service."[12] A second son, Michael, was commissioned in the company, and in 1648 he too got a grant of forty crowns a month; perhaps the pension formerly paid to his father, who was now dead, was still being paid to the son. Delahydes still figure in the service of the Spanish army in Flanders but it is not possible to pinpoint their relationship to the house of Moyglare. One Richard Delahyde of the regiment got a licence to go to Ireland "on business concerning his estate" in 1660. He may have been the Richard Delahyde who had been Luke's grandson and heir at Moyglare. Judging by the surviving records, Richard had no success in obtaining land in Restoration Ireland. Soon afterwards this regiment was disbanded.[13]

In the wars of the three kings, from 1689 to 1691, a lieutenant colonel Michael Delahyde appears as a combatant, and a Colonel Delahyde died at the battle of Aughrim. By this time the Delahydes had gone forever from Moyglare, and though one or two appear in the eighteenth century French army lists – one Richard Delahyde was in the duke of Berwick's regiment in France – it is not possible to trace a direct connection with the house of Moyglare.[14]

The life and work of Walter Delahyde, his brother and his sons reveal the radical side of the Delahydes, their backing of many horses to ensure that the family survived, but also the complicated web of tribal and family loyalties which bound their tenants and followers to them. These reflect the theme of Robert Louis Stevenson's "The Master of Ballantrae", and echo also in the quatrain attributed to an Old English Darcy who lived outside Navan in 1690, and was accused of hypocrisy for having entertained King James and King William on successive days:

"Who'll be king
 I do not know
 But I'll be Darcy
 Of Dunmoe"

Another member of the Moyglare family, James, of Moygaddy, obviously took the other side in the O'Neill wars. He was mentioned as petitioning for lands which the government had for sale in 1609. He was then in receipt of a pension of two and six per day "granted in respect of his maim in one of his legs in service." He was still receiving it "during pleasure" in 1623.[15]

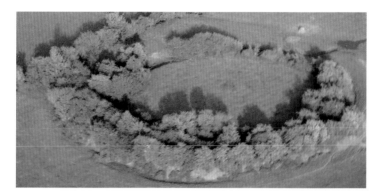

Collistown Ringfort

Rodanstown Earthwork

Moyglare Gateway

Moygaddy Tower House

Opposite page:
Down Survey map

Mulhussey House
and Tower

ii

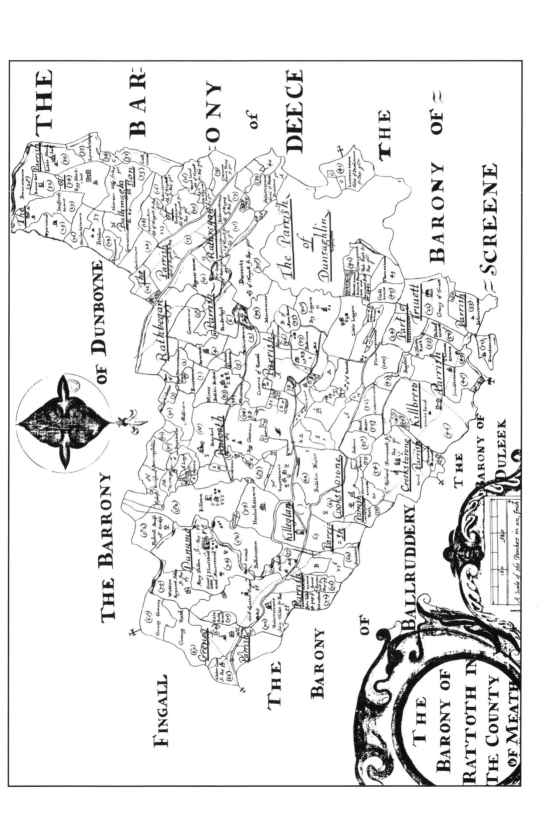

THE BARONY OF RATTOTH IN THE COUNTY OF MEATH

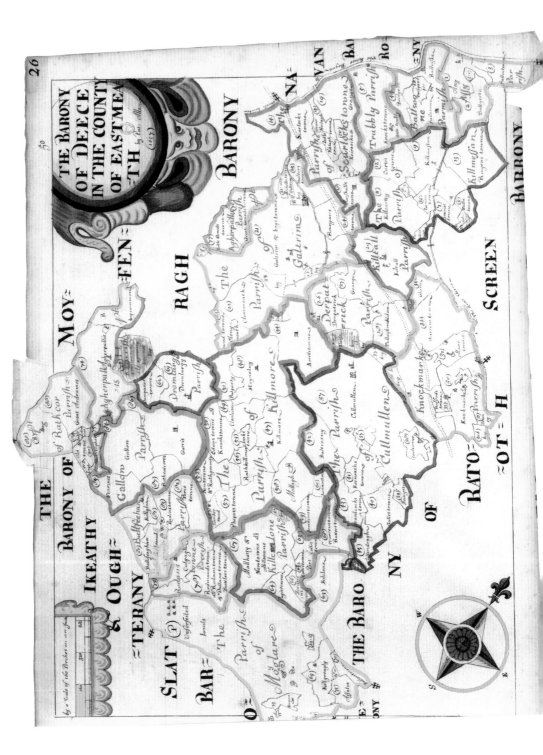

THE BARONY OF DEECE IN THE COUNTY OF EASTMEATH (167) by Petr Gallozay

THE BARONY OF RATHCOR IKEATHY OUGH & TERANY

SLAT BAR O

MOY= =FEN=

RAGH

NA

THE BARONY

VAN BAR RO =NY

SCREEN

RATO= =OT=H

NY OF THE BARO

THE BARO =ONY E

Opposite page:
The Barony of Deece

The Synod of 1216
Bishop Simon
deRochfort
1194 – 1224, first
Norman Bishop of Meath

The Decrees of Synod
David Wilkins, Concilia
Magnae Brittaniae et
Hiberniae a Synodo
Verulamiensi AD
CCCCXLVI ad
Londinensem AD
MDCCXVII (Londini:
sumptibus R. Gosling,
1737). 4v.

Constitutiones Simonis episc. Midensis. 547

Papae Rom.	Archiep. Cantuar.	Anno Christi	Reg. Angliae
Honorii III. 1.	Steph. Langton 10.	1216.	Henric. III. 1.

Constitutiones factae in ecclesia cathedrali SS. Petri et Pauli Novae Villae juxta Athrumiam, per Simonem, Dei gratia episcopum Midensem, in synodo ibidem tenta anno MCCXVI. Ex MS. penes Joh. episc. Klogherensem.

CUM dominus Johannes Paparo, presbyter cardinalis tituli S. Laurentii in Damaso, summi pontificis et domini nostri Eugenii III. legatus in Hibernia, in synodo generali tenta apud Kenanas in Midia, anno gratiae MCLII. inter alias salubres constitutiones, tunc et ibidem factas, ordinaverit, ut decedentibus chorepiscopis, et exiliorum sedium episcopis in Hibernia, in eorum locum eligerentur et succederent archipresbyteri a dioecesanis constituendi, qui cleri et plebis solicitudinem gerant infra suos limites, et

nobis vel officialibus nostris impositas delinquentibus debite, et ea, qua decet solennitate, peragi, et perimpleri in ecclesiis infra suos limites, quibus ipsi cum presbyteris parochialibus intersint, tanquam testes, ut qua humilitate et devotione poenitentiae laboribus defuncti sunt, testificare possint.

VII. Item, ut in admissione ad officium, juramentum praestent de fideli executione sui officii. Item, de inquirendo et praesentando nobis et officialibus nostris nomina et cognomina om-

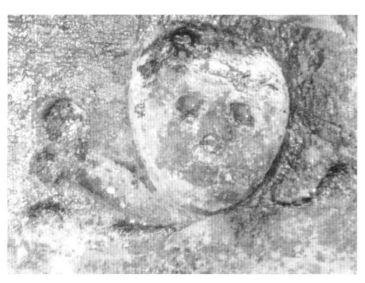

**Balfeighan Church
Stoneworks**
15th Century

Opposite page:
**Newtown Trim
Cathedral**

Rodanstown Church

Rathregan Earthworks

Ruins of Rathegan
Stone House

Ruins of Church
at Rathegan

Sunken Way
at Rathegan

The Husseys Crest
Mulhussey

Opposite page:
Soldiers Arming
Themselves
Jacob Duck
1600 – 1667, Dutch
oil on panel

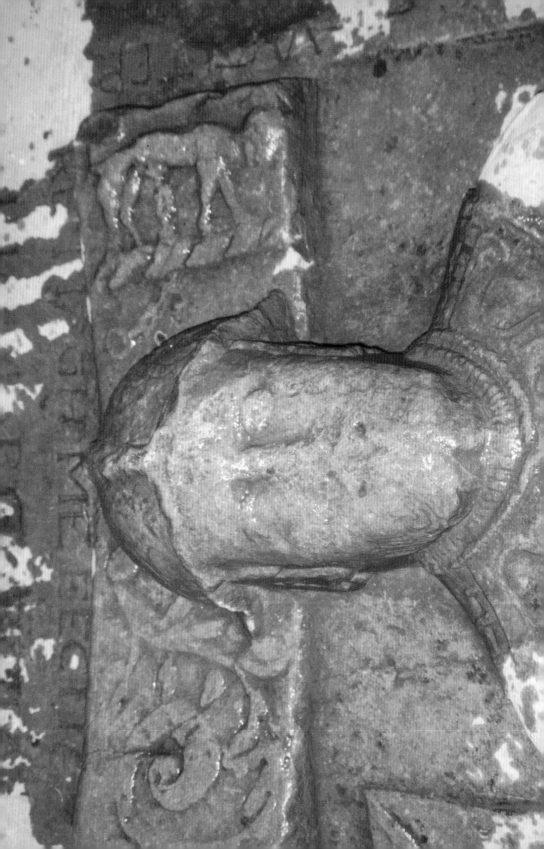

Footnotes

The Delahydes 1350 to 1534

1   Genealogical Office MS 182, p170, 177.

2   St. John Brooks, Knights' Fees in Wexford, Carlow and Kilkenny, passim.

3   C.D.I – 1252-1284, 696 William de Trubleville, marshal of the king's household, complained of being impleaded by John Delahyde, who had married a daughter of Valerian Wesley. Trubleville claimed Ballemadun as he had got it for a pair of "cowhide greaves" from the king before the king granted Ireland to his son. He claimed three carucates of land and nine marchates of rent but had not obtained justice because of Valerian Wesley's influence. The king ordered two discreet men to investigate and report under seal to him. What happened is not recorded but John Delahyde and his family kept the manor of Ballymadun for nearly another century.

4   St. John Brooks, p25.

5   St. John Brooks, p25, note 6

6   36 report, P.R.O. appendix 62, Edward I, 1272 to 1307.

7   c.f. Calendar of Inquisitions, p401: in the reign of James I the family still kept up contact with the Delahydes of Moyglare, Among the most prominent scholars of his day was David Delahyde. He was of the Moyglare family, perhaps a nephew of Sir Walter. Born in county Kildare, some say at Carbury, one of the estates of the Moyglare family; went to Oxford, made fellow of Merton college (1549) M.A. (1553) and B.C.L. (1558). Imprisoned for refusing to accept the Elizabethan changes in religion, he was described in a report of the commissioners enforcing the changes in Oxford, "David Delahyde, an Irishman, late scholar of Oxford; at his liberty saving that he is restrained to come within twenty miles of either university. Very stubborn, and worthy to be looked into."Stanihurst, who wrote the History of Irelande for Holinshed, describes him as "an exquisite and profound clerke... Verie well seene in the Latine and Greeke toongs, expert in the mathematicals, a proper antiquarie, and an exact diuine... I gather that his pen hath not beene lazie, but is dalie breeding of such learned bookes as shall be available to posteritie. "He wrote many books, most of them published abroad where he went into exile at Rouen; none of them seems to have survived. He left his library to the city of Dublin when he died in 1588. Before that he was among the promising ecclesiastics put forward for vacant bishoprics in Ireland. He was one of four "in literis valde eminentes. "John Brady, "Eminent Irish Scholars of the sixteenth century" in Studies, 1948, p227. In the reign of Henry VIII Richard Delahyde was chief justice and Christopher a justice of the king's bench. They both seem to have been brothers of Sir Walter and both lost their positions as a consequence of the rebellion of Silken Thomas.

8   Pipe Roll of Edward III, 1342,1345,1346, when Walter Delahyde was sheriff of Meath, P.R.I.E. p51 to 57.

9   Rotulus Clausus, de Anno 48, Edward III, Analecta XXXV, p118.

10 Rotulus Clausus, de Anno 48, Edward III, Analecta XXXV p118 (8th June 1374).

11 Chartularies of St. Mary's Abbey, Vol. 2, p283; Calendar of Carew 1, p168.

12 Rotulus Clausus, de Anno 48, Edward III, Analecta XXXV, p152.

13 Gormanston Register VIII, 139, Guide to English Financial Records for Irish history, Anelecta X, p19.

14 Guide to English Financial Records for Irish History, Analecta X, p14.

15 Guide to English Financial Records for Irish History, Analecta X, p32.

16 Christ Church Deeds, 100.

17 C.S.P.I. 1509 to 1573, p2. The dowager countess complained that her stepson, (Garret Óg) had let lands of his brother fall into the hands of the "wilde Irish" except for the piece that fell to Sir Walter Delahyde.

18 Cal. Carew, 1515 to 1575, p39.

19 C.S.P.I. 1509 to 1573, p11.

20 Patent and Close Rolls, Henry VIII, p3 (1533 to 1534).

The Delahydes and the Rebellion of Silken Thomas

1   Earls of Kildare, the Marquis of Kildare, p145 quoting state papers, Vol.2, 226.

2   C.S.P.I, 1509 to 1573, p11; Justice Delahyde despite efforts to disengage himself from the rebellion (he even wrote to Thomas Cromwell in London offering to send him a goshawk) lost his position as chief justice of the court of common pleas. He was succeeded by Thomas Luttrell of Luttrellstown who managed, though a Catholic and half brother of Robert Luttrell, a prominent Catholic cleric in Meath, to remain chief justice through the reign of Edward VI and he died still chief justice in the first year of the reign of Mary Tudor. Justice Richard Delahyde was Sir Walter's brother; another brother, Christopher, was a justice of the king's bench from 1527 until 1535 (Liber Munerum, p32,35).

3   STANIHURST, Richard, The Historie of Irelande, in Holinshed's Chronicles p269.

4   Quoted in Earls of Kildare, p298, 299.

5   STANIHURST, Richard, The Historie of Irelande, Holinshed, p281.

6   Earls of Kildare, p146 (The reference is to state papers 2, p226).

7   STANIHURST, p282.

8   Ibid, p283.

9   Comerford, Collections: the dioceses of Kildare and Leighlin, Vol.1, p25.

10   Earls of Kildare, p150.

11   Fiants, Edward VI, p134

12   Notes on the Rise and Fall of a great Meath estate, Ellison, Riocht na Midhe, Vol.3, No.4, 1966, p318.

13   Fiants, Edward VI, p639.

The Survey of 1540

1   Crown Surveys of Lands, 1540 to 41, with the Kildare rentals begun in 1518, ed. G.McNiochaill, p226 ff.; The Civil Survey, Vol.5, Meath; Griffith, Union of Celbridge (1851), Union of Dunshaughlin, (1854).

2   Christ Church Deeds, p348, 350.

3   Mason, The History and Antiquities of the Collegiate and Cathedral church of St.Patrick near Dublin (Dublin 1820) p96.

4   Christ Church Deeds, p866.

5   Christ Church Deeds, p866; Fiants Edward VI, p134; Wentworth Papers N.L.I., A coppy of Sir George Wentworth's Clayme to Moyglare, 1654; Civil Survey, Vol.5 (Meath) p153 ff.

The Delahydes – 1534 to 1638

1   He was succeeded in Kilberry by Robert Luttrell, The Church Establishment, Vol.2, p97.

2   Fiants, Edward VI, p134.

3   Fiants, Elizabeth, No.281.

4   Fiants, Elizabeth, 3232.

5   The Periott Papers, Analecta XII, p13; C.S.P.I. 1574 to 1585, p546.

6   Fiants, Elizabeth, 4927.

7   Fiants, Elizabeth, 4926.

8   Fiants, Elizabeth, 5206, No.9

9   Patent and Close Rolls, Elizabeth (1600) p567.

10   Fiants, Elizabeth, 6416. Among the terms of the wardship was that he "be maintained and educated in English religion and in English apparel in the College of the Holy Trinity from his twelfth to his eighteenth year". The terms proved ineffective. The lord deputy, Chichester to Council 1612, Analecta VIII, p121; Cal. Patent Rolls, James I, p292.

11   Calendar of Carew Papers 1601 to 1603, p449; Moryson's Ireland, Vol.1, p71 (1735 ed.)

12   C.S.P.I. 1598, 1599, p340.

13   Calendar of Carew Papers, 1589 to 1600, p298.

14   Fiants Elizabeth, 6557.

15   Fiants Elizabeth, 6777.

16   C.S.P.I. 1606 -1607, p297. C.S.P.I. 1660-1662 p353. The King renewed in 1661 the pension granted in 1616 and confirmed in 1625 but not paid during the Commonwealth years.

17   Wentworth Documents, N.L.I.

18   Office book belonging to Paul Rycart, Secretary to the Earl of Clarendon, Rawlison, 481, letter in the name of James II, 1685, Analecta, I, p107.

19   The Transplantation to Connaught, 1654 to 1658, ed. Simington, p78,169.

20   Bishop Dopping's Visitation Book, 1682 to 1685, ed. Ellison, Riocht na Midhe, Vol.5, No.2 (1972) pg3; O'Hart, Irish Landed Gentry, p310.

21   O'Hart, Irish Landed Gentry, p510.

The Wild Geese from Moyglare – 1600 to 1650

1   This essay is based largely on Grainne Henry's The Irish Military Community in Spanish Flanders and on Brendan Jennings ed. Wild Geese in Spanish Flanders. 1582-1700

2   Fiants, Elizabeth 6557,6777. The pardon was somewhat controversial. One of the Dublin Council in a letter to Sir. Robert Cecil wrote "There are of the Delahydes, a gentleman, born not far from Dublin, and a man very civilly brought up, who hath been a chief and principal traitor, and one who hath done great hurt and committed many murders and outrages upon her majesty's subjects. This man's pardon and protection hath not only been procured by Sir Oliver Lambert, but he hath now professed the traitor to be lieutenant unto Captain Guest and fifty of the traitors, which are his men, to receive her majesty's pay and to be of the same company". Obviously Delahyde was not only a competent soldier but could deliver on the loyalty of his followers from Moyglare.

3   C.S.P.I. 1603 to 1606, 23rd June 1605, p298.

4   C.S.P.I. 1603 to 1606, 23rd June 1605, p298; H.M.C. Salisbury Papers, pt. XVIII, p449, ff.

5   C.S.P.I. 1606 to 1608, p642.

6   C.S.P.I. 1603 to 1606, p579.

7   HENRY, p90, 111; Jennings No.535 (612).

8   C.S.P.I. 1625 to 1632, p73; Jennings, p535 (1612); P.R.O. Sp. 77 – 11 ff 351,352, 20th June, 1613.

9   In 1599, George, with many other Delahydes in Kerry and Westmeath was pardoned (Fiants Elizabeth, 6314); P.R.O. Sp. 77-11, ff, 351-2 (20th June 1613); Jennings, 878 (1625).

10 C.S.P.I. 1615 to 1625, p393, Analecta II, p13 "Recruiting soldiers for service of Spain,...Captain Delahyde of that service whose neighbourhood the deputy liked not had his four hundred or five hundred men quartered up and down the county Dublin".

11 Calendar Carew, 1601 to 1603, p449; C.S.P.I. 1615 to 1625 (1622), p393; Jennings No.878 (1625), 736, 821.

12 JENNINGS, 1885, 1640.

13 JENNINGS, 2658.

14 O'Hart, Irish Landed Gentry, p529,510.

15 Fiants,Elizabeth 1602, 1603, 6777; C.S.P.I. 1608 to 1610, p325, 337, 511; C.S.P.I., 1615 to 1625, p12, 447.

Chapter 15

The Manor of Mulhussey or Kilclone – 1350 to 1655

In 1406 Matthew Hussey, baron of Galtrim, was licensed to set up the manor of Mulhussey as a discrete manor to be held from the lordship of Trim.[1] It was an inheritance for his second son, Nicholas, and his family. The manor comprised most of what is now the civil parish of Kilclone, though by 1550 the townland of Kilclone itself was part of the Hussey manor of Rodanstown, also held by a branch of the Hussey family. In time the Husseys of Mulhussey acquired substantial estates in neighbouring parishes so that by 1640 the head of the family, Edward, held over two thousand five hundred plantation acres, roughly seven thousand five hundred acres in modern or statute acres. (See illustration of the Hussey crest, a 15th century sculpture formerly at Mulhussey, p xii). In the fifteenth century the Husseys built a tower house, still to be seen there in ruins, as their manorial centre. (See illustration of Mulhussey house and tower, p ii). They built a church near it, as the parish church of Kilclone was four miles away, and besides it was like the four neighbouring parishes, a chaplaincy depending on Galtrim. Presumably the chaplains were appointed by the baron of Galtrim or by the abbot of St. Peter and Paul at Trim who, with the bishop of the diocese, held the advowson for most of the 15th century. And the Husseys of Mulhussey preferred to have a chaplain of their own.

For the first century and a half of their ownership of Mulhussey, the Husseys kept a low profile. Only twice does the name reach the records which have survived. In 1465 with many others, Nicholas Hussey was required "for the preservation of the good rule, weal and prosperity of the county of Meath", to present himself at Dublin Castle to answer grave charges unspecified, under pain of being attainted and having all his goods confiscated. That Meath was not the most peaceful of places towards the end of the fifteenth century is indicated by the next act of parliament and perhaps it is a pointer to the charges at least alleged against Nicholas, son of Patrick Hussey.

"That whereas divers great robberies, thefts and murders were committed from night to night by thieves, upon the faithful liege people of the king within this land of Ireland, especially and most commonly in the county of Meath, which have caused and make great desolation and waste in the said county: it is ordained and established by authority of the said parliament, that it be lawful to all manner of men who find any thieves robbing by day or by night, or going or coming to rob or steal, in or out going or coming, having no faithful man of good name and fame in their company, in English apparel, and upon any of the faithful liege people of the king, that it shall be lawful to take and kill them and to cut off their heads without any impeachment of our sovereign lord the king,... And for any head so cut off in the county of Meath, that the cutter of the same head and his assistants to him there, cause the said head so cut off to be brought to the portreeve of the town of Trim, and the said portreeve to put it on a spear upon the castle of Trim,...and it shall be lawful...for the said bringer of the said head and his assistants to the same, to distrain and levy by their own hands from every man having a plough land (120 acres or about 400 statute acres) in the barony where the said thief was so taken, two pence and from every man having half a plough land in the said barony, one penny, and from every other man having a house and goods to the value of forty shillings, one penny, and from every other cottier having a house and smoke a half penny."[2]

Though presumably the picture presented here of Meath in the late fifteenth century is exaggerated, as acts of parliament tend to be in description of the context of legislation, the savage and public penalties for crimes against property, the presumed incursion from beyond the marchlands, the giving of draconian powers of life and death to ordinary citizens especially over those not dressed in the English fashion, all point to a lawlessness that the tower houses and the Pale ditch were intended to counteract.

But the act does point to cavalier attitudes to the private property of others being the motivation of the sanction against Nicholas Hussey and the other thirty-eight summoned with him (most of whom had Norman names). Nicholas, with two others, was spared by a separate act from having to go to jail in Dublin, for they

"are gentlemen of the land, having lands and goods sufficient within the same and are amenable and justifiable at the common law, and are also ready in their own persons to answer to all manner of matter which shall be alleged or sufficiently proved against them or any of them."[3]

Two years later Nicholas Hussey figured in a similar list of people made up of a mix of "idle men" and "gentlemen" (about 110 in number from Meath and Louth) which included Wellesley of the Dangan, Hussey of

Gallo, and John Plunkett of Beaulieu near Drogheda, who were to present themselves for distraint at Dublin Castle, accused of "divers and many extortions, oppressions, larcenies, robbery and taking of pledges."[4]

What happened in this instance does not appear in the subsequent acts of parliament; evidently the businesses were settled to the satisfaction of all.

But again, in 1471-72, another list of names (21 in all) appears in an act of parliament; it also includes Nicholas Hussey, William Wellesley of Dangan, Henry Plunkett of Beaulieu, Edmund Deshe of Rathbeggan, and Baldwin Fleming of Culmullen. They were once again required to present themselves for jail in Dublin Castle, and in 1476, another list of 70 names appears in an act of parliament, again requiring the listed to appear for jail while answering charges of crimes against property. This time special acts were passed by which a number of people, including Wellesley of the Dangan and Nicholas Hussey of Mulhussey, were no longer obliged to appear in Dublin jail if each of them appeared before "the king in the chancery of Ireland," gave their surety for good behaviour and restored any goods unlawfully taken.[5] It seems as if common law, which handled ordinary cases of alleged crimes against property, or differences having to do with ownership thereof, had broken down in the reign of Edward IV and special provision in parliament was needed to handle important cases.

The Husseys of Mulhussey do not figure in the records again until the reign of Mary Tudor, 1553 – 1558. In 1554 Meiler Hussey was on a commission.[6] for jail delivery and in 1558 he was on a commission with Gerald Wellesly of Dangan and Patrick Hussey, baron of Galtrim to execute martial law in Kildare.[7] The newly restored earl of Kildare made Meiler his chief steward sometime before 1562;[8] he had granted him his large townsland in Moyglare parish, Newtownmoyaghy, in 1556. In 1558 he granted Meiler the manor of Moynalvy for eighty pounds sterling and two hundred pounds Irish. The Husseys kept this townsland of three hundred and thirty eight plantation acres until the Cromwellian plantation.[9] In 1563 Hussey was the earl of Kildare's messenger to Shane O'Neill, advising him to submit to the government, which he did, and go under the earl's protection to England. In 1567 the earl granted Meiler eighty pounds, with two hundred pounds more to come, for handling some delicate business in England.[10] Though the family remained Catholic and had not shared in the monastic plunder of Henry VIII's days, Meiler Hussey of Mulhussey arrested Richard Creagh, Catholic archbishop of Armagh, in 1567, and handed him over to the lord deputy Sydney on condition that his life would be spared. Hussey sent back the forty pounds reward for the archbishop's capture and asked that his condition be observed. In one way it was fulfilled, as Archbishop Creagh died in the Tower of London in 1585. His death has been accepted as that of a martyr and his cause for beatification has been proceeding recently to its close in Rome. Rumours spread among contemporaries that he had been poisoned in prison.

Meiler was succeeded by Walter, and Walter was of similar mind in political matters as his father had been. In 1591 he wrote to the Lord Chancellor reporting on the rumours circulating around Mulhussey on various political matters: the Spaniards were to invade France, the king of Navarre (the Huguenot who a few years later became Henry IV of France) was set to flee with his people to England, and "further he (Hussey) said that next Christmas, naming what day, her majesty should die and all England be overthrown." The comment of the good lord chancellor was: "It were well to sift this matter out very circumspectly, as it no doubt proceeds from some bad cause."[12] Of course, the letter proved to be a nonsense but its existence does emphasise the insecurity of the government in Dublin and the commitment of the Husseys of Mulhussey to the crown which made them report on local public opinion and rumour. Fines Morrison, secretary to the lord deputy, Mountjoy, in the O'Neill wars, gives a shadowy sketch of conditions in Mulhussey as he passed through in 1601." We passed the Liffey, and came to Mulhussey, one master Hussey's castle, passing by some pleasant villages, and by Menuth, a faire house belonging to the earls of Kildare, now in the hands of the Countesse Mabell, an old widow."[13] When Walter died in 1602 he held a substantial estate; not only Mulhussey, Milltown, (?) ton, Pagestown and a messauge in the "villa of Kilclone" bordering on Cullendragh, all in the manor of Mulhussey (Kilclone) but also Portane in Rathregan, Barna Kittyn, Galstown, Woodcockstown, Cullendragh in Cullmullen, Clarkestown in Gallo – one castle, twenty messauges, and one water mill, and four hundred plantation acres – and in Moynalvy four messauges with one hundred and twenty acres with Culcor in Gallo (ten messauges and two hundred and eighty five acres), Warrenstown in Knockmark, Jenkinstown in Kilmore and a number of others impossible to place – Vernockstown, Dranoghton, Oughterillaghe and Ballycollagh.[14] The estate was one of more than two thousand plantation acres – at least seven thousand five hundred statute acres. Walter was succeeded by Thomas, who died in 1629, and he was succeeded by Edward, then twenty two years old and married.[15]

For Edward's activities during the confederate wars, see chapter 23. He lost the estates in the Cromwellian plantation and despite carefully exiling himself at the court of Charles II in the Low Countries when Cromwell ruled England, and receiving a decree of innocence when Charles was restored, he never got his lands back. He, or his son, seems to have been a tenant in Mulhussey afterwards. One Meiler Hussey of Mulhussey was outlawed in 1691 and soon afterwards the Husseys disappeared from the parish and manor of Kilclone. They surfaced in an estate in Roscommon called, nostalgically, Mulhussey.[16] One of them, Ignatius, conformed to the Established Church in 1718. He was a grandson of Edward Hussey and son of Walter of Donore, County Kildare. From him descended the famous orator – Hussey Burgh, who immortalised himself in a lapidary phrase in the Irish parliament in the 1780's: "England has sown her laws as dragon's teeth and they have sprung up in armed men." It was an allusion to the legend of Jason and his argonauts and their search for the Golden Fleece.[17]

Footnotes

1   Holding on: The Husseys of Galtrim, p8. quoting Bernard Burke, The Landed Gentry of Ireland (1904) p337.

2   Statute Rolls of Ireland, Edward IV, ed, Berry, p289, 445, 721.

3   Statute Rolls of Ireland, Edward IV, ed, Berry, p425.

4   Ibid, p443.

5   Statute Rolls of Ireland, Edward IV, Part 2, p357.

6   Cal. P. and C. Rolls, 1554-5, p347.

7   Cal. P. and C. Rolls, 1558, p409.

8   Maynooth Castle, Walter Fitzgerald, J.K.A.S. Vol.1, p231.

9   Calendar of Inquisitions, Elizabeth I, 41; Maynooth Castle, Ibid. p231.

10 Ware, quoted in The Earls of Kildare, p205.

11 C.S.P.I. 1509 to 1573. p354.

12 C.S.P.I. 1585 to 1592, p467.

13 Ormond Papers, Vol.1, p49; Moryson's Ireland, Vol.1, p201 (1735 ed.)

14 Inquis. in Officio rotulorum Cancellanae Hiberniae, Vol.I, Lagenia, Meath, Charles I, p63.

15 Ibid. 63.

16. Burke's Family Records, p343.

17 Ibid. p343; The Convert Rolls, Ed. O'Byrne, p140

Chapter 16

The Manor of Balfeighan – 1350 to 1655

Just as the barons of Deece, the Husseys of Galtrim, were reluctant to see Kilclone, Balfeighan and Rodanstown become separate parishes, so they were equally reluctant to give them independence and manorial status before the 15th century. Sometime before the middle of the 15th century, the manor of Balfeighan became part of the estate controlled by Thomas Fitzgerald, the 7th Earl of Kildare; perhaps it was leased from the Husseys in the 14th century, but the surviving records are silent about the names of the lords of Balfeighan from the Norman conquest until sometime in the mid years of the 15th century, when the 7th Earl of Kildare granted two manors from his inheritance to his second son Thomas. They were the manors of Lackagh, Co. Kildare, and of Balfeighan.[1] Both these lands were manorial residences and both were lived in by successive generations of the Fitzgerald family. In 1642 Balfeighan was a "town and castle fit to receive 100 men".[2] It does seem as if there was a tower house on the site of what is now the ruins of Balfeighan House, perhaps built by Thomas Fitzgerald when he took over his inheritance. The nearby church was reconstructed too in 15th century style; perhaps it also marked an effort to give prominence and status to the junior branch of the Fitzgerald family. It is also possible that all this happened after the death of the 7th Earl in 1478 when the rest of his estates were inherited by his son Garret Mór, 8th Earl of Kildare.

The reign of Edward IV, from 1460, was marked by occasional efforts, some of them extremely ruthless, to free his governance of Ireland from the necessity of ruling through one or other of the great Anglo-Irish magnates. The Earl of Ormonde and Wiltshire had backed the Lancastrian King, Henry VI, and when that cause was lost at the Battle of Towton in 1461, he was executed. The next Anglo-Irish lord who came to prominence in the reign of Edward IV was the Earl of Desmond who was Chief Governor of Ireland 1463 – 1467. The necessary tension between the usefulness and threat of such a local magnate was broken when in 1468 a new governor sent from England, Sir John Tipcroft, nicknamed The Butcher, seized Desmond, Thomas 7th Earl of Kildare and Edward Plunkett of the Meath Plunkett family, and accused them of treason for breaking the Statutes of Kilkenny in associating with the King's Irish enemies in the North. Desmond was executed but the other two were kept captive for further use.

In 1470, when he regained his throne after a brief Lancastrian interlude, Edward once again turned to an Anglo-Irish magnate to rule those parts of Ireland which accepted his authority. The only obvious candidate was Thomas, 7th Earl of Kildare, because the Desmond Fitzgeralds were still nursing the injustice of 1468 and the head of the Ormonde family was an absentee in England. The Crown tried to mark the Earl by having his enemy, the English-born Bishop of Meath, William Shirwood, occasionally as Chief Governor, Chancellor or Treasurer but when Shirwood's tenure of the Governorship lapsed in 1478, Garret Mór, now 8th Earl of Kildare since his father's death in the same year, was selected by the Irish Council as temporary governor. Garret evidently intended that his hold on the position would be permanent and when a newly appointed deputy governor arrived in Dublin he got no co-operation from the resident council which was obviously controlled by a clique gathered by Garret's father in the last years of his life when he was governor of Ireland; and Garret became lord deputy. This same clique was to rule Ireland with occasional and temporary gaps for the next 40 years. One of the most prominent of them was Sir Roland FitzEustace of Portlester, near Athboy, sometime Chancellor but more regularly Treasurer of Ireland for most of the years of Garret Mór. His daughter, Alison, was married to the Earl. Another daughter, Janet, was married to Sir Walter Delahyde of Moyglare.[3]

Another of the clique was of course Thomas Fitzgerald, lord of Lackagh and Balfeighan, who became Chancellor of Ireland on the death of Bishop Sherwood in 1482. In the same year he was granted for life the royal manor of Ardmulchan (near Navan) and Belgard in Dublin, provided his income from them did not exceed forty-four pounds a year.[4] The new king, Richard III, tried to oust him from his office in 1483 but was unsuccessful.

When the Yorkist King Richard was overthrown by Henry Tudor of the house of Lancaster in 1485, the sympathies of the Fitzgeralds and indeed of most of the Anglo-Irish magnates were with the deposed house of York. When in 1487 a young boy, Lambert Simnel, was brought to Ireland purporting to be a nephew of the last two Yorkist kings, he got substantial support there. Garret Mór, probably sympathetic, was prudently silent. The main role in rallying support for the pretender was taken by his brother Thomas. In time, Kildare became more overt in his support for the young man. In 1487, five thousand German mercenaries arrived in Ireland, sent by Margaret, Duchess of Burgundy, sister of the last Yorkist King, to prepare for an invasion of England. Ireland rallied to the cause. The young man was crowned king in Christ Church with a crown taken from a statue of the Blessed Virgin, and a parliament was summoned by Kildare. A substantial army, made up of the German mercenaries, and Anglo-Irish and Gaelic troops, invaded England in 1487 but they were comprehensively defeated at the Battle of Stoke, June 16th. At that battle, Thomas Fitzgerald of Lackagh and Balfeighan was killed.[5]

Thomas was succeeded by his son Maurice, who in 1519 was appointed deputy by his cousin, Garret Óg, when he went to England to answer charges made against him. In 1520, as the Annals of the Four Masters records, "Maurice, the son of Thomas, the son of the earl, the choice of the English family of the Geraldines, was slain by Conn, the son of Melaghlin O'More, as were many others along with him". His son was another Thomas. The family does not appear in the records again until 1533, when, with judicious timing, just before the rebellion of Silken Thomas, in which the family was bound to have been involved on the losing side, the head of the house, Sir Thomas Fitzmaurice Fitzgerald, died and his heir, Maurice, a minor of five years, became a royal ward of court and was sent to the convent of Odder near Skyrne to be reared.[6]

Succeeding generations of the family were not involved in politics except for occasional forays into local government, acting as organisers of the troop musters in the County of Kildare. Maurice Fitzgerald does not appear in the records except for his role in local hustings in Kildare.[7] He seems to have fixed his normal place of residence at Lackagh, but he did not take any part in politics and received none of the monastic plunder which was the reward for those who did, though in 1552 he did get a grant of the bridge of "Bealyne" in O'Dempsey's country on the Barrow. Presumably, he was to guard the Pale from the incursions of the native Irish from what is now Offaly and Laois. He died in 1575 in Lackagh.[8] (See front cover and illustration of head and shoulders of Sir Maurice Fitzgerald, p xvi). A possible ambiguity in the attitude of the family to the government is hinted at in the career of Gerald, Maurice's younger son, known as Captain Garret, a "well-known rebel" who was hanged as such in 1581.[9] The Fitzgerald estate was a substantial one. The involvement of his grandfather and great grandfather in the councils of government at the highest level had left Maurice with an estate of about two thousand contemporary acres, which is the equivalent of about five thousand statute acres to-day. He did receive a lease from the Queen in 1573, two years before his death, of rectories of O'Regan, Rossenalis or Wyemore, Killaghan, and Castle Breche, in "O Doyne's country" in Queen's County, and others in Offaly or King's

County. But the rent was never paid and the patent was declared void.[10] Evidently the real price of the grant was the strengthening of the Government presence in the march lands and when that did not take place there was no income for Fitzgerald from his rectories. Maurice's son, Thomas, died about 1611[11],. to be succeeded by his son, Maurice, who died in Balfeighan in 1637 and was buried in the cathedral of Kildare.[12] It was Maurice who leased the townsland of Kilglin to George Booth, a Protestant, who lived in a stone house there.[13] His heir was his son, James, who became an outlaw for his support of the Confederation of Kilkenny and lost his lands as a result.[14] In the Civil Survey of 1654, Balfeighan is noted as owned in 1641 by Eleanor Butler. She was Maurice's widow and whether the ownership derived from dower rights or from a seemingly prudent move to keep the property from the confiscation inherent in James's outlawry is not known. The lands went in any case to the adventurers in 1655 and the Fitzgerald connection with Balfeighan was permanently broken.[15] A last whisper of their presence there is on a broken headstone in Rodanstown graveyard.

It commemorates Sir Thomas Fitzgerald who died in the reign of Charles II. It was recycled by a Protestant minister in the 18th century and placed in the interior of the church with the side containing the Fitzgerald inscription plastered to a wall. Time and vandals have removed the stone from the wall and left it in fragments on the floor.

Footnotes

1   The Fitzgeralds of Lackagh, Walter Fitzgerald, Kildare Archeological Journal, Vol.1, p248.

2   Ormond Papers, Vol.1, p49.

3   c.f. Cosgrave, Late Medieval Ireland, 1370 to 1541, p54.ff.

4   Calendar of Patent Rolls, 22 Edward IV, p34; Guide to English Financial Records for Irish History, 1461 – 1568, Analecta X, p22.

5   c.f. Late Medieval Ireland, 1370-1541, Cosgrave, p63, 64.

6   Calendar of Inquisitions, ed. Griffith, Henry VIII, 113-118; 114-119.

7   The Fitzgeralds of Lackagh, Walter Fitzgerald, Kildare Archeological Society, Vol.1, p253. In 1556 he was a justice of the peace and in 1562 sheriff of County Kildare.

8   Calendar of Inquisitions, ed. Griffith, 1991, p84; "The Fitzgeralds of Lackagh", Kildare Archeological Society, Vol.1, p252.

9   C.S.P.I 1575 – 1585, p293, 319, 336, 338. Captain Garret was involved with the Eustaces of Baltinglass who revolted in 1582. He was hanged by the Wicklow man, Feach M'Hugh O'Byrne, at the instigation, it was reported, of the Earl of Kildare.

10   Calendar of Inquisitions, 260-173; Fiants, Elizabeth, 2208.

11   Inquis. in Officio rotulorum Cancell. Hiberniae, Vol.I, Lagenia, Meath, James I, 111 , The Fitzgeralds of Lackagh, Kildare Archeological Journal, Vol.1, p258.

12   Inquis. in Officio rotulorum Cancell. Hiberniae, Vol.I, Lagenia, Meath, Charles I, 143 (1638). Ibid, p258.

13   Inquis. Lagenia, Meath, Charles II, 5.

14   Gilbert, History of Affairs in Ireland, 1641 to 1652, Vol.3, p364.

15   Civil Survey, Vol.5, Meath, p158; Books of Survey and Distribution, MSS, National Archives, Parish of Balfeighan. James Fitzgerald was regranted two thousand plantation acres at Lackagh in 1668. He died in 1671. In the family tradition, his eldest son was called Maurice, and seems to have been the last of the Fitzgeralds of Lackagh.

Chapter 17

The Manor of Rodanstown – 1350 to 1655

As we have seen, Rodanstown has a very large earth work, thirty nine metres in diameter, with a triple ditch, which seems to have been of Norman construction. (See illustration of earthworks at Rodanstown, p i). It seems to date from the early years of the Norman conquest and can reasonably be associated with the Husseys, barons of Galtrim. Rodanstown never became a discrete manor and, until the late fifteenth century, seems to have been resolved into three fee farms involving a branch of the Hussey family, and the Boyce family who lived at Calgath and at Dollanstown. The parish is small, of no more than fourteen hundred and eighty statute acres, but successive tenants had often substantial properties in fee farm in other parishes as well.

The Boyces first appear in the records as settled in Kildare, probably in Boycetown, near Kilcock, about 1298.[1] The reference is to a law case in which a James de Boyce was charged with killing one Adam, son of Ralph, a robber: James claimed Adam slew a kinsmen of his and was outlawed and that he, James, had a license from the officers of the liberty of Kildare to slay him wherever he could be found. James was fined one hundred shillings (being poor) and the jury testified that the deed was done in a time of disturbance. The pledges for payment of the fine were given by John le Bret, Henry de Boyce, Robert de Boys, and another John le Bret, all names associated with Moyglare and Rodanstown. In 1312, in another court case, two Husseys and one Henry Arnold were convicted of robbing "nine heifers, a brass pot, a brass posnet, five and a half marks of silver, rings, brooches and divers cloths of the value of ten shillings." They were pardoned "for all trespasses done by them in Carbury, County Kildare except homicide and arson", and a fine of twenty marks (sixteen pounds thirteen and fourpence) was imposed. Those who pledged for their payment were Peter de Tuit, for five marks, Henry de Boys, for five marks,

Will de Cane and Hugh son of Richard of Balyrodan, for ten marks. The case marks the first definite appearance in the records of inhabitants of Rodanstown.[2] It does seem as if they were Husseys. In 1381 Henry Boyce granted the pieces of land made up of a messuage and curtilage which eventually went to Christ's Church in 1485, to Nicholas Sex, chaplain: they were formerly owned by Edmund Boys and were in Rodanstown. In 1390 Joanna Cane appointed John, son of Robert Hussey, and Henry Boyce of Ballyrodan to deliver control of a messauge and land in Balrodan to Peter Boyce of Calgath. In 1398, Thomas, son of William Boyce released to Nicholas Sex, chaplain, a messauge, curtilage, arable land, wood and pasture in Bryanstown – he had acquired it in 1379 from Richard Feelde, vicar of Moyglare.

These references are from the deeds in Christ's Church which were preserved because of Francis Estrete's gift in 1485 of lands in Balrodan and Bryanstown (in Moyglare manor) to the canons of the cathedral. They reveal a complex and frequent series of land transfers, usually involving chaplains (unbeneficed clergy) and also families which had been in the area since the Norman conquest. Among them are Boyces, Husseys, Seys (Sexs), Canes, Delahydes and Brouns. In 1467 John Boys of Dollanstown had committed to his custody "all the manors, land, tenements, rents and services, with all their appurtenances which were lately of Andrew Hussee in Balrodan", but even in the sixteenth century the Husseys of Galtrim had rents from Dollanstown (ten shillings per annum), Balrodan (six shillings and eight pence), and Calgath, (thirteen and fourpence – one mark). In other words, the Husseys of Rodanstown and the Boyces of Calgath and Dollanstown were still fee tenants of the lordship of Galtrim as late as 1579, and their properties had not become discrete manors.[5] Boyces held Dollanstown and Calgath; sometimes there was a different Boyce family in each, but eventually one man, Boyce of Calgath, held both. There were two tower houses built there, one in Calgath and one in Dollanstown. Both have long since disappeared on the ground but are referred to in the 1654 Civil Survey and in a report of 1642.[6]

The Boyces of Calgath were also involved as clients of successive earls of Kildare, Garret Mór and Garret Óg. James Boyce was a collector of rents on at least part of the Kildare estates, in Newtownmoyaghey in the lordship of Moyglare and in what is now Laois.[7] He was appointed by Silken Thomas or by his father, constable of Maynooth castle, and in March 1535 when Maynooth castle was taken and the goods contained there forfeited to the crown, he wrote to the chancellor of the exchequer that when the rebellion broke out he had surrendered his office and had refused his services to Silken Thomas. Thomas, Boyce explained, had, in September last (1534) *"conveyed thence into a castell in the Irishry, called the castell of Ley as well as all the countasis apparayll and rayment, as all the substance, in effecte belonging unto the late earle so as, at the receipt of your letter, remayned nothing of the premisess in my custodie; and if ther had I wold not have failed to the utmost of my letle power to have fulfilled the tenour of your letter...".*[8]

And Boyce, with adroit footwork, avoided the fate of the Fitzgeralds and the Delahydes consequent on the rebellion and kept his lands intact.

In the first part of the sixteenth century (1529) James Boyce of Calgath acquired property in Westmeath, Wilianston and Ballyloghloe, from Lord Dunsany (the Plunketts had acquired it in 1429)[9] but in 1582 Peter Boyce, James's son, sold it to Awley and William McGawley who lived near the Boyce holding there.[10] The Boyces also acquired land in County Kildare, Clonfert, "als Talbots is Grange" (sic) and Cappagh in Kilmacredock but never rose above the level of middling sized landlords.[11] That was an advantage in that they never suffered from association with the great but it was a distinct disadvantage, when, after the Cromwellian plantation in which they lost their land, they were declared innocent in 1661. They had not the legal or pecuniary resources to follow the decree with a restoration of their properties. As late as 1689 they were still trying to get their land back, but in that year "Thomas Boyce and Nicholas Hussey were enjoined to permit Richard Noyse and his heirs to hold peaceful possession of Radanstown, Colgrife, Bridewell and Longstowne in Radanstown parish, County Meath".[12] Soon afterwards, with his legal expertise and capacity for unscrupulous machinations, William Connolly, known as the Speaker, and builder of Castletown House at Celbridge, acqured not only the whole parish of Rodanstown but much adjoining property as well (chapter 31), these being the first acquisitions which he built into the biggest estate in eighteenth century Ireland. The fact that a number of Boyce deeds survive in St Patrick's College, Maynooth, is a measure of the efforts made to assert ownership of their traditonal holdings: the efforts, of course, were in vain. Of interest is the fact that three eighteenth century houses surviving in the parish are at Calgath, Dollanstown and Rodanstown, an eloquent witness to the phenomenon that centres of even minor estates and major tenancies remained as centres of large holdings in Kilclone until these were broken up in the forties, fifties and sixties of the twentieth century.

In 1474 there appears for the first time in the records a definite reference to Husseys in Rodanstown, though the reference in the court case of 1303 to Hugh, son of Richard of Balroddan, may well have been to them. In 1474, as we have seen, Boyce of Dollanstown was confirmed in possession of properties in Rodanstown formerly held by Adam Husse.

As late as 1579 the three townslands which, with part of Newtownmoyaghey, make up the parish of Rodanstown, were still held by fee tenants of the baron of Galtrim owing him dues of ten shillings, half a mark (six and eightpence), and one mark (thirteen and fourpence) per year. By 1620, Rodanstown (the townsland) was held by Robert Hussey in capite, i.e. directly from the king. He also held the townsland of Kilclone, as perhaps his family had done since the manor of Mulhussey was set up in 1406.[13] When Robert Hussey died in 1620 (his heir, John, was twenty-two years old and unmarried) he held, with Rodanstown, rights over the townsland of Kilclone and other places in Kildare. In 1620 Kilclone was leased for sixty-one years to Maurice Fitzgerald, lord of Balfeighan and Lackagh, who in turn leased it to John Walsh of Shanganagh, County Dublin. He leased it to Philip Ffernsley, a Protestant army officer, with a reversion to Robert Hussey and his heirs. Ffernsley obviously intended to build up a presence in the area. He leased land in Moygaddy held by Andrew Forde, a Protestant, in 1641[14] and in the 1633 visitation of the diocese it was recorded that he held the advowson of Ballymaglassan.[15] Needless to say, Robert Hussey's heir, John, got nothing despite efforts in the 1660s to get the lands of his ancestors back when he was declared innocent at the court of claims. As with the Boyce estate, the holding was too small to finance the political and legal action necessary to assert his rights. Like the Boyces, this branch of the Husseys disappears from the list of landowners after the Cromwellian plantation.

Footnotes

1   Cal. Jus. Rolls 1295-1303, p195

2   Cal. Jus. Rolls, Ireland 1305-1307, p490.

3   Calendar of Christ Church Deeds, 744, 762, 790, 929, 930, 933, 949, 350, 348, 100.

4   Statute Rolls Ireland, Edward IV, ed. Berry, Part I, p569 (1467/8)

5   Cal. Inquisitors Ed. Griffith, Elizabeth 124/87

6   Ormonde Papers, Vol.1, p49

7   Crown Survey of Lands 1540-41 with the Kildare rentals begun in 1518, Ed. Mc Niochaill, p142.

8   C.S.P.I. 1507-73, p12

9   Irish Genealogist Vol.IV, p527.

10   Cal. Inquis. James I, 85

11   I.E.R. Vol.48 (1936), p666, Boyce papers No.10.

12   I.E.R. Vol.48 (1936), p665.

13   Inquis. in Offic. rotulorum Cancell. Hib., Vol.I, Lagenia, Meath, Charles II, 67.

14   The History & Antiquities of the Collegiate & Cathedral Church of St. Patrick, Mason, p96

15   Visitation of 1633, N.A.

Chapter 18

The Manor of Rathregan – 1350 to 1700

The Plunketts were a Dublin family who rose in the world through law. John Plunkett, a professional lawyer, practised as a sergeant in the king's court in Ireland. He specialised in property law which, through fees and through land acquired, brought him substantial wealth. As was customary in the fourteenth century, he married an heiress, in his case Alice, daughter of one John of Trim, who brought with her to the marriage the manor of Beaulieu, outside Drogheda. John had two sons, John the elder, who became lord of Beaulieu, an ancestor of the family who became the Lords Louth.[1] The second son, Richard, also specialised in law. In his role as legal go-between he facilitated the transfer of property in Kildare from Hugh le Whit (or Blount) of Rathregan, to Walter de Birmingham, lord of Carbury in Kildare, in 1359.[2] The Carbury lands, as we have seen, were swapped for the Delahyde manor of Ballymadun by the Prestons of Gormanston, when by a whisker, Robert de Preston succeeded to the Carbury estate through the fact that his wife, Matilda Birmingham, had outlived her surviving sibling by a short head in 1361. Soon after 1360 Richard Plunkett became lord of Rathregan and it seems that he acquired it by purchase from Hugh le Whit, or Blund, the last le Blund lord of the manor.

The Plunketts were not to live there too long either. They were set to move to greater things. Richard, and his son Richard, were called to parliament and to the great council of 1374, one as baron and the other to the "concilio regis".[3] Before 1399 Richard's son and heir Christopher married the heiress of Killeen, Joan Cusack, and henceforth the family settled at Killeen, though they held onto the manor of Rathregan until the nineteenth century.[4] Christopher was one of the most upwardly mobile of the family. He became sheriff of Meath and was rewarded by Henry VI for services rendered and expenses incurred in the wars. In 1426 and in 1432 he became deputy to the lord lieutenant of Ireland, Sir Thomas Stanley. Of his four sons, one, John, succeeded him at Killeen, Christopher became first of the lords of Dunsany, Thomas of Rathmore, following family tradition, became lord chief justice of Ireland and Roland held a manor in Dunshaughlin.

Because they held Rathregan through the various catastrophies attending on the old English landowners in the seventeenth century, there is scant appearance of the manor in the records, except in inquisitions on the deaths of successive lords when the Rathregan possessions are enumerated.[5] Sir Christopher died in 1445 and was succeeded by his son John, who in turn was succeeded by his son Christopher. Christopher had two sons; one succeeded him and the other, like Thomas Fitzgerald of Balfeighan, fell at the battle of Stoke in 1487 when Anglo Norman hopes of putting the Yorkist pretender, Lambert Simnel, on the English throne were dashed by the first of the Tudors, Henry VII. When the Reformation took place, the then Lord Killeen did not figure in the share out of monastic property, and the family remained Catholic throughout the religious persecutions. James Plunkett, eighth Lord Killeen, entered the house of peers in 1585 and his son Christopher was a prominent member of the opposition in the parliament of 1613. He died soon afterwards and was succeeded by Lucas Mór as tenth lord who was belted an earl as Lord Fingal in 1628. Lucas died in 1637 and his eldest son, the second earl, was a prominent figure in the rebellion of 1641. Captured by parliamentarians at the battle of Rathmines, he died in prison in Dublin in 1649. His son Luke succeeded him and leaving Ireland in 1650, he wisely chose exile at the court of Charles II in France. His prudence paid off and he was restored to all his estates, including Rathregan, when Charles II was recalled to the English throne in 1661. The family naturally supported James II in 1688 and fortunately for it, Luke died in 1690 before King William could outlaw him. Though he was outlawed by name in 1691, his young son Peter had already succeeded him and he had been with his mother in the Low Countries out of the way of trouble in Ireland. The outlawry was reversed in 1697 and so by great good fortune the family held onto its ancestral acres, including Rathregan, through the penal days until the land acts of the nineteenth century.[6] Fortuituously the family papers are intact from 1700 onwards, and it is possible for the first time to see in them details of the quality of land in Rathregan, its leaseholders and their rents. The first comprehensive land report that has survived was drawn up in 1702 by Peter Lacy, the land agent of Peter, the fourth earl of Fingal.[7]

Though the senior branch of the family, descendants of John Plunkett, lost their properties at Beaulieu, outside Drogheda, at the Cromwellian plantation, Lord Louth got some of his estates back in the reign of Charles II. The descendants of Richard Plunkett, being rich in male children and hence available for marriage to heiresses, became large landowners all through County Meath and all remained Catholic in the times of persecution. Among them was Oliver Plunkett, 1625 – 1681, archbishop, martyr and saint, from the Loughcrew branch of the family, and Bishop Patrick Plunkett of the house of Killeen who became bishop of Ardagh in 1647 and eventually died as bishop of Meath in 1668. The Plunketts never returned to live at Rathregan, though a stone house was built there of which ruins still remain and also what seems to be a fifteenth century church, now in ruins, which has the same large dimensions as the other Plunkett churches at Killeen, Dunsany, Rathmore and Loughcrew. (See illustration of the Ruins of the Church at Rathregan, p xi). Presumably the stone house mentioned in the Civil Survey of 1654 replaced the buildings on the earthworks, made of wood and clay, constructed by the le Blunds at the Norman conquest. There are, opposite the church, the traces on the ground of a vanished medieval village with a central sunken way between a series of rectangular houses on either side.

The stone house was presumably for the Plunketts' steward who represented family interests on the ground there. (See illustration of the Ruins of Rathregan stone house, p xi). There was a captain Richard Plunkett of Rathregan, outlawed in the Williamite wars, whose outlawry was eventually lifted.[8] But from at least 1680 the Corbally family were major tenants there and remained as such until well into the nineteenth century. Monuments to members of the family can be seen in the old graveyard, in one of the church walls, and inside Batterstown church to which the family made a substantial contribution when it was built about 1838. Their main seat was in Corbalton Hall, in Skyrne parish, and in the nineteenth century a Corbally was an M.P. for Meath and a staunch supporter of Daniel O'Connell. Like their landlords, the family remained Catholic all through the penal days.

Footnotes

1   Paul Brand in "The Formation of a Parish: The Case of Beaulieu", County Louth (Settlements and Society in Medieval Ireland, ed. John Bradley, p261 ff.) gives a full account of the origins of the Plunketts of Beaulieu.

2   Calendar of the Gormanston Register, p139, 140.

3   Abraham Appendix, IV, p491.

4   Burke's Peerage, 1853.

5   Calendar of Inquisitions, James I, 24; Charles I, 137; Calendar of Patent Rolls of James I, p408, (1619).

6   Irish Jacobites, Analecta, XXII, p133.

7   The Papers of the Fingal Family are in the National Library of Ireland.

8   Irish Jacobites, Analecta, XXII, p22, and 101.

118

Chapter 19

The Manor of Ballymaglassan – 1350 to 1655

After the Crues verus Bacun lawsuits, Ballymaglassan next appears in an act of parliament passed in the reign of Edward IV in 1463.[1] Evidently his father, the Duke of York, then lord of the liberty of Meath, had let to Robert Rochford "Cookstown, Harlockstown, Brownstown and Molcronesland" (it seems to have been a name for Staffordstown or Waynestown, or for both) for thirteen marks, sixteen shillings and eight pence" which lands and tenements were wasted by the great intolerable charge of the chief rent and of no value". The lands were repossessed by the duke and given back to Robert Rochford for forty shillings rent. The king, now the lord of the liberty, let them in 1463 to Roger Rochford for the same rent (Roger and Robert seem to have been brothers). The properties were then rented at twenty shillings per annum, for twenty years, provided they "build the said town of Brownstown" and they were discharged of the chief rent mentioned above. This is the first time there is mention in the records of the presence in Ballymaglassan of the Rochfords of Kilbride, a connection which was to last until the end of the seventeenth century. It is not recorded if a village was ever built in Brownstown. If it was, it became soon enough one of the plethora of villages all over Norman Ireland deserted for various reasons at the end of the Middle Ages.

Robert Rochford's grant of 1463 was confirmed in 1470. The acres of the townslands are given, and their names. There were twelve acres in Mulcronesland, twenty-five in Little Fidorf, but Roanstown and Waynestown are not mentioned, which were Rochford lands in succeeding centuries. Strangely, the land is deemed "for the most part uncultivated", another indication of unsettled conditions even in the Pale, in the second half of the fifteenth century. Robert Rochford became constable of the castle at Trim and received land grants to sustain it, together with eight pounds of silver annually and customary "fees, wages and emoluments". Roger, his brother, received the chief rent of the town of Trim, and local taxes and petty customs, and the fines imposed on those who brewed bad ale.[2]

The family seems to have been high in the favour of the earls of Kildare and to have had benefited from their influence by tax remissions. The Rochford connection with Ballymaglassan lasted until the Cromwellian plantation and though most of its property in Ballymaglassan was restored in the reign of Charles II, the Rochford connection with Ballymaglassan ended about 1700.

The survey of 1540 reveals that the Kildare family had been overlords of much property in Ballymaglassan. The fassagh, or wastelands, of Ballymaglassan itself provided grazing for a herd of the earl's cattle, and "the vill" of Ballymaglassan, a Kildare tenancy, was rented for six shillings and eight pence to William Wesley of Dangan.[3] This is the first mention of a Wesley connection with Ballymaglassan: the survey reference implies a presence there back before 1540, and dating perhaps from the fifteenth century. The Wesley connection with Ballymaglassan was to last until 1816, when with Dangan and Moygare, (near Trim), the two other Wellesley estates, together making up 12,800 statute acres, it was sold at auction.[4] Sometime in the sixteenth century, a junior branch of the family inherited the Ballymaglassan estates and lived at Blackhall, but early in the seventeenth century, with the death of three generations of their family in quick succession , the estate reverted to the senior branch of the family at Dangan in Summerhill.[5] Both branches of the family had remained Catholic and the head of the family in 1641, Valerian, was active in the confederate wars with his half brother Patrick Cusack of Blackhall (chapter 23), but his son William died before his son Gerald was born in 1637, and William's wife Margaret died in 1646. A Colonel Axell was granted the estate in 1655 but, through his guardian, Dr. Jones, Gerald took a court case which he won in 1657 to have it restored.[6] Dr. Henry Jones, formerly dean of Kilmore and then quartermaster of the Cromwellian army, had been guardian of the young man since 1652 and Gerald was educated in TCD and reared as a Protestant. The Wellesley estates, including Ballymaglassan, survived intact in the family until the sale of 1816. Gerald's son, Gerald, inherited the estate but died childless in 1728, leaving as his heir, his cousin Richard Cowley or Colley of Castlecarbury who succeeded to the estates on condition that he change his name to Wellesley. He did so, and it was his descendants who became marquises of Wellesley, and in the junior line, the dukes of Wellington.

Footnotes

1   Statute Rolls of Edward IV, 1st to 12th year, p65.

2   Ibid, p363, 705, 813.

3   Crown Survey, ed. McNiochaill, p228.

4   Ellison, Dangan, Mornington and the Wellesleys, Riocht na Midhe, Vol.5, No.1, 1967, p14.

5   Calendar of Inquisitions, James I, 71; Patent Rolls of James I, p496, 579.

6   C.S.P.I. 1625 to 1660, p655. A petition to the lord protector (Oliver Cromwell) of Gerald Wesley, an orphan, aet. 18, by Dr. Henry Jones, his guardian.

Chapter 20

The Churches of Moyglare, Rathregan, Ballymaglassan – 1350 to 1560

Very little survives in the records about religious life in Kilcloon in the years 1350 to 1540. Very few names of serving priests survive, except in the deeds of the property in Moyglare and Rodanstown which in 1485 was given to the canons of Christ Church in Dublin. The system set up at the conquest, and ratified in bishop de la Corner's time, whereby the monasteries got both income and the right to present vicars or chaplains to the six parishes of Kilcloon, seems to have worked out fairly well on the ground. At least no complaints have survived in the records. From the outburst of energies which characterised the early days of the Norman colony, new structures were quickly set up in manor and parish, but once set up and accepted there seems to have been no radical change called for or passionate objection to prevailing conditions, until the Reformation, imposed from the outside, changed things completely. In the wider level than the parish, the church structures were very much subordinate, at least in Norman areas, to the state. Bishops were appointed in the colony, often Englishmen, for their talents in administration of church and state, rather than for any evangelical leanings they may have had. In fact, the church provided a career opportunity for those younger sons of families, English or Irish, who had no taste for a military career and for those with exceptional talent of high but illegitimate birth. Perhaps nationally it could be said, as was said about the French Revolution afterwards, that the Reformation was necessary to save the church in Ireland from its unhealthy liaison with the state. But going on the surviving records again, the comment of the visitators at Ballymaglassan in 1377 , that they know nothing but what is good about it, is relevant to much of the faith life of the six parishes in the late Middle Ages.

Just as the fifteenth century was a time for building tower houses – they evidently answered a need and indicated a certain prosperity – so too the fifteenth century was a time for refurbishing churches to reflect the ambitions or confidence of new landowners. Rathregan, Mulhussey, and Balfeighan are examples. In the other parishes, Ballymaglassan, Moyglare and Rodanstown, nineteenth century Protestant churches have obliterated the remains of pre-Reformation churches. It is impossible to date the surviving ruins at Kilclone itself; they are only low wall foundations with no identifiable sylistic features. A holy water font, formerly in the old parish church of Kilcloon, has some crude decorations of an Ionian type, dating it to perhaps the seventeenth century.

Very little evidence survives to allow us to see the way the people of Moyglare lived the life of faith in the late Middle Ages. One small incident has survived in the records about Moyglare which gives some insight into the medieval Norman attitudes to morality. It dates from sometime in the sixteenth century, before the rebellion of Silken Thomas in 1534 and concerns the Delahyde family.[1] The incident and its sequel were treated of in a law case in 1544. Sir Walter Delahyde had married one of the four independently minded daughters of Robert Fitz Eustace, of Portlester, near Athboy. Fitz Eustace had been treasurer of Ireland in the years of Garret Mór and was a prominent member of the Earl's governing circle. His family had married well. One of them, Alison, married Garret Mór, who with intervals, was ruler of Ireland for many years. She died in 1496, a friend of Irish poets it was said, for they bitterly lamented her demise. The romantic cause of her death was the shock of her husband's imprisonment in the Tower of London. Their mother Margaret, the widow of Fitz Eustace, married a second time, and evidently made an agreement with her second husband that the property inherited from her first husband would go to the children of her second family, specifically her eldest, Eleanor, married to Thomas Fitzwilliam. She died, and the sisters, with their husbands and with their brother in law, met in Dublin at the offices of one Golding, a lawyer, who held the family chest of deeds. Sir Maurice Eustace, one of the brothers in law of Sir Walter Delahyde, slipped a key document into his pocket and the family, minus Fitzwilliam, went to Sir Walter Delahyde's town house.

There the sisters proposed to burn the document which left the property to their half sister. Sir Walter demurred (at least he said so at a subsequent legal hearing), and on hearing the " sacryng bell", went off to hear Mass. Meanwhile, the ladies and their husbands asked for a fire and burned the document. Sir Walter on his return voiced his disapproval (so he stated afterwards) and when he and his wife went to confession for Easter to the Grey Friars (Franciscan) monastery, they were told by the good friar that they had to give the land to the true owner and tell him what had happened. Sir Walter, with a mixture of guile and virtue, approached the Earl of Kildare, his nephew, who had Fitzwilliam the heir as a client, and offered to go public with his wife on what had happened, on condition that the heir freely allowed him the property his wife had acquired by deceit. The business was not resolved until after the death of Silken Thomas Fitzgerald, the young earl's heir, when Lady Delahyde was dead and buried in the Grey Friars' Church in Dublin, beside the Delahyde town house. Sir Walter got the property, and it proved very useful when the Delahyde estates were forfeit as a consequence of the Geraldine rebellion.[2] The incident shows a manipulation of law and a concern for personal morality not untypical of the Anglo Irish lords of the Pale.

Sir Walter's son, Edward, became parson of Kilberry; he was himself involved in the rebellion of Silken Thomas, and declared a traitor, but died before the state could punish him.[3] The income from his parish was eighteen pounds Irish per annum which put it tenth in income out of one hundred and five parishes mentioned in the list of incomes in the diocese of Meath, made in 1540.[4]

Only two vicars of Moyglare from the sixteenth century appear in the records. One Walter Walsh, parson of Moyglare, was pardoned in 1578, with John Gilsenan, parson of nearby Culmullen. Lawrence Delahyde of Moyglare was pardoned at the same time too; presumably all three had been attainted for their joining in the general opposition to the cess, a tax then being imposed by the Dublin government. There was also at that time a question mark over the loyalties of the earl of Kildare which involved arrests and questioning in London of the earl's steward, Meiler Hussey of Mulhussey. This may have involved Lawrence Delahyde and some people about Moyglare.[5] The government did not help matters by adopting permanently – though gradually – a policy excluding the Anglo Irish lords from participation in national government. The other Moyglare vicar, John White, was dead by 1596 when his name appears in a Delahyde will: the terms of the will and the web of relations and neighbours mentioned make it pretty clear that all were Catholic.[6] It was only in the early seventeenth century that Moyglare got a parson of the state church who, even if he wished to evangelise, was hobbled by the fact that the Catholic Delahydes had the right to appoint to the living, and there were very few Protestants in the area.

Nothing survives from the records about church life in Ballymaglassan from 1350 until the Reformation. The appointment of a chaplain and the right to parish income was still in the hands of the Augustinian monks of St. Thomas in those years. Perhaps, not unreasonably, we can repeat about the faith life of the parish the lapidary phrase used about it in 1377 by the Armagh visitators: "they know nothing but good about it."

As we have seen, the income from Rathregan did not suffice for a vicar in 1300. Income seems to have improved by 1400, for in 1409 Thomas Wellys (perhaps Wesley) was vicar of Rathregan.[7] He is the only priest who served Rathregan in the Middle Ages whose name has come down to us. The next one in the records is that of William Kenne, who in 1538 is reported absent from his parish since 1536.[8] The vicarage was then worth twenty marks, or thirteen pounds six and eightpence, which is hard to square with the income enjoyed by his predecessor in 1300, the income of eight pounds, eight shillings enjoyed by the tithe farmer in 1540[9], or the six pound rent paid by the tithe farmer Sir John Barnwall in 1537.[10] Kenne's Irish name puts him among those priests of the Irish nation, or the king's Irish enemies, as they were variously termed, who were increasing in numbers, not only in the Gaelic west of the diocese of Meath but also in the Old English Pale.

The church at Rathregan is the biggest in the parish of Kilcloon, at twenty-two metres in length. (See illustration of the Ruins of the Church at Rathregan, p xi). It bears comparison in size with the Plunkett churches at Killeen, Dunsany, Rathmore and Loughcrew. It has a chancel externally separated from the nave and seems to date from the fifteenth century. It was probably built by the Plunketts after they became lords of the manor of Rathregan, in the last quarter of the fourteenth century, and reflects their wealth and their concern to assert themselves as one of the new families in Meath who moved from law to nobility in the latter half of the Middle Ages. The church was associated with the manor and with the castle or manorial centre nearby. Both the castle and the nearby village have disappeared, leaving only some traces on the ground. (See illustration of the Sunken Way at Rathregan, p xi). The Plunketts left Rathregan in the very early years of the fifteenth century for Killeen, when Christopher Plunkett married the Cusack heiress to Killeen and its associated manors. But they retained the manor of Rathregan until the nineteenth century.

Footnotes

1   Calendar of Patent Rolls Ireland, Henry VIII – Elizabeth, Vol.1, p98.

2   In 1540 Walter Delahyde held a messauge and 15 acres in the manor of Raynoldstown, Co. Dublin "in right of Jenetta his wife". Extents of Monastic Possessions, ed. White, p105. It was in the Villa of Heathtown, parish of Clonalvey, Co. Meath.

3   The Church Establishment, Vol.2, p97; C.L.P. Henry VIII, part II, 1537, p458, No.30; "goods and chattels of outlaws, Simon Walshe, vicar of Rathbeggan, James Delahyde, Edward Delahyde, clerk, rector of Kilberry".

4   COGAN, Vol.1, p377.

5   Fiants, Elizabeth, 3232.

6   Calendar of Inquisitions, Elizabeth, 219-145.

7   McCleneghan Papers, p350.

8   Calendar of Inquisitions, Henry VIII, 129-127.

9   Extents of Monastic Possessions, ed. White, p296.

10   The Dissolution of the Religious Orders in Ireland under Henry VIII, Bradshaw, p55.

Chapter 21

The Churches of Galtrim – 1350 to 1560

As we have seen, the remains of the churches which survive in Kilclone, Balfeighan and Rodanstown, have features which date at least a substantial renewal of the fabric of two of them, to the fifteenth century. In both Balfeighan, and the small chapel near the tower house of Mulhussey the windows had High Gothic ogee arches. A chancel arch fragment at Balfeighan seems to indicate that a separate chancel was built there, sometime in the fifteenth century. (See illustration of Balfeighan, p viii). The nave of the church was the responsibility of the local parishioners and it seems reasonable to connect the rebuilding at Balfeighan, and the building at Mulhussey, to the Fitzgerald and Hussey families, who were granted these manors in the fifteenth century by the senior branches of their families.

No record survives of any chaplain at any of the three parishes, but there does survive substantial material from the papal and royal archives about those who looked for, and got appointment to, the rich rectory of Galtrim, on which the three chaplaincies, together with those of Gallo and Drumlargan, depended.

One of the most interesting of these rectors of Galtrim was John Swayne, whose career in the papal curia in Rome eventually brought him to the see of Armagh.

John Swayne – Rector of Galtrim and Archbishop of Armagh

John Swayne was born probably in the decade between 1360 and 1370 in the diocese of Kildare.[1] He was illegitimate, but must have come from a family connected with the church, for he made his way to Rome towards the end of the fourteenth century and first appears in the records in 1399 with a dispensation from illegitimacy, so that he could acquire benefices in Ireland. He was technically described as cleric, but that did not mean that he was ordained a priest, but rather that he had taken tonsure, the first of the minor orders, and so had entered the clerical state. His presence in Rome meant that he represented Irish interests at the papal curia and had influence on the policies of the papal curia which concerned Ireland. His dispensation from illegitimacy was not to be mentioned in any future promotions which could (and in time did) involve all the offices in the church except the papacy itself.

Galtrim had been a bone of contention among high flying clerics and their Roman representatives. When a cleric with a benefice, or a number of benefices, was appointed bishop, the benefices were automatically rendered vacant and the appointment to them devolved on the Roman curia. In 1399 Thomas Snel was appointed bishop of Waterford and Lismore, automatically making his archdeaconry of Glendaloch and the rectory of Galtrim vacant. One Maurice O'Brien, a clerk of Limerick, got both. In 1400, Thomas Bath was made archdeacon of Meath (this involved his being rector of Kells also) and evidently rector of Galtrim by episcopal appointment. Someone in Rome reported the irregularity; the appointment in Galtrim should have devolved there since Thomas Snel, former occupant, had been made a bishop. In 1400, one John Teyr, rector of the free chapel of St Mary, Ambusden, in the diocese of Ferns, was appointed by Boniface IX to Galtrim. Thomas Bath was to remain archdeacon of Meath and rector of Kells, but was to lose Galtrim because technically he had no right to it. Teyr was treasurer of Dublin, occupying a key and lucrative position in the government of the archdiocese, but his right to it was challenged by John de Swyndon and the matter went on appeal to Rome. Teyr's was a Roman appointment facilitated by John Swayne: John de Swindon's was one which had its origin in the Dublin chapter and with the regal authorities in Dublin and London. As often happened in these rows, death intervened, and the two candidates for the position died fighting for their rights.[2]

John Swayne, Teyr's agent in Rome, was well positioned to obtain the rectory of Galtrim, which he did, and he was in line for the treasurership of Dublin, but when one Nicholas Fleming was appointed archbishop of Armagh, Swayne got not only two livings held by Fleming, one in Ferns diocese, Taghcomshan, the other in Dublin, Newcastle de Lyons, but he also became Fleming's proctor or representative in Rome.[3] Technically, Swayne was called an abbreviator of letters, one who processed letters to and from the papal chancery.

There are some hints that he was rector of the University of Siena but his name does not appear in the official lists. Certainly he collected doctorates in canon and civil law, perhaps in Siena, and having been an abbreviator under Gregory XII and John XXIII, he moved upwards to become one of John's papal secretaries.

All sorts of privileges came his way. He was entitled to his own confessor, could have Mass said for him, even before daybreak, and in places under interdict (he was evidently involved in diplomacy too) and even though a cleric, he had the power to dispose by will of all his goods, even those derived from ecclesiastical sources. Still a mere cleric (he had received only the order of tonsure), he was dispensed for ten years in 1413 for holding his benefice without receiving full ordination to the priesthood.[4]

These Roman years of John Swayne were dominated by the great schism which saw two claimants to the papacy, and three after 1407. Swayne made the first part of his career serving the Roman pope Gregory XII. After the Council of Pisa, which unsuccessfully tried to unite the church in 1407, he switched allegiance to John XXIII, the so-called Pisan pope. It was under John that he became a papal secretary, an examiner of candidates for papal notaries and generally a person well placed to expedite Irish businesses at the curia, including his own. He became archdeacon of Meath (and so rector of Kells) the office next in importance to that of the bishop and was allowed keep his other rectories including his first at Galtrim. Besides, he exchanged his Dublin benefice, Newcastle, for that of Swords, the richest benefice in the cathedral chapter of Dublin, and was able to hold it against rival claimants. Perhaps he felt that as an unordained cleric in minor orders he was going to have to face strong opposition to his control of Irish benefices, especially when his mentor, John XXIII was having difficulty maintaining his position in Italy. In any case, Swayne was ordained priest in London in 1415. At the Council of Constance, called to reunite the church in difficulties, Swayne was present and had to accept the loss of his influence at the papal court when his mentor John XXIII was deposed. (John XXIII in church history is reckoned as an anti pope and so Cardinal Roncalli was free to take his name, John XXIII, in modern times). Very quickly, a new pope, Martin V, was elected, acceptable in time to the universal church. In 1416 Archbishop Fleming of Armagh, for whom Swayne had acted as proctor in Rome during the early years of his rule, died. The chapter of Armagh selected a Dublin canon, Robert Fitz Hugh, as their candidate, but John Swayne, though technically unemployed in Rome, was not without skills or influence, and he secured the position for himself from the new pope, Martin V, sometime before January 14, 1418.

Technically he had to dispose of all his benefices when he was consecrated archbishop, and so the connection with Galtrim, albeit only a one way financial one since before 1404, was broken. Swayne became a reforming archbishop of Armagh and put a stamp of his own on the archdiocese until he retired because of old age in 1439. He died in 1441 and was buried in the old St Peter's church in Drogheda. One presumes that the legal expertise picked up in his Roman years served him well in the complicated problems of Armagh and its division between the English lands of what is now Louth and the Irish area north of what is now the border. In any case, the income from Galtrim, his first benefice, had enabled him to study and speculate in Rome until he became successively abbreviator of papal letters, one of the papal secretaries and eventually, by deft switching of allegiance at the proper time and by having a web of contacts and allies built up over a lifetime in Rome, archbishop of Armagh, an office he discharged with vision and with zeal.[5] Galtrim is reported as going by papal provision to a cleric of the diocese of Meath, Thomas Prys, in 1425.[6] He was already rector of a parish in Lincoln, England, archdeacon of Bangor in Wales and a prebendary of Lusk since 1411. It is next heard of in the episcopate of Thomas Sherwood in 1480 when history takes it in a different direction.

Galtrim and its Chaplaincies – 1480 – 1533

Bishop William Shirwood of Meath, an Englishman appointed through royal influence to Meath, was expected to involve himself in government and political affairs as much as in the administration of his diocese. Highhanded and ruthless, he locked horns with the former abbot of Navan, John Bole, then archbishop of Armagh. There were reconciliations at times and at other times excommunications were thundered from Termonfeckin, where the archbishop lived, to Ardbraccan which was Sherwood's residence. But eventually a reasonable modus vivendi was worked out before Bole died in 1471.[1] His successor Octavian, an Italian, was not appointed until 1479. At a provincial council held at St Peter's in Drogheda in 1480, Bishop Sherwood with three other bishops of the northern province was present and, one presumes as a gesture of peace and good will to the new primate, he gave, in perpetuity, as an alms "for the good of his own soul and the souls of his predecessors and successors the parish church of Galtrim", to the monks of St Peter's at Trim, the Victorine canons, who also held the rectory of Rathregan and a number of other rectories in the diocese. When they were granted Galtrim, they were, of course, granted the rights of patronage over its chaplaincies at Kilclone, Balrodden, Balfeighan, Gallo and Drumlargan.[2] They had the responsibility of serving the diocesan cathedral, then the largest in medieval Ireland, which was obviously an expensive charge on any monastery. Sherwood died in 1482 and was buried at the cathedral in Trim, where a stone effigy is pointed out to the present day as his tombstone.

So things rested until 1533. Robert Luttrell, an able and ambitious cleric, the illegitimate half brother of Thomas Luttrell of Luttrellstown, who was soon to be chief justice of the common pleas, had graduated with two degrees from Oxford in 1532, one in canon the other in civil law,[3] and was now looking for appointment to a parish in Ireland which would enable him to finance a clerical career in law. There must have been something less than compelling in the handing over of the rectory in Galtrim to the bishop of Meath in the early fourteenth century, for Nicholas Hussey, citing his ancestral claim to nominate to Galtrim brought an action of 'quare impedit' against the monks of Trim, evidently because they could not prove that Galtrim had been properly handed over to bishop St. Leger in the early fourteenth century.[4]

The rights over Galtrim were returned to the Hussey family who appointed Robert Luttrell, vicar of the parish, and one John Tuyte as its rector.[10] The monks naturally objected, citing their obligations to provide divine service and hospitality and their need to sustain the brethren and the cathedral of the diocese. Both sides accepted arbitration from a group which included the lord deputy, Sir William Skeffington, John Alen archbishop of Dublin, and chancellor of Ireland, Sir John Barnwall, lord of Trimleston, and Thomas Luttrell, the king's sergeant at law in Ireland.[5] The perpetual vicar was to have all the income from the glebe lands in Galtrim, the manse, the altarages, oblations and yearly offerings, one third of the tithes of turf of the parish, all the tithes of corn, hay, from Clonemeath, other tithes to the yearly value of eight marks (five pounds, six and eightpence). The advowson (right to present to the parish) was to go to the monks, together with "all other manor of tithes, oblations and altarages, chapels and free chapels that pertaineth to the same 'except what had already been decided as belonging to the vicar". So the monks won the rights to present to and take the income from Kilclone, Balrodden, Balfeighan, Drumlargo and Gallo. In a flourish, at the end of the document, which settled the matter, the monks guaranteed "to pray for the souls of the antecessors of the said Nicholas, and for the prosperity of the said Nicholas and his heirs and sequel, for their souls after they pass this transitory life". When, in 1537, the monastery with many others was suppressed, it was found that the tithes of many of the parishes impropriate to it had been farmed out by the good abbot, who anticipated the suppression. Kilclone and Balrodden had gone to Peter Lynch of the Knock (Summerhill) and Balfeighan to one William Dixon, who with his brother Edward, had the ongoing income from the rectory of Galtrim itself. Not without significance is the fact that Lynch was paying four pounds rent in 1537, and the two parishes were worth four times as much in 1540. Balfeighan, leased out for two pounds in 1537, was worth four pounds to the leaseholder, Dixon, in 1540.[7] It seems as if ready cash must have changed hands when the property was leased out, at a time when the abbot evidently saw the writing on the wall. Not without interest was the annuity of one mark (thirteen shillings and four pence) to be paid for life from 6th June 1532 to Thomas Luttrell of Luttrellstown, gentleman, for legal advice tendered to the abbey.[8]

Galtrim still appears in the records after the Reformation, but the connection with Kilclone, Balrodden and Balfeighan was effectively broken at that time.

Robert Luttrell – Rector of Galtrim and Archdeacon of Meath

Robert Luttrell was another vicar of Galtrim who played a key role in national church affairs. He was half-brother of Thomas Luttrell, chief justice of common pleas (Thomas succeeded Sir Walter Delahyde's brother, Richard, who had been dismissed because of associations with the Kildare rebellion in 1534).[1] Robert went to Oxford where he graduated a bachelor in canon and civil law in 1532.[2] Like John Swayne, he was obviously destined for an influential career in the church, and also like Swayne, he had to get a dispensation from illegitimacy. In a court case of 1533 the Hussey baron of Galtrim was given back the patronage of the rectory of Galtrim and immediately he nominated Luttrell to the office of perpetual vicar and Luttrell was instituted by the bishop of Meath.[3] In 1535 when Edward Delahyde "parson of Kilberry" died, Luttrell got that rectory also.[4] And when a new archbishop, George Dowdall, was appointed to Armagh in 1543, he immediately appointed Robert Luttrell as officialis or chief law officer in the archdiocese. He presided over two Armagh synods, one in 1544 with the bishop of Raphoe, and one in 1548 with the bishop of Kildare.[5] In 1548 Robert Luttrell, and his half-brother Thomas, and the vicar of St Peter's in Drogheda, were invited to hear the archbishop of Dublin, George Browne, denounce a Scottish Protestant brought over to Ireland to further the Reformation by preaching against the Mass and other religious ceremonies. Presumably they were invited because of their Catholic sympathies and Brown wanted them to hear his.[6] It is obvious too that Robert Luttrell was looked on as one of the leading clerics in the Irish church. Brown was reprimanded by the government and went along with the Protestant changes brought in after Henry VIII died. The chief justice held onto his position until his death in 1554, but did not involve himself publicly in the state church which was then adopting an increasingly Protestant character. Of his private Catholic convictions there is no doubt. When his son died in 1557, he made provision in his will for one John Scurlock "confessor to the testator and to his father and brother for many years". Robert Luttrell was the overseer of his brother's will and of that of his nephew.[7] Though his thoughts on the religious changes must have been publicly known, his name does not appear on the records until 1553, when he appears as archdeacon of Meath and rector of Kells by papal provision.[8]

He was appointed to a commission set up during the reign of the Catholic Queen Mary to restore Catholicism in Ireland. He served with William Walsh, new bishop of the diocese, Thomas Leverous, new bishop of Kildare, and George Dowdall, restored archbishop of Armagh, Luttrell's patron in the 1540s. All these were associates of Cardinal Pole, new archbishop of Canterbury and papal legate for England and Ireland. With them served bishops Walsh of Waterford, and Devereux of Ferns, and Bartholomew Fitzsimons, rector of Clongill near Navan in Meath.[9] Luttrell was at the forefront of the Marian revival of Catholicism, especially in the diocese of Meath. It was his business, as it was that of the commission, to restore to the churches the vestments, the vessels, the altars and all the other trappings of the old Catholic faith and also to remove those clerics who, like bishop Staples, had married and had "sewn heresies and schisms away from the true Catholic faith". But the restoration of the old faith lasted only a few years, until the death of the Catholic Queen Mary in 1558. In 1559 Elizabeth passed the Act of Supremacy and made the state church once again Protestant. Luttrell was offered the Oath of Supremacy, and he refused to take it. In 1559 he was deprived of his archdeaconry which was given to an up and coming Protestant, John Garvey, who made a very successful career for himself, first as bishop of Kilmore and then eventually as archbishop of Armagh.[10] Luttrell's name appears in a document dating from 1566 surrendering "a parcel of the rectory of Galtrim"; it had been leased in the time of Henry VIII and was now surrendered by "Robert Luttrell, clerk, Thomas Fleming, vicar of Rathmolyn, Thomas Fitzsimons of Rath by Grinshe and Nicholas Luttrell of Clonsilla".[11] By then Robert had been stripped of all three of his benefices, Galtrim, Kilberry and Kells, and was imprisoned like his bishop, William Walsh, presumably for preaching against the new Protestant doctrines. There is a shadowy reference to his death in prison in 1578, a year after Walsh died in Spain, still a champion of the old faith he had helped restore, albeit temporarily, in the reign of Queen Mary. In Nicholas Sander's book on the Anglican Schism, published in Cologne in 1585, just seven years after his putative death, archdeacon Luttrell is saluted for his witness to the faith[12], and his name appears in the Analecta of bishop Rothe of Ossory, published in 1616, as one of those who were imprisoned for their faith.[13] His name does not appear on the list of Irish martyrs drawn up and published in 1903, but obviously his life and his contribution made him a witness to the faith, a martyr in fact, who deserves high honour in the diocese of Meath.

Footnotes

John Swayne- Rector of Galtrim and Archbishop of Armagh

1   Calendar of Papal Registers, Papal Letters, Vol.V, p203.

2   Calendar of Papal Registers, Vol.V, p312.

3   Calendar of Papal Registers, Vol.V, p614.

4   Ibid. 1405 to 1415, p375

5   His career can be traced in the Papal Registers of John XXIII, (Cal. Papal Registers, Papal Letters, vol.vii) p349, 374, 375, 442, 448. It is treated fully in "The Roman Career of John Swayne, archbishop of Armagh, 1418 to 1439", Katherine Walsh in Seanchas Ard Mhacha, Vol.2, No.1, p.1 ff.

6   Calendar of Papal Registers, Papal Letters, Vol.viii p317. 1417 to 1431. There survives in "Early Statutes of Ireland, John to Henry V", ed. Berry, p.583 another example of the legal differences of opinion on the respective rights of the king and pope in Irish clerical appointments. One "poor orator" John Randolf, parson of Our Lady of Galtrim, sued for "himself and his most sovereign lord the king." Evidently the seizing of the temporalities of the bishop of Meath into royal hands had coincided with the vacancy of Galtrim caused by the appointment of John Swayne to Armagh. Hence the king presented the suitor, John Randolf, to the vacant benefice and he was inducted by the ordinary of the diocese "not withstanding that one Thomas Prys, chaplain, procured a papal bull in which no mention was made of the royal title and right". Thomas and others in Rome responded that the king had no right to present to any church, the temporalities being in royal hands (because of a vacancy) unless by reason of the death of the bishop. This they claimed, Randolf alleged, to "the disherison of your crown and (one presumes) a greater misdeed, to the great damage and injury of the said John". A suitable remedy was required "with a view to preservation of the rights of your crown." Who won out in the end does not become apparent from the records. These rows took place on one level between those who could afford to go to law with one another and knew the ropes in Dublin, London and Rome. The income of Galtrim was at issue. One presumes that oblivious of all this, chaplains there and at Kilclone, Balfeighan, Rodanstown, Gallo and Drumlargan continue to look after their flocks and make available the parochial sacraments.

Galtrim and its Chaplaincies – 1480 – 1533

1   Register of John Bole, ed. Anthony Lynch, Seanchas Ard Mhacha, 1991, p61.

2   Ibid, p61. Register of Octovian, No.604.

3   Alumni Oxensis, Luttrell Robert, BCL, 8th July 1532, B. Can. Law, November 1532, c.f. Douai Register of Cardinal Pole, BMD,MS, 922, 111, fos, 61V – 32, where Luttrell, despite illegitimacy, holding without papal dispensation the rectory of Kilberry, in addition to a benefice in the cathedral and the vicarage of Galtrim, for which he had papal provision, and getting royal dispensation instead, now receives dispensation through Pole to hold these benefices legitimately. (10 July 1555)

4   Trim Castle, Butler, p232, 233, 234, 235.

6   Trim Castle, Butler, p235.

7   Extents of Monastic Possessions, ed. White, p297.

8   Extents of Monastic Possessions, ed. White, p298.

Robert Luttrell – Rector of Galtrim and Archdeacon of Meath.

1   Liber Munerum Publicorum Hiberniae, Rowley Lascelles, 1824, List of Chief Justices. Delahyde was deprived 7th October 1534 and Luttrell held the office until he died in 1554 at the beginning of the reign of Mary Tudor.

2   Alumni Oxensis, Robert Luttrell, BCL, 8th July 1532, B.Can Law, November 1532.

3   National Archives, d 17006 "Commission from Staples per proxy to J. Chambre, archdeacon of Meath, to William Cusack, treasurer of St. Patricks, Dublin, to give possession of the vicarage of Galtrim to Sir Robert Luttrell (on the presentation of Nicholas Hussey, Baron of Galtrim,) and to institute John Tuyte, chaplain to the rectory of Galtrim, both being vacant, August 10th 1533."

4   The Church Establishment, Vol.2, p97;

5   Dowdall Register, part 1, p15, 89, 68, 69 (61), 92 (78).

6   Original Letters and Papers, ed. E.P.Shirley, p19.

7   Calendar of Inquisitions, Philip and Mary, 24 -26, 24th April 1558.

8   Douai, Register of Cardinal Pole, BMD, MS 922, 111, fos 6, IV – 38.

9   Cal.P.Rolls, P+M, (1553-4), p71.

10 A member of the State Church, one William Brady, perhaps a relative of Bishop Brady, became rector of Kilberry in 1561 (Liber Munerum Publicorum Hiberniae, 1824, year 1561); Fiants Elizabeth 236, "Sir Robert Luttrell, Chaplain, Archdeacon of Meath", refused the oath of supremacy "affirming his conscience to be his let" 20 April 1560; Fiants Elizabeth 262, John Garvey appointed archdeacon of Kells, there being no bishop, 14th July 1560.

11 Fiants Elizabeth 854 (1566).

12 Cited in Murphy, 'Our Martyrs', p106.

13 Analecta, Rothe, p386.

Henry VIII: Changes in Religion
in Kilcloon 1536 to 1640

Chapter 22

The Reformation in Kilcloon

When Henry VIII declared himself head of the church in his kingdom and consequently required people in authority to accept this declaration under oath, the whole business did not really impinge on the people of Kilcloon. Most people in the days before mass communication lived and died within a few miles of their place of birth, and the daily efforts to sustain themselves and their families took up most of their attention and energies. They went to Mass on Sundays in one of the six parish churches and were served there by a vicar or chaplain appointed by the religious order to which the parish income from tithes had been given by the Norman founders of the churches. The religious order appointed a vicar who may have appointed a chaplain; both of them were supported by an income from the monastery and from the altarages or customary fees payable on the occasion of reception of the Sacraments or at funerals. If the religious order was tardy or mean about paying the salaries of the parochial clergy or about keeping the chancel or altar area of the church in good repair, then there was the yearly episcopal visitation through the rural deans, or the triennial visitation of the archbishop of Armagh personally or through nominated commissioners to contend with. One result, as we have seen regarding the Middle Ages, was, at least, in those of the six parishes of Kilcloon from which substantial ruins have survived, a massive building programme, in the fifteenth century at any rate, when the churches of Balfeighan and Rathregan were renewed in the fashionable High Gothic style to be seen in more detail in the ruins of the Plunkett churches at Killeen, Dunsany, Rathmore and Loughcrew. The nave or body of the church was the responsibility of the parishioners, and that presumably meant principally the lord of the manor.

While the oath of supremacy accepting Henry's claim to be head of the church did not impinge on the religious life of Kilcloon (it did impinge on political life as it contributed, among other developments, to the course of the rising of Silken Thomas of the house of Kildare, in which Kilcloon was intimately involved) the suppression of the monasteries after 1536 certainly did. That may seem strange as there were no monasteries in Kilcloon, but the take-over by the crown of the monasteries involved taking over control of the parishes, all six of the parishes in Kilcloon, where the Augustinian monastery of St. Thomas in Dublin and the Victorine monastery of St. Peter and Paul in Trim had the right to parish income and to appoint their serving priests. The ultimate effect of government policy was a collapse in parish structures. The policy was to retain a small amount of the value of monastic rights in the form of a rent, set the property or income to a layman for a fixed period of years, generally about twenty five years, to bind the interests of the lay grantee and the state together, and thereby expand the influence of the crown both on the frontier with the lands of the king's Irish enemies west of Kinnegad and on the Kildare/Offaly border and also in the settled and loyal lands of the Pale.

The result was that the obligation to keep the chancels of the churches (the altar area) was ignored. The salaries of the serving priests were not paid because there was no sanction imposed on those whose obligation it was to do so, or if they were paid it was because of the generosity and commitment of the impropriator or layman who held the properties. The advowson or right to appoint vicars fell to the crown but with little or no salaries attending the clergy, recruitment of priests with education and training was difficult, especially as the Protestant character of the state church, which had appeared briefly in the reign of Edward V1 (1548 – 1551), became the dominant one in the reign of Elizabeth from 1560 onwards. The recruitment of educated Protestant ministers from England or from Ireland, with commitment to the new Protestant teachings and practice was, of course, in these circumstances, practically impossible: the exceptions were the relatively well endowed offices of bishop, archdeacon or dean in the various dioceses. The impropriators, as the laymen who got the tithes were called, neglected the upkeep of the church chancels and in all the parishes of Kilcloon the churches soon fell into ruins. Obviously when the priests did not receive an income from the laymen to whom the parish incomes had been granted, when the monasteries which had formerly owned them were suppressed, they depended on local people, chiefly the local landlords for support. When these were traditional and Catholic in outlook, and not involved in the new scheme of things, the tendency was to continue with the old rhythms of worship and practice.

In the six parishes of Kilcloon none of the major or minor landlords appears in the surviving records as benefiting from the monastic confiscation. The Delahydes of Moyglare obviously did not do so; they had been involved in the Kildare rebellion and had had their lands confiscated. The Fitzgeralds of Balfeighan and Lackagh got none of the properties of the abbeys when these were first confiscated. Thomas Fitzmaurice Fitzgerald had died in 1533, leaving as his heir, his son, Maurice, a boy of five. He was a ward of the King and was handed over to the nuns of the convent at Odder, near Skyrne, to be reared.[1] The Plunketts of Killeen, who were the lords of Rathregan, received nothing of the monastic properties; neither did the Wesleys of Dangan, who were lords of Ballymaglassan, or the Rochfords of Kilbride who had substantial interests there as well. The lords of Kilclone itself, as such in effect they were, were the Husseys of Mulhussey, and they got no property either. The Husseys of Rodanstown and the Boyces of Calgath, the Fosters of Kilgraigue and the Husseys of Moygaddy, all minor gentry, likewise got no grants then or in subsequent reigns; all this is an indication that whatever they felt or thought, they took no active part in government religious policies. The Husseys, Barons of Galtrim, who had appointed to Galtrim and its chaplaincies, briefly in the 1530s before the rights of the Abbey of St. Peter and Paul's of Trim were partially restored in 1533, received no confiscated properties either. The King indeed held the right to appoint to all these vicarages and chaplaincies, but by 1622 that right of appointment had been transferred into the hands of the Husseys (Galtrim and its chaplaincies), the Delahydes (Moyglare) and the Plunketts (Rathregan).[2] By then the landlords were actively Catholic. Even the pardon in 1600 for involvement in the O'Neill rebellion of 1594 – 1603 of the twenty three or so people from about Moyglare, the list headed by Walter Delahyde of Moyglare, is an indication of where the loyalties of the ordinary people lay in matters of religion. It is clear that the population of the parish was almost exclusively Catholic all through the 16th century.

Four of the parishes of Kilcloon were chaplaincies, Ballymaglassan, Balfeighan, Kilclone and Rodanstown. The income of the priests serving there had been negotiable with the rectors, the abbot of St. Thomas's for Ballymaglassan and the abbot of St. Peter and Paul's in Trim for the other three. That the income was reasonable was guaranteed by the yearly visitation of the rural deans and the triennial visitation of the archbishop of Armagh. But when the rights of the abbeys were impropriated to laymen, there was no sanction to compel the impropriator to fulfil his duty to chaplaincies or vicars, though the latter in Moyglare and Rathregan had customary rights in law to a specific portion of the parish income.

In the Middle Ages chaplaincies were served by priests newly or recently ordained who had not obtained a permanent benefice. As we have seen Robert Luttrell, recently (1532) graduated in law, canon and civil, from Oxford was a chaplain for a short time, perhaps in one of the chaplaincies attached to Galtrim, before Nicholas Hussey acquired again for his family the advowson of the parish in 1533 and nominated Luttrell to the office of perpetual vicar.

Those who acquired the monastic income in Kilcloon are an interesting bunch of people.[4] In the first division of spoils there were government officials from England, locals from County Meath who in one way or another had proved to be useful, or were connected to the Dublin government, and the gentlemen of the Pale who had high office and took lightly, for the time being at least, the new dispensation that required taking the oath of supremacy which accepted the king as head of the church. Things began to be different when this acceptance of the "true religion as by law established" involved more and more Protestant ideology and practice, briefly and temporarily in Edward's reign, but permanently after 1558 in the reign of Queen Elizabeth.

Peter Lynch was an example of a relatively small local landlord – he came from Knock in Summerhill – who did well out of the confiscated properties. He had been collector of the income from the diocese of Meath due to the archbishop of Armagh, and, at least in 1537, of the income due to the Crown from Moyfenrath, Rathcore, Ballyregan and Balskeagh. In the years before the confiscation of Thomascourt in Dublin and of St. Peter and Paul's in Trim, the abbots in each, seeing the writing on the wall, quickly disposed of much monastic property on long leases to various associates in return for ready cash. Peter Lynch was a willing collaborator and a financial beneficiary in at least two transactions. In 1536 the abbot of Thomascourt leased the rectories of Laracor and Kilmore to John Lawless, chaplain, and Peter Lynch of Knock, for forty-one years. Lynch also had part of the vicarage income from Carbeston, impropriated to the College of the Blessed Virgin at Maynooth, where obviously he and his three companions had negotiated the lease before the college was suppressed. Incidentally he was on the jury which examined all the college property at Rathmolyn on 4th October, 1540 and the property of the Thomascourt monastery in the same place on the 6th October of that year. That property included the vicarage income from Kilmore and Laracor.

Lynch and companions had negotiated with the abbot of St Peter and Paul's in Trim a lease on the tithe income from Kilclone, Balrodden and Gallo for forty years, at a rent of eight pounds thirteen shillings and four pence, and of course that lease survived the suppression of the monastery. When he came to die in 1554 he "desired to be buried before the image of the Blessed Virgin" in his parish church of Laracor and instructed his wife to maintain a priest during her life from his goods and leases.[5] In 1540 he had substantial properties owned by the monastery itself around Trim and may well have had them on lease before it was suppressed. Two brothers, William and Edward Dixon, described as yeomen, negotiated a lease from the abbot of Trim on the rectory of Galtrim and Walterstown, Ranganstown and Ferrans and the two chaplaincies of Galtrim not held by Peter Lynch, Balfeighan and Drumlargan, for twenty one years. In 1540 they also held the rectories of Robertstown and Kilbeg. Their lease was renewed for a further twenty-one years in 1554.[6] They also held property of the former Carmelite House of Cloncurry in County Kildare, and in 1553, together with other New English people, they held lands worth fifty six pounds thirteen and four pence in the west of County Kildare. By 1570 William Dixon was dead and his interests in Galtrim were assigned to Henry Brante of Castle Rickard, together with a chapel of Our Lady, "now a bake house", near the north end of the bridge of Dublin. Judging by his name, Brante was probably of New English origin as the Dixon brothers seem to have been also.[7] The tithes of Moyglare were leased by the abbot of Thomascourt in 1538 to Thomas Alen to hold for forty one years from the death of his brother John Alen. Sir John Alen, who received the property of the first monastery to be suppressed in 1536, St Wolsten's in Celbridge (his family held this until the end of the eighteenth century), was Lord Chancellor and had obviously got a lease on the tithes of Moyglare from the abbot of Thomascourt before his brother's reversion lease in 1538. By 1540 Sir John was in possession, paying four pounds fifteen for an income estimated at over fourteen pounds. Thomas, his brother, held the tithes of Moyglare until his death in 1587. The tithes of Moyglare were obviously a lucrative prize. In 1570, Edmund Fitzalexander was granted a twenty-one year lease on them, again for four pounds fifteen and a fine of four pounds fifteen, the lease to run from the time the other one ran out. He had to wait for seventeen years for his income until the death of Thomas Alen.[8]

Ballymaglassan tithes had belonged to the Abbey of St Thomas as well. They went to one Barnaby King, who had been receiver of the property of Thomascourt. He served on the jury determining the properties of Thomascourt in 1540 and, presumably, as a reward for his services, got some minor pickings in the share out. He got a tenement in the parish of St. Nicholas within the walls of Dublin, worth eight shillings, another tenement in the parish of Cookstown, Ratoath, worth six shillings, an income from the altarages of Confey in Leixlip, and the tithes from the rectory of Ballymaglassan. The income from all these was six pounds thirteen and four pence for which King undertook to pay a curate and repair the chancel of the church and pay a rent of four pounds and four pence. By 1622 the church was in reasonable repair but the chancel was in ruins.[9] One presumes the curate fared no better in recovering his income. The tithes of Rathregan, which formerly had gone to the monastery at Trim, went to Sir

John Barnwall. He had been Lord Chancellor, one of the prominent Palesmen who were high in the favour of the Dublin government. He got substantial income from monastic properties, and when he died in 1538 the tithes in Rathregan were granted to one Nicholas Fre, a merchant in Dublin. By 1580 these tithes were granted to John Foster, Alderman of Dublin, for twenty one years at eleven pounds thirteen and four pence per annum.[10] He lived in St. Werbergh's Place and was lord mayor in 1597. In 1559 Sir John Elliott, a government official who had acquired the estate of Balreask, outside Navan, rented land from Gerald Wesley from Dangan who had most of the land in Ballymaglassan and acquired the advowson of Rathregan.[11] By 1622 it was in the disposal of the Plunketts of Killeen who owned the manor of Rathregan as well.[12]

Obviously the alienation of church properties to lay impropriators did not have an immediate effect on church life, though it did make a few people substantially richer than they had been. But it did begin a process which impoverished the church, and effectively through that process it made the Reformation, which took energy and shape and permanence only in the reign of Queen Elizabeth 1558 to 1603, impossible of success on the ground. A real Reformation was to take place at the beginning of the seventeenth-century but that was of a resurgent Counter Reformation Catholicism which filled the vacuum left by the decayed medieval structures and the failure of the state church to make any substantial inroads in the faith life of the people.

The bishop at the time of the changes in Henry the VIII's reign was Edward Staples. He was an English man appointed to Meath in 1530. He was appointed, as many of his predecessors had been, to serve as a civil servant and as a member of the Dublin government, conducting its secular business. He had no problem with accepting the King as head of the church; few in Ireland had as it did not seem a matter of much practical significance. Ordinary church life went on as before. Bishop Staples did not object when the monasteries were suppressed. Au contraire, he enjoyed his share of the spoils. But he was not an enthusiast when various practical reformed policies like abolishing pilgrimages, dismantling shrines and forbidding various rituals honouring the dead were introduced. He knew that the theories were one thing and the practical implications of introducing them were another. He urged caution. People obviously were not hostile to changes as long as the immemorial rituals of their ancestors were left alone. In a letter to the lord deputy's secretary in 1548, Staples sketched out his direct experience of public opinion:

*"One Jentilwoman to whom I did crysten a man childe which berith my
name, came in great councell to a ffrende of myne desiringe howe she*

myght ffinde meanes to change her childe's name, and he asked her whie? and she said because I wold not have him bere the name of an heryticke, a Jentilman dwelling ny unto me forbeadd his wif whiche wold have sent her child to be conformed by me so to do, sayenge his childe should not be conformed by him denyed the Sacrament of the Autor (altar). A frinde of myne rehersing at the marks that I wolde preache this next Soundaie at the Novam (Navan), dyvers answered they wolde not come there at lest they shoulde lerne to be hereticks, one of or lawers declared to a multitude that it was a great pitie that I was not burned for I preached herysie so was I worthie therfor"... "a benyfyced man of myn owne promotion came to me weepinge"... and My Lord, said he, before ye went last to Dublin ye were the best beloved man in yo r dioses that ever came in it, and now ye are the warst beloved that ever came here. I asked whie. Whie saith he for ye have taken open part wh the State that false herytick and preached agaynst the Sacrament of the Autor and deny saints and will make us worst than Jews where if the Countrie wiste how, they wold eat yow... and I advyce you for Christe sake not to preache at the Novam. "[13]

In the short reign of Edward V1, 1547 to 1553, things got worse. The young King's regents introduced practical Protestant practices whereby the Mass was abolished, the service conducted in English and communion received under both species, bread and wine. These practices imposed from the outside, by outsiders, cut into the rhythms of traditional religious observances and did not go down well in Meath, or in Kilcloon. It does seem as if the Anglo-Irish lords of the Pale, untroubled by royal supremacy (it was only opposed by the ordinary clergy in convocation) or by the assumption of the crown of Ireland by Henry V111 (they had urged it on him when he was reluctant to take on the responsibilities involved in extending jurisdiction to the whole island) or even by Papal opposition to the changes in the nomination of bishops, gradually jibbed at the practical implications of the Reformation. Allegiance to the Catholic church gradually joined other attitudes of opposition to policies elaborated in England, implemented by Englishmen and adversarial in character especially towards the powerful native Irish chieftains. It did not help that government taxes called the cess increased in Elizabeth's reign and sparked much opposition among the Old English lords.

The clergy, as we have seen, were increasingly dependent on the good will of their parishioners in order to survive. On paper, it looked as if the vicars and rectors at least were guaranteed a reasonable income. Their income appears again and again in the inquisitions or enquiries about estates of those who had died, or into the absence of clergy from their parishes or whether they kept schools in their parishes where English was taught. But when the comments of the Protestant Bishop Brady, (1562 – 1586) on the church of Meath in Elizabeth's reign are taken into consideration, it is obvious that the new lay owners of church incomes did not fulfil their obligations to pay priests to make available the parochial sacraments. The physical deterioration of the church fabric in Elizabeth's reign is merely another practical and easily measured indication that the financing of the parochial structures did not figure in the plans of the so-called lay impropriators, especially when at first and for some time (until the reign of Charles the First) there were no sanctions anyone, government or bishop, could apply that were in any way effective. The clergy were thrown back on the support of their parishioners, especially of their more prominent ones.

In the parishes of Kilcloon no local landowner seems to have been involved actively in any way in implementing government policy in politics or in religion, and we must assume that lay influence in the matters of religion was on the side of Catholicism. The close relationship between clergy, rectors, vicars and chaplains and the landlords is traceable up to the end of the reign of Elizabeth in 1603, in the inquisitions into property ownership made at the time of death of a landowner. Again and again, the executors of the wills of the Anglo Irish lords were their neighbours, their relations and above all the priests in neighbouring parishes, just as they had been in the years before the Reformation in the early years of the 16th Century.[14] Then the local clergy as well as neighbouring landowners, were the group which executed wills and ensured that when death struck a family, the property would be handed on in accordance with the landowner's wishes to keep the estate intact, and to ensure that the new head of the family was no less influential than the one who had drawn up the will. It was only towards the end of Elizabeth's reign that the clergy no longer appear in such documents. It was a sign that Protestant clergy, native or English born, had taken over or had been given the benefices, nominally, at least, and that the Catholic clergy, now frequently educated in the Counter Reformation seminaries on the continent, had to all intent and purposes gone underground; their names no longer appeared on legal documents and their support derived from the Anglo Irish lords and landowners privately in the areas where they served.

Another reason for the failure of the new religion in Meath is more difficult to assess; that is the influence of the bishop of Meath , William Walsh.[15] His predecessor, Edward Staples, an Englishman provided to the see in 1529, went along with the various changes in religion taking place in government circles. He took the Oath of Supremacy, accepted the new and Protestant liturgy in the reign of Edward V1, married, and was deprived of his see in 1554 in the reign of the Catholic Mary Tudor for refusing to put his wife aside and abjure his heresy. He was succeeded by

William Walsh, a native of Dunboyne, who seems to have had close connections with Kilcloon. He had been a monk in Bective before the suppression of the monasteries. When Bective was suppressed with other smaller monasteries, he transferred to St Mary's Abbey in Dublin, the premier Cistercian abbey in the country. Then in an extraordinary move for an Irish priest, not to say for a Cistercian monk, he moved to Rome.

There seems to have been a Kildare dimension in his decision. The Walshes of Tircroghan (near Enfield) were hereditary standard-bearers to the House of Kildare. One of them, Richard Walsh, parson of Ballymore Lough Seudy, in Westmeath, was a prominent supporter of Silken Thomas and went to Spain to obtain help for him, only to be told, with James Delahyde of Moyglare, when they met the emperor, Charles V, that Silken Thomas with his uncles had been executed at Tyburn. Richard Walsh's brother, Simon, was vicar of Rathbeggan, near Dunshaughlin, and was taken and executed at the capture of Maynooth castle in 1534. One Walter Walsh, clerk of Moyglare, was pardoned in 1578 and the whole web of relationships seems to have included William Walsh, the Cistercian who went to Rome. Even in 1534, Henry the V111's cousin, Reginald Cardinal Pole, seems to have become the focus in Rome for Henry's subjects who opposed his changes in religion, his divorce from his wife Catherine, and his reduction to illegitimacy of his eldest daughter, the Catholic Mary. Pole is mentioned in one of the reports about the rebellion. A letter sent in 1538 by someone, not accustomed to writing, is a nonsense: he proposed to defect to the league protecting Gerald, Silken Thomas's half-brother, the young heir to the house of Kildare and so betray him to the government; "wherefore it is best that ye send for Gerald and Delahyde and cause them to bring O'Nell and O'Donell's letters with them to the bishop of Rome and to the cardinall Poull that and he would come with sarten ordnance and powder that the said O'Nell and O'Donnell, O'Bryen and James of Desmont, with divers others Irishmen, shall meet the said cardinall in any place in Munster or in the borders of Galway and that they shall take the strong towns in that parts and deliver them to me."[16] Though obviously a bizarre flight of fantasy, it does reflect the place in Irish public opinion of Cardinal Pole as a focus for opposition to his cousin Henry VIII.

Pole was a central figure too in the government of the church. He was one of those who explored the possibility of congruence (unsuccessfully as it turned out then) between Catholic doctrine being defined at the Council of Trent and the theories on justification put forward by Martin Luther.[17] It was no coincidence that when the young Gerald, stepbrother of Silken Thomas, and heir to the House of Kildare, avoided capture by being smuggled abroad, it was to the household of Cardinal Pole in Rome that he was brought by his tutor, Thomas Leverous, who was soon to be bishop of

Kildare when the Catholic Mary Tudor succeeded her Protestant half-brother in 1553.[18] When Mary became queen the Protestant legislation of her predecessor was repudiated and she recalled her cousin, Cardinal Pole, to be her archbishop of Canterbury. He was also appointed Papal Legate to reform the church in England and in Ireland and make it Catholic once again. To restore Catholicism effectively in Ireland Pole depended principally on three men, Thomas Leverous, George Dowdall and William Walsh. It was no coincidence that all had been associated with Pole. Leverous was the tutor to the heir of the House of Kildare in Pole's household. Dowdall, archbishop of Armagh in Henry the VIII's time, had been in exile in Italy since his rejection of the Protestant liturgy of Edward VI. And William Walsh was a member of Pole's household in Rome.

Walsh implemented Pole's policies in Meath. He had succeeded Edward Staples, who had both married and implemented the Protestant liturgical changes. In 1554 Walsh and Bishop Leverous of Kildare, with Robert Luttrell, parson of Kilberry, vicar of Galtrim and archdeacon of Meath, Bartholomew Fitzsimons, formerly a canon of St. Patrick's Cathedral, and prebend of Tipper in 1536 in the archdiocese of Dublin and now rector of Clongill near Navan, were appointed to a commission to restore normal Catholic religious life.[19] They deposed clergy who had married in the years of Edward V1, 1547 to 1553, restored the vestments, vessels and furnishings to the churches where they had been removed under the Henrican Act of 1540, and reversed the Protestant liturgical practices introduced in the reign of Edward V1. But time was not on the side of the Catholic restoration. After a brief reign of five years, Mary died in 1558; her cousin, Cardinal Pole, died the same day at Lambeth Palace.

Immediately on the accession of Mary's half sister, Elizabeth, the Catholic restoration was halted and put into reverse. The supremacy of the queen over the church was asserted and had to be subscribed to under oath by the leaders of church and state. Those who refused to take the oath were deposed. Most government officials complied, as did not a few bishops in Ireland. William Walsh's opposition was uncompromising. A number of bishops left Dublin before the oath could be presented to them. Walsh stood his ground and refused to take it; he was deposed in 1560. So was his second in command, Robert Luttrell, archdeacon of Meath, parish priest of Kells, parson of Kilberry and vicar of Galtrim, who as we have seen was one of the chief actors in the restoration of Catholicism under Mary. (In 1561 William Brady was appointed vicar of Kilberry before becoming dean of Armagh in 1562; John Garvey was appointed archdeacon and rector of Kells in the same year).[20] Walsh preached against the Protestant changes at Trim and in the diocese of Meath so much that he was imprisoned in 1561. Released after a few months, his effective opposition to the religious changes caused him to be arrested again in 1565. This time he was kept in prison because of his influence over his people. Compliments to the effectiveness of his ministry are contained in some letters from the Dublin authorities to London.

In July 1565, urging his re-arrest, Loftus, the Anglican Archbishop of Dublin wrote to Cecil, the queen's chief minister in Westminister: "He hath manifestly condemned and openly showed himself to be a misliker of all the queen majesty's proceedings. He openly protested before all the people the same day he was before us that he never would communicate or be present by his will where the (Anglican) service should be ministered…. He is one of great credit among his countrymen and upon whom, in the cause of religion, they totally depend". He "fell to preaching against the common prayer." While arrested in 1565 Bishop Walsh was too prominent and popular for martyrdom and he was left a prisoner in Dublin Castle. In 1565, in the same letter quoted above, Loftus advised a change: "If it shall seem good to your honour, and the rest of her majesty's most honourable council; in mine opinion, it were fit he should be sent into England and per adventure by conferring with the learned bishops there he might be brought to some conformity." In other words, by his presence in prison, Bishop Walsh was encouraging disaffection with the Protestant religious changes and had become a focus for loyalty to the old ways and to the old faith. He had been one of those nominated to the vacant see of Armagh by the Apostolic Delegate, Fr. Wolfe, S.J.[21]

In prison, he was able to communicate fitfully by letter with the outer world, and in 1569 was one of the signatories to a document sent to the Court of Spain by leading Irish ecclesiastics and lords, offering to the king of Spain the right to nominate a new king for Ireland (whether of the House of Spain or Burgundy) as long as he was acceptable to the Holy See.[22] The bishop went into exile with the connivance of the authorities who found his presence in Dublin, even in prison, an embarrassment. He kept up correspondence with Ireland, and died in Alcalá de Henares, north of Madrid, in a Cistercian monastery in 1577.

Such a man, especially in his years of liberty from 1561 to 1565, after he had been deposed by the state in 1560, must have done his best to ensure that as far as possible the priests in the 225 parishes of his diocese were orthodox. The future was uncertain, and there was a talented and energetic Anglican bishop in his place, and he must have been concerned to ordain those who supported and understood the old faith.

In any case, the picture of religious affairs in Meath is fully sketched out in the correspondence with ministers in London from the Church of Ireland bishop who was appointed in 1563 to succeed Bishop Walsh. Bishop Brady was talented and energetic and a believer in the state church. In 1566, the Lord Deputy Sussex in a letter to Cecil summed him up. "For his sufficiency in preaching… he is equal to the best of the bishops her (sic) and for his grave judgement in counsel he far exceeded the rest."[23] Other bishops who had accepted the various changes in religion associated with the short reigns of successive monarchs were not so committed to the changes of Elizabeth as to be enthusiastic in their propagation. Hugh Brady was, like William Walsh, a native of Dunboyne, and in fact one who perhaps was his father, Donald, sat on various juries determining in Dunboyne the extent of monastic possessions in the area. Donal, with one Patrick Burgess, was the occupier of the lands in Rathregan, Belshamstown, Parsonstown, Cremore and Woodland from which the tithe was paid to the tithe farmer, Nicholas Fre, the Dublin merchant, in 1540.

Hugh Brady's experience of his new diocese was not encouraging. After his first three months he gave his initial reaction to Cecil, one of the Queen's council in London: "The ragged clergy are stubborn and blind…. the simple multitude through continual ignorance hardly to be won." To another of the Queen's counsellors, Walsingham, he wrote that within the church things had gone "from evil to worse."[24] To Cecil, "Storms rising at every side, the ungodly lawyers are not only sworn enemies of the truth, but also for lack of due execution of the law the out throwers of the country."[25] In other words lawyers (who formed part of the web of the Anglo Irish landlords closely related to each other by blood and marriage) were using their skills to subvert the government laws on religion. This state of affairs merely got worse in Meath as the years went on. In 1566 the Lord Deputy, Sidney, wrote to the Privy Council in London of "very small stipends as entertainments for vicars or curates." By 1576 he was writing that there were neither parsons nor vicars but merely a sorry curate in the parishes.[26] Another government official, Pelham, wrote to Walsingham pointing out there was "Not one house standing for any of them (curates or vicars where there were vicars) to dwell in." Pelham wrote in 1579 that he knew of one tithe farmer with sixteen benefices and no suitable clergy in any of them.

In 1575 Bishop Brady made a visitation of his diocese. Though the detailed observations on each parish have not survived, a general comment on his diocese has. It revealed that there had been simply no effective reformation on the ground. Out of 224 parishes, 105 were impropriate, that is leased out to the tithe farmers to whom "much benefit" accrued above the rent reserve to the Queen: "No parson or vicar resident in any of them and a very simple or sorry curate, for the most part appointed to serve them. Among which number of curates only eighteen were found able to speak English, the rest Irish priests or rather Irish rogues, having very little Latin, less learning and civility….all these live on bare altarages as they term them (which God knows are very small) and were wont to live upon the gain of Masses, dirges, shrivings, and such like trumpery goodly abolished by your majesty. No house standing for any of them to dwell in. In many places the very walls of the churches down, very few chancels covered, windows and doors 'ruined and spoiled'.[28]

Even interested and committed officials like bishop Brady, and John Garvey, his archdeacon of Kells, dean of Christ Church in Dublin and subsequently bishop of Kilmore and then archbishop of Armagh, did not let their commitment to the new religion extend to handing on episcopal lands intact to their successors: often they were leased out for long terms at small rent in return for immediate payment. The reformation did not impinge on life in the parishes where an impoverished church with no buildings relied upon a congregation and ministers who clung only to the old faith. The Reformation did not fail in Meath; it was never seriously tried.

Obviously there was no success in tempting married English and Protestant clergymen, to a diocese where there was no house for them to live in and the principal and sometimes total income from tithes had been given to buy government support, or establish English civil servants in Ireland. The priests of the old religion obviously lived, as their successors have done ever since, on the Mass stipends, funeral offerings and offerings given on the reception of Sacraments. The churches dependent on the tithe farmer fell quickly to ruin. The people again and again appear in reports to London. Sussex in 1562 wrote: "Our religion is so abused, as the papists rejoice… the people without discipline, utterly void of religion, come to a divine service as to a May game".[29]

Loftus wrote to the queen in 1565: "We found by their own confession that the most part of them (the lords) have continually since the last parliament frequented the Mass…very few of them ever receive holy communion or used such kind of public prayer and service as is presently established by law."[30] In 1581 Brady wrote to Walsingham "We have so many lets and stays of religion as everything therein groweth from evil to worse."[31] When bishop Brady died in 1583, he was succeeded as bishop by Thomas Jones. He was the son of a London alderman, and when he took orders after graduating from Cambridge, he came to make a career in the Irish church. He quickly married the sister in law of the archbishop of Dublin, and whether by coincidence or not, soon afterwards was elected dean of St. Patrick's in Dublin. For his speed and efficiency in alienating much of the patrimony of the deanery, he was immortalised by one of his successors, the acerbic Dean Swift, as "that rascal Dean Jones".

He was part of the dominant puritan faction in the Dublin government and while his sermons, for which he was rebuked by more moderate officials, were strong in word, he was weak in deed. By 1600, bishop Jones was accused of what he himself had been complaining of in 1586, the utter ruin of the fabric of churches in Meath. "For as much as her Majesty is credibly informed that the most part of the churches within the two large diocese of Dublin and Meath are utterly ruined, in so much as between Dublin and Athlone which containeth sixty miles and is through tracks of the English Pale, there are so few churches standing as they will scarcely make a plural number, and so few pastors to teach or preach the word, as in most of them there is not so much as a reading minister…that the lord deputy let these two bishops know how greatly her majesty is offended with them for their remiss and unchristian like carriage in their spiritual callings, whereby idolatry is grown to that height as it is the very strength and heart of rebellion, and Jesuits and other Rome running priests do so swarm both in cities and country, within the realm, who for due want of looking to in time, have got such an awe over the people that the poor subjects (who otherwise are sound in their loyalty) dare not but yield to those Romish priests in matters of conscience and faith."[32]

While little enough evidence survives to indicate the faith life of the people in the six parishes of what is now Kilcloon, there are enough indications that little of the new religion impinged on the lives of the people. As we have seen, none of the landlords were involved in the Dublin government. None of them shared in the division of monastic properties in the beginning or consequently. The Delahydes of Moyglare, of course, were tainted after their involvement in the Kildare rebellion and although treated leniently, and eventually given back their Moyglare estates, they did not play any part in government during Elizabeth's reign. Neither did the Plunketts of Killeen, who owned Rathregan, nor did the Wesleys of Ballymaglassan and their cousins and namesakes of Dangan. The Rochfords of Kilbride, who had substantial interests in Ballymaglassan, were not active in government affairs. Neither were the smaller landowners like the Fosters of Kilgraigue, the Boyces of Calgath, or the Husseys of Rodanstown and Mulhussey, though in 1567 Edward Hussey betrayed Archbishop Creagh to the government for a reward of forty pounds. A letter survives from Hussey offering the reward back if the archbishop's life was spared. Not surprisingly, his belated offer was not taken up.[33] Archbishop Creagh died in prison in 1587; his cause for beatification as a martyr has been introduced at Rome. The Fitzgeralds, who had settled in Belfeighan and Lackagh, were not involved in government either, though they did take part in army hostings and in local Kildare politics in Elizabeth's reign.

The names of a number of local priests occur by accident in the records. For Rathregan, one William Kenne was absent from his benefices without leave in 1538, as was Cormac Canne in 1575 and 1578.[34] Both these names are Gaelic in origin and probably placed the priests among those of native Irish origin who in increasing numbers appear in the parish appointments in the Pale, especially in Louth, Meath and Kildare, in the first two thirds of the century. In 1578, one Walter Walsh, parson of Moyglare, was pardoned for treason, together with John Gilsenan of Culmullen. His name puts him probably among that web of the Walshes of Dunboyne and Tircroghan which included parson Walsh of Lough Seudy and his brother Simon who had been executed in Maynooth. Bishop Walsh seems to have been part of this extended family also. In a 1591 will of a junior member of the Delahydes, great grandson of Walter of Moyglare, who had property in Dublin and Meath, the name of one John White, vicar of Moyglare, then dead, appears. The will made provision for a priest in St. Catherine's chapel in Dunshaughlin to pray for the soul of Richard Delahyde, his ancestors and descendants. Other chaplains were mentioned and the whole circle of family and witnesses and guarantors seems to have been Catholic.[35]

In any case, we have the word of Bishop Jones in his report on the diocese in 1605. "With the greatest number of churches in the diocese of Meath (about 120) belonged to the suppressed abbeys and religious houses and so the tithes are come to his Majesty's hands and are for the most part granted to Papists by lease for years, or in fee farm, who placed curates of their own choosing, without sufficient maintenance; neither do they keep in repair (as they are bound by their estates) the chancels of their churches, which is a thing the bishop cannot remedy, being debarred to sequester the fruits of their impropriet parsonages".[36] These, curates deemed unsatisfactory by Bishop Jones, could well have been priests placed by the tithe improprietors in the area, or more likely, by those who had the patronage of the churches, like the Husseys of Galtrim, the Plunketts of Rathregan and the Delahydes of Moyglare.

*   *   *

The Visitations of 1615, 1622 and 1633.[1]

The Visitation of 1615

Giving local habitation and name to Bishop Jones's comment is the regal visitation of 1615. A regal or episcopal visitation produced a detailed report on church property and personnel commissioned by the government or local Protestant bishop. In the parishes of Rathregan, Ballymaglassan, Moyglare, Kilcloon and Rodanstown the churches were repaired but all the chancels were in ruins. Balfeighan was alone in having both church and chancel in repair.

This visitation reveals both the efforts of the Church of Ireland to provide the parish with ministers and the quality of the ministers provided. There was one minister in the area, a graduate of TCD, Robert Cook, who was ordained in 1607, and who, by 1618 was rector of Culmullen, Gallo, Balfeighan and Drumlargan. William Fitzsimons, a deacon from 1615 to 1623 when he was ordained, had influence with the Delahydes of Moyglare, as he was vicar there in 1611, four years before he became a deacon. He must have had a reasonable education, as he is listed as a preacher in Rodanstown and Kilclone where Edward Doyle was curate; Doyle was also "a reading" minister in Rathregan and in Killeen, appointed to both by the Earl of Fingal. It is hard to resist the conclusion that his repaired rectory and cure in Rathregan, far from Killeen allowed Lord Fingal, the patron of both parishes, to support a priest undisturbed in the college of Killeen. Robert Cook was preacher for Nicholas Fferens in Gallo, Balfeighan and Drumlargan. The income of the parishes was very small. For example, Fferens got thirty shillings per annum each from Gallo and Drumlargan, and forty shillings from Balfeighan, minus whatever he had to give to Robert Cook for his occasional services as a preacher.

It does seem as if the presence of the state church in most of the various parishes was thin enough and, in any case, there were probably very few Protestants living in the area.

A minister serving in the area before 1607 was one James Kyan or Keane (was he a relation of Cormick Canne, Vicar of Rathregan who was there in 1578 and William Kenne, there in 1538, who was still there in 1570?) ordained deacon on 12th July 1592 and full minister in 1597. He certainly seems to have been of the family of Kean who held tenancies there in 1586. At the suit of Meiler Hussey, Teige Kean of Rathbeggan and John Kean, farmers, "Thomas Cullen of the same and...Edwin Flyn of Rathbeggan were pardoned in that year.[2] He was presented to the rectory of Rathbeggan in 1600 when the previous occupant, John Laghlin, died; it was no coincidence that Thaddeas Keane of Rathbeggan – presumably his father or brother, was patron of the parish with the right of appointment.

By 1615 Kyan was still in Rathbeggan but Garret Moore of Drogheda is given as patron and impropriator. In the notes on Rathregan it was commented that the clerical income was "sequestrated in the hands of J. Keyan."[3] Kyan was still rector in 1641 and so must have been very young indeed when he was inducted into the cure in 1600. Perhaps in his career we can see the transition from a church when the official incumbents in the area were in fact Catholic priests, to one when the state church had begun to establish a set of its own adherents in the parishes. If that premise is acceptable, then John Laghlin was the last of the old religion to serve officially as a parish priest of Rathbeggan. Things went the other way in nearby Galtrim. At the end of the sixteenth century, Owen Cahill was vicar of Galtrim and a tenant of Valerian Wellesley of Dangan in Clonymeath. He was succeeded as vicar by one James Daly, a reading minister in Kilmessan, Kiltale and Galtrim where he lived in 1622. He was recognised as an Anglican priest by bishop Ussher. But about 1630, through the influence of Thomas Messingham, head of the Irish college in Paris, one of his pupils there, Patrick Cahill, afterwards a rather turbulent priest in Dublin, was made rector of Galtrim by papal provision. He was probably a relation of Owen, who had been vicar there just before 1600.[4] It seems as if it was only at the turn of the century that the division between parson and priest became irrevocable and permanent, though as late as 1615, the state bishop of Meath, George Montgomery, deprived one of his incumbents for being a Catholic priest.

The Visitation of 1622

The state church in Kilcloon had progressed somewhat in the seven years since the last visitation. In Rathregan Edward Doyle, a native and reading minister, "now verie aged and sickly", lived in a rectory which, with the other houses of office, were well repaired. The church and chancel were both ruined. Robert Cook had replaced Baldwin Shepherd who had been curate at Ballymaglassan in 1615. Cook lived in Culmullen, and was curate in Gallo, Balfeighan and Drumlargan as well. Apart from Ballymaglassan where, though the chancel was still ruined, the church was repaired, all the churches and chancels in these parishes were either "ruynous" or "ruinous". By 1622 William Fitzsimons, now a deacon, lived at Moyglare and held the rectory with the curacies of Kilclone and Rodanstown. The church and chancel of Kilclone was "ruined", and though the naves of Rodanstown and Moyglare were repaired, the chancels were ruined.

The Visitation of 1633

By 1633 John Wilson was vicar of Rathregan. Ordained in 1620, he became curate in Monkstown, Staffordstown, Ffolletstown and Brownstown in 1622; in 1626 he added Rathregan where he subsequently lived, and, in 1630 in Grenock. John Smith was curate of Ballymaglassan and Philip Ffernsley, a Protestant army officer, was the patron. Robert Cook was still at Culmullen, and was curate of Balfeighan, and Drumlargan.

William Fitzsimons, ordained since 1624, was living at Moyglare, probably since 1611. He was curate in Kilclone (worth £30 to the impropriator Sir

John Netterville and forty shillings to Fitzsimons) and Rodanstown, where the income was the same as that in Kilclone. In 1632 Cook was replaced in Gallo by John Sterling M.A, who had been ordained in 1627. He got the rectory of Kilbrew the same year: Sterling fixed his residence in Gallo. By 1641 then, most of the ministers of the state church in our area were fairly well paid as they generally had a plurality of benefices though the impropriators, with the exception of Sir John Dungan of Celbridge, who held the tithes of Moyglare, worth forty pounds, where Fitzsimons the rector got a relatively generous ten pounds, did not allow much to the rector, vicar or curate of each parish. The clergymen were better educated too, and did not, as in 1615, need the assistance of preachers to make some stab at meaningful liturgy but it still seems most likely that there were very few Protestants on the ground. Certainly in the depositions of 1641 – 1642, made by Protestants driven off from the parishes of Kilcloon – there is only mention of Sir George Wentworth of Moyglare who was arrested by the rebels and allowed to go free in December 1641 to bring messages to Dublin, and of two other farmers, one in Brownrath, and one in Barrocks. The man who gave evidence of the robbery of Moyglare castle in 1643 was another, as was John Wilson, the rector of Rathregan.

The impropriators of church income in the parishes had only a financial interest in them. By 1613 the great tithes of Moyglare were in the hands of Frances Gofton, one of the auditors of the exchequer in England, with the small tithes reserved for the Anglican vicar.[37] By 1622 the tithe farmer was a Mr. Kenrdye of Dublin and the vicar was a deacon, William Fitzsimons, "born in the country", of good life and conversation. He was still there in 1640. The church then was well repaired but the chancel was ruined. There was a rectory , a garden and an orchard, three messauges (houses with gardens) four crofts, and there were three more acres of land and one of meadow detained by the patron, Luke Delahyde. Peter Lynch of the Knock had died in 1556, and the tithes of Kilclone and Balrodden which he then possessed were granted on by the Crown. In 1594 Thomas Poore of Powerstown, Co Tipperary was granted them, with very substantial parcels of land in various counties, reward no doubt for services rendered in the O'Neill wars then raging.[38] By 1613 Edward Medhopp, an English government official, held them together with the tithes of the other Galtrim chaplaincies, Kilclone, Balrodden, Gallo and Drumlargan.[39] By 1622 Lord Netterville of Dowth, near Drogheda, was tithe farmer. His family had not gained in the 1540 share-out and had not been involved in government in the meantime. Obviously tithe farming by then was a purely commercial proposition. By 1622 the church and chancel of Balfeighan were "altogether ruinous", as were the church and chancel of Kilcloon. In Balrodden the church was repaired but the chancel was in ruins. William Fitzsimons held the curacy there with that in Kilclone.

In 1540 one Nicholas Fre, a Dublin merchant, had acquired the tithes of Rathregan when John Barnwall of Trimbleston died in 1538. In 1579 a government official, John Elliott, who had established his family on an estate in Balreask near Navan, acquired from Gerald Wesley of Dangan a lease on substantial property in Ballymaglassan and was granted the right to present to the vicarage of Rathregan.[40] By 1622 the patron was Luke Plunkett, afterwards Lord Fingal, who owned the manor of Rathregan and was a Catholic.[41] In the same survey Luke Delahyde, of Moyglare was patron of Moyglare and Hussey of Galtrim patron of the vicarage there. Obviously, the Queen had ceded to local and Catholic landlords her rights to nominate to the rectories and vicarages formerly impropriate to the monasteries. Perhaps this was to underline the obligation of the parish community, led by the lord of the manor, to keep the nave or body of the church in repair.

There was a downside to this on the government side. The case of Rathregan illustrates it. In 1622 the incumbent at Rathregan, Mr. Doyle, a native, a reading minister (he was just able to read the service and did not preach) now "very aged and sickly", was also incumbent of Killeen of which Lord Fingal was also patron. Doyle lived at Rathregan in a rectory with the other houses of office well repaired, including "an haggard and a backside". The church and chancel were in ruins, but over at Killeen, where Doyle was also incumbent, the church and chancel "is reasonably repaired" and there was a rectory, and houses of office, and haggard and backsides and sixty acres of arable land. It is probably no coincidence that a report from circa 1622 in the papers of Sir Nathaniel Rich, an English-man sent to sit on a commission to investigate Irish affairs, stated that "Sir Richard Lee, priest (lives) in the college of Killeen". That same report lists priests all over the diocese of Meath. Oliver Warren was a priest at Knockmark (the Warrens owned Warrenstown in that parish near Rathregan) and there was another at Ratoath, but in the south east of the diocese the parishes of Dunshaughlin, Dunboyne, and the parishes of Kilcloon are not mentioned.[41] One can presume, however, that there were priests there, especially when a report of 1615, drawn up by the Anglican Bishop Montgomery, referred to "Robert Fitzoliver Nugent, Jesuit, cousin german to the Lord of Delvin, with whom and the Countess Dowager of Kildare, he ordinarily remaineth".[42] Though the Kildare family had been Protestants since the beginning of Elizabeth's reign, they were sympathetic to their Catholic relations, and in 1615 the widow of the Earl was a Nugent from Delvin, staunchly Catholic and a very competent businesswoman whose husband had died young. She controlled the family estates which included Little Moygaddy and Newtownmoyaghey as guardian for her young son.[43]

In short, it is obvious, that by 1622 that there had been efforts to cover the diocese of Meath, and indeed Kilcloon, with a network of Church of Ireland clergymen. Most of the churches were in ruins and the description by the Anglican Bishop Usher, himself from an old Anglo Irish family long established in Balsoon near Bective, of the characters and talents of the incumbents, did not give much promise of evangelical activity or even of worship.

There was one thing both the Protestant bishops, Brady and Jones, and the Roman authorities agreed on – the lack of knowledge among the ordinary people of even the rudiments of their faith. The papal nuncio in Paris was Archbishop Bentivoglio. Successive rectors of the Irish College there (the first three were from Meath, John Lee from Drogheda, Thomas Dease and Thomas Messingham) were the main means through which information on the Irish church was channelled to Rome. In an early seventeenth century report to Rome the nuncio summarised his information about the country, "though the inhabitants are all Catholics, they are mostly steeped in a profound and blind ignorance of any faith they may possess".[44]

But things were changing, as we have seen, in Ireland, in Meath and in Kilcloon. One of the first changes that we can see from the perspective of our own time is the gradual disappearance, complete by the end of Elizabeth's reign, of the local priests from the wills and estate settlements as executors or guarantors of the properties of local lords and landowners.

They were never replaced in this role by their successors, the official incumbents of the parishes, the often English-born and Trinity College educated Protestant clergymen. It is as if the priests went underground, as in fact most of them did. Another change is obvious too. In the 1530s, 40s and 50s, the rectors, vicars or chaplains were chiefly from one or two backgrounds, either Old Irish or from the families of minor landlords or substantial tenants. The new class of priests, at the end of the century, came from the families of the leading lords of the Pale. Formerly these lords had sent their children to Oxford or Cambridge for legal education. They were now being sent abroad to France, Spain and to the Spanish Netherlands where there were substantial numbers of Irishmen who had fought in the O'Neill wars and had joined after 1603 the armies of the arch dukes. Among these were at least two Delahydes from Moyglare and a Preston from Gormanston. Many of the children became priests, both secular and religious; those from Meath who joined religious orders were generally attracted to the new orders formed after the Counter Reformation in the spirit of the Council of Trent, the Jesuits and the Capuchins.

In 1578 John Lee from Drogheda, rector of the church of San Severin, which is still to be seen near the south bank of the Seine in Paris, where it faces Notre Dame Cathedral, gathered the stray Irish students at the University of Paris into one house. It became a college under Thomas Dease from Coole, County Westmeath, a member of the extended family circle of the Nugents, barons of Delvin. He had been ordained in Douai in 1591. In 1592 the Irish college of Salamanca was founded, and one of its first graduates was James Plunkett of Killallan, near Oldcastle, who came from a junior branch of the Plunketts of Killeen and Rathregan (he became vicar apostolic or administrator of the diocese of Meath in 1613).[45] In the 1590s Cornelius Stanley, administrator of the archdiocese of Dublin, acted as administrator in Meath too. Jesuits from the leading Meath families came back to work in Meath and Westmeath, and James Archer, S.J., in a report written in 1598, talks of having been invited to Meath by Cornelius Stanley where "he converted ten priests who were living in sin and concubinage".[46] Obviously, for the first time since the imprisonment of bishop Walsh, diocesan structures were being renewed again. Successive letters and reports from the Dublin officials to London reflect an awareness of a new vitality in the Counter Reformation Catholic church, especially in the Pale and their inability to do anything about it.[47]

The first Catholic bishop of Meath since Bishop Walsh was deposed in 1561 was appointed in 1622. He was Thomas Dease, then rector of the Irish College in Paris, capable, dynamic and with a clearly focused mission. (See illustration of Bishop Thomas Dease, 1569–1652, p xv). That was to implement the decrees of the Council of Trent of seventy years before, which were intended to reform completely the structures of the local churches.

At the centre of the reform was the bishop: he controlled absolutely the provision of the parochial sacraments, Baptism, Confirmation, Extreme Unction and the ceremonies attached to funerals. He alone could licence those whom he wished to serve in his diocese. In this the local bishop had both flexibility in orchestrating the human resources available to complete his mission and was also accountable to the authorities in Rome. From 1622 onwards, in the case of Ireland, that meant control by the Roman dicastery (or department) dealing with areas where the church was not established, the Congregation of the Propagation of the Faith, called in short, Propaganda.

In this the Catholic bishop had a decided advantage over his Protestant counterpart, who was lumbered with the structures of an unreformed medieval church with its income in hock to people with no interest in the state church or in its mission. The problems were compounded for the state bishop by the policy, seemingly introduced sometime in Elizabeth's reign, of granting to local landlord the rights of presentation to the churches, to encourage them to keep the naves of the churches in repair. The result in Kilcloon was, as we have seen, that the Catholic Delahydes, Plunketts, and Husseys had the right to appoint the vicars of Moyglare, Rathregan and Galtrim and the chaplains in Balfeighan, Rodanstown and Kilclone. They would hardly favour evangelical Protestants, even if these were available for appointment to the parishes; in any case the actual control of all the lands of Kilcloon by the Catholic lords ensured that evangelical activity on the part of the local clergyman of the state church was not encouraged. The new class of Catholic clergymen that Bishop Dease had at his disposal were the products of the seminary system, another innovation of the Council of Trent. It produced both secular and regular priests, who were disciplined, theologically literate and subject in their work to the bishop himself. Dease even took the precaution of having secular priests appointed by the Datary in Rome as titular priors or titular abbots to vacant abbeys in his diocese, which in the Middle Ages had controlled the appointments to many parishes. He did this to prevent any attempt of old religious orders to reorganise their priories and abbeys and claim the rights they had had in the Middle Ages to appoint to half of the parishes in the diocese.

The secular priests appointed were often from the families of the lords who had acquired the properties of the abbeys in the previous century and did not wish to have their titles to them questioned.[48] It seems likely that they contributed to the income of their relations who were the titular abbots and priors. By 1630 the diocese was divided up once again into parishes. Then, as now, a number of medieval parishes were joined together in one union. No name of a priest or priests active in Kilcloon has survived from the first half of the seventeenth century, but we can be sure that the normal parochial life re-established by Bishop Dease, was lived here in Kilcloon at least in the 1630s.[49]

Of course these structures were no sooner set up than they were disrupted by the rebellion of 1641 and levelled to the ground in the years associated with Cromwell – 1649 to 1660. A tribute to the work of Bishop Dease and the often nameless clergy who worked to re-establish the church in those short years from 1622 to 1641, is the survival of the Catholic church after Cromwell, and after the penal laws of Queen Anne, as the church which attracted the loyalty of the vast majority of the people of the area.

Footnotes

The Reformation in Kilcloon

1   Cal. Inquisitions, Henry VIII, 113-118; 114-119.

2   Ussher's Visitation in "The Whole Works of the Most Rev. J. Ussher, DD", ed. Elrington, Vol.1, appendix V, p41.

3   Fiants Elizabeth, 6557.

4   c.f. Extents of Irish Monastic Possessions, 1540 to 1541, ed. White, p34, 36, 47, 294, 296, 297, 321.

5   Cal. Inquisit. vol.i, Lagenia, Meath, JI , 61-61; C.S.P.I. Henry VIII, 1509 to 1573, p458, No.1310 (1537).

6   Fiants Philip and Mary, 56; Patent Rolls, Mary, 301.

7   Fiants Elizabeth, 1663.

8   Fiants Elizabeth, 1627; 5343. In fact the tithes were given in 1589 (Fiants Elizabeth 5343) to William Monynges "the altarages to vicar and curate excepted" for twenty one years at the rent of four pounds thirteen and fourpence which had been the vicar's income in 1300. The lease to Alexander was forfeited for non payment of rent.

9   Extents of Irish Monastic Possessions, ed. White, p34, 47, 321; Ussher's Visitation of 1622, the complete works of Ussher, appendix V. In 1576 Michael Kettelwell got Ballymaglassan for twenty one years at twenty pounds rent; he was at different times collector of customs at Wexford, engrosser of the exchequer, a clerk of works, surveyor of ordnance, constable of Dublin castle, and on the commission examining land confiscated from the Eustaces after the rebellion of 1582. When he died in 1596, Sir Henry Wallop got the income from Ballymaglassan. Both men were civil servants.

10   Fiants Elizabeth, 3980.

11   C.P.R. James I, No.49. The Wellesley property of Ballymaglassan were made up of forty messauges, twelve tofts, sixty gardens, five hunded and forty arable acres (perhaps about two thousand five hundred statute acres), sixty acres in meadow, thirty in pasture and forty in woods at Ballymaglassan, Blackhall, Brownrath, Garres and Coldermine (both these names cannot be now identified).

12   Ussher's Visitation.

13   Shirley, Original Letters, p24.

14   c.f. Cal. Inquisitions, ed. Griffith, passim.

15   For his life, c.f. Hogan, Riocht na Midhe, 1977, p3 to 15.

16   C.S.P.I. 1509 to 1573, No.1516.

17   c.f. Fenlon, Heresy and Obedience in Tridentine Italy; Cardinal Pole and the Counter Reformation, Cambridge, 1972.

18   History of the Archbishops of Dublin, Moran, p58.

19   Ware, "Annals of Ireland" 1544; C. P.C.R, 1 and 2, Philip and Mary, Nos.3, 4, 5, 13, 14.

20   Fiants, Elizabeth, 262; Liber Munerum Hiberniae (1561); his bishop, Hugh Brady, writing to Cecil, the Queen's minister, called him "a sharpe preacher in the Irish tongue", S.P. 63-13-39. Fiants, Elizabeth, 236. Sir Robert Luttrell, Chaplain, archdeacon of Meath refuses the Oath of Supremacy "affirming his conscience to be his let" 20 April 1560.

21   Loftus to Cecil, 16th July 1565. C.S.P. 63-14-22, cited in the life of Bishop Brady by Helen Coburn Walsh.

22   WALSH, William, bishop of Meath, Hogan, Riocht na Midhe, Vol.6, 1977, p11 and note 51.

23   Specilegium Ossoriense, Vol.1, p59, 61.

24   Sydney to Cecil, 1566, S.P. 63 – 17 – 31, cited in Coburn Walsh.

25   Hugh Brady to Walshingham, "The clergy of his diocese are of abysmal quality so as there is left little hope of their amendment" Brady to Cecil, 14th March 1564, S.P – 63-10-30, cited in Coburn Walsh.

26   Civil Survey, Vol.5, Meath, p399.

27   Sydney to the Queen, S.P. 63-67-46; S.P. 65-55-38.

28   Pelham to Walsingham, S.P. 63-69-46; S.P. 63-67-46; S.P. 65-55-38.

29   Brady's visitation of Meath, 1575, S.P. 63-55-38.

30   Sussex to Cecil, 1562, S.P. 63-6-57.

31   Brady's visitation of Meath, 1575; Loftus to the Queen, 1562, S.P. 63-6-57.

32   Brady to Walsingham, S.P. 63-85-39.

33   C.S.P.I. 1600, p273.

34   C.S.P.I. 1509 to 1573, p354.

35   Cal, Inquisitions, Elizabeth, 71-52; Ibid. Henry VIII, 129-127.

★ ★ ★

The Visitations of 1615, 1622 and 1633

1   The second of these visitations is published in "The Whole Works of Most Reverend James Ussher", ed. Elrington, Vol.1, appendix V, p111. The first and third are in manuscript in the National Archives.

2   Cal. Inquis. Elizabeth, No.3651.

3   Civil Survey, Vol.5, p386 and 388. Keane had been vicar of Dunboyne and Kilbride since 1622 at least. History of the Diocese of Meath, ed. Curran, vol III, p1128.

4   Patrick Cahill seems to have been somewhat adversarial in character (c.f. O'Connor, Thomas Messingham, Riocht na Midhe, Vol.11, 2000, p96, ff.). He was eventually appointed dean of St. Patrick's by the Roman Datary in 1644 to hold along with the parish of St. Michael which he had held since 1628(Arch. Hib. Vol. 1, p34.) The habits of acquiring Roman appointments to Irish benefices, one of the unfortunate characteristics of the Middle Ages as we have seen, died hard. By 1644 Cahill could not have had either influence, income or life in Dublin. His life was spent in Dublin before 1641; where he lived and worked after the rebellion broke out is not recorded. Perhaps he went home to Clonymeath near Galtrim. In 1600 Wesley of Dangan renewed a lease of property in Walterston, parish of Galtrim, to Shane Cahill of Galtrim, brother of Owen Cahill, vicar of Galtrim, in as ample a manner as Owen Cahill held it for thirty years at one grain of wheat, consideration thirty pounds. One of the witnesses was James Daly, vicar of Galtrim. In 1602 Wesley leased to Oweyn Cahill, late vicar of Galtrim and John his brother and Owyn, William, Connor, and Hugh, John's sons, lands in Walterston "with turbary rights in Clonymeath for a hundred years...twelve pounds paid by Owen Cahill to Gerald Wesley".

★ ★ ★

36   Cal, Inquisitions, Elizabeth, 219-145.

37   Healy, History of the Diocese of Meath, Vol.1, p217.

38   Calendar Patent Rolls of James I, p340.

39   Fiants, Elizabeth, 5873.

40   Cal. Patent Rolls of James I, p509.

41   c.f. Episcopal Visitation of 1633, National Archives; Cal. Inquis. vol. I, Lagenia, Meath, James I, 49.

42   Ussher's visitation, The Complete Works of Most Reverend James Ussher, Vol.1, appendix V, p411.

43   History of Diocesce of Meath, Healy, Vol.1, p236.

44   The Leinster Papers, p417.

45   Archivium Hibernicum, Vol.3, p300.

46   For his career, c.f. Attitudes to the Counter Reformation in Meath, 1600-1630, Rice, Ríocht na Midhe, Vol.5, No.2, 1972, p57, ff.

47   c.f. Gams, pg. 230; Wadding Papers, ed. Jennings, p65; The Diocese of Meath, Healy, Vol.1, p286.

48   C.S.P.I. 03-06, p58, 65, 212.

59   Thomas Messingham (C. 1575 -1638 ?) and the seventeenth century church, T.O'Connor, Ríocht na Midhe, Vol.11, 2000, p95, 96.

50   Collectanea Hibernica, No.14 (1971), p11. John Roche, bishop of Ferns, passing through Meath in 1629, reported to Rome: "There are but few heretics there, whilst there is a numerous clergy, and the parochial district are admirably arranged", cited in Moran, Archbishops of Dublin, p397.

Cromwell and Kilcloon

Chapter 23

Prelude to Oliver Cromwell:
The Rebellion of 1641

The decade of 1640 to 1650 began as a decade of hope and ended in despair. In 1640 the Old English, as they were called, inhabitants and lords of the Pale, and of most of Munster, Leinster and Connaught around Galway, descendants of the Norman conquerors of five hundred years before, the traditional supporters of the crown and its government in Dublin, were disaffected, alienated from the Dublin government circles, excluded from involvement in government and persecuted in the practice of their religion. Their loyalties were to the crown in England, and their opponents, the so-called New English, came from families who had immigrated to Ireland in the previous century. As civil servants and high government officials these had become substantial landlords by acquiring monastic and other confiscated properties, and formed a class, Protestant in religion, which had replaced the Old English in the central administration of the country. The final threat to the security of the Old English was from the policies of the Lord Deputy, the soon to be Lord Lieutenant, Thomas Wentworth, subsequently Earl of Strafford, who came to Ireland in 1634 to make Ireland pay for itself, and contribute to the king's treasury in England. King Charles was locked increasingly into a quarrel with his parliament over his need for additional taxation and its demand for more power as the price for granting it. Wentworth began to question the titles under which the Old English had held their properties since the Norman conquest, so that the plantation policy, which had heretofore been implemented against the Old Irish in Ulster, Laois, Offaly, and Longford and against the gaelicized Normans like the Earl of Desmond in Munster, was now to be used against the Old English themselves to acquire additional income for the crown. Another grievance was religious. The Old English had negotiated a voluntary tax in return for the so-called "graces" – concessions on the anti-Catholic laws against the practice of their faith. The cash was levied by themselves and was paid, but the graces, for one reason or another, were never given a promised legal status in parliament. Even in 1640 when Wentworth called a parliament after a gap of six years – he was not fond of parliaments, as they were inclined to question his high-handed methods and policies – he delayed in allowing the graces become law.

The Old Irish in Ulster, spotting differences between the king and parliament in England which they could exploit – these differences would eventually lead to civil war – decided to rebel in 1641, and seize Dublin. It was a way of highlighting their grievances, partly religious but mainly arising from the confiscation of their properties and the planting of their lands at the Ulster plantation only thirty years previously. They set off a decade of turmoil, and eventually of despair. Wentworth had been called to London to answer the charges of all parties in Ireland, the Old English, the Old Irish, the Presbyterians in the north, who were being pressurised into joining the state church, and even the New English whose opportunities for personal and illegal enrichment were severely curtailed by the deputy. His impeachment in parliament led him to the executioner's block. In Ireland, the Lords Justices who succeeded him, supporters of the parliament, and puritans in religion, saw the Ulster rebellion as an opportunity to squeeze the Old English lords into rebellion. The Lords Justices refused repeated requests for arms from the Old English lords. When the social unrest which accompanied the rather shapeless uprising and the sporadic acts of vengeance for the plantations and the persecution of the Catholic faith, grew in intensity, the leaders of the Old English decided to make common cause with the Ulster rebels and eventually formed a confederation which would rule most of the country for the next nine years. It was the first time in Irish history that Old English and Old Irish came together in a form of home government. Their initiative was imitated by the inhabitants of the island who in succeeding centuries by parliamilitary or violent means tried to set up some kind of national government until they succeeded in so doing in the twentieth century.[1]

In any case, by the beginning of 1642, most of the country – apart from the capital and chief ports, and some areas in the north of Ulster – was in the hands of the rebels who came together in Kilkenny to set up a confederation of the Old Irish and Old English to form a government and rule the country. The chief rebel in Meath was Lord Fingal who owned the manor of Rathregan. At a meeting in Duleek early in 1642, captains were chosen to raise military forces in each of the baronies of the county. For Deece Hussey of Galtrim was chosen together with Edward Hussey of Mulhussey. Valerian Wesley of Dangan was involved in Kilcloon also because of his interest in Ballymaglassan.[2] From the beginning it seems as if all over Ireland there was a movement to expel all New English, together with Protestant church ministers, from their homes and to confiscate their goods. The tale of robbery, violence and death is furnished only by a not unbiased source, the depositions, given mostly in Dublin by those who had fled there, as to the events that had taken place, and the compensation expected. In our own parish a coherent pattern in these matters seems to have emerged.

The New English seemed prudently to have fled or were expelled from their properties. Sir George Wentworth, who had owned Moyglare since 1638, was taken briefly by the rebels and released in late 1641. Protestant ministers fled to Dublin. All the activities in what is now Kilcloon were associated with Edward Hussey of Mulhussey and Valerian Wesley of Dangan (through the latter's half-brother, Patrick Cusack of Blackhall). In view of the urgent need for horses to form a rebel cavalry and a subsequent decree in Kilkenny confiscating enemy property to support the war, events in Kilcloon seemed to have anticipated the Kilkenny decrees in the first months of the rebellion. No one was killed or injured and only property, goods or animals were involved. Obviously, those who fled from the provinces to Dublin were anxious that the story of their experiences be recounted. The authorities were anxious to oblige, so that public opinion in England would be inflamed with tales of Irish atrocities. Naturally, Moyglare, now owned by Sir George Wentworth was a prime target. The deponent, one Thomas Kirby of Ballymagillin, testified on 4th May 1643 to events of two years previously. Edward Hussey, he claimed, had seized the house of Moyglare, robbed the contents of goods and chattels, seized on arrears of rent, cows, horses, mares, geldings and afterwards through the agency of Garret Talbot, brother of Sir Robert Talbot of Carton, burned the house and four outhouses. All told, Wentworth was declared deprived of 2,956 pounds, two shillings sterling and was deprived of 485 pounds in profits from the land. Ralph Gill of Moyglare testified that at the end of November 1641, he was deprived of cows, garranes to the value of 35 pounds, household goods worth 20 pounds, coin and valuables worth 80 pounds and suffered "loss and hinderment of the benefit of my land" (160 pounds) and that his losses were effected by Edward Hussey and Walter Hussey. Altogether he calculated that he was deprived of 212 pounds.

On January 15th 1642, Bartholomew Newton of "Barrigge, a British Protestant", complained that on the 26th November last about twelve of the clock on the night and about ten the next day, he was robbed by means of Edward Hussey of Mulhussey, the Baron of Galtrim and Edward Barnwall and their tenants. He claimed they took cows, horses and mares worth 73 pounds, household goods worth 44 pounds, corn and hay worth 32 pounds, the lease of a farm, clothes worth 14 pounds, debts to the value of 16 pounds and timber worth 4 pounds. He also claimed – the only harm to persons reported in Kilcloon – that Edward Hussey and his followers stripped the deponent, his wife and children, of apparel, "exposing them to be harmed by the cold". In another deposition, one Thomas Johnson of Brownrath wrote to Lord Ormond complaining that " Mr. Wesley of Dangan" and his half-brother, Patrick Cusack of Blackhall "hath moved your honour for arms and aid" while robbing him of goods worth 60 pounds in Brownrath and moving them to Cusack's house. The vicar of Gallo, John Sterlinge, claimed that corn, turves and hay worth 120 pounds, cattle worth 20 pounds, and household goods worth 60 pounds, were taken on 30th November 1641 by Edward Hussey, who, Sterlinge claimed, told him that he would save these goods for the use of the rebels. Sterlinge claimed that Edward Hussey, Nicholas Hussey of Gallo, Patrick Barnwall of Kilbrew, James Mooney of Garradice and Kathleen Bennett, among others, owed him, between them, 481 pounds. It is as if he was alleging both personal and political reasons for the robbery. John Wilson, the vicar of Rathregan, fled before anything happened "fearing to stay in ye house myself by reason of the daily threatenings which – I credibly heard – were given out against my person." He claimed that on the 24th November 1641 "the rebels being the poorer sort of parish dwellers and others" took household goods worth 7 pounds and cows worth 30 pounds. He also lost "in ye hands of one Mr. Patrick Cusack of Blackhall whom I trusted" two mares and a colt worth at least 8 pounds, and likewise "ye oversight of haggard corn and hay worth at least 58 pounds". He also claimed he placed his books, brass, pewter, bedding and household goods among neighbours in the village whom he trusted, but they were all pillaged from where they were left. He also claimed cash to the amount of 100 pounds, being made up of tithes and "church duties" and of money loaned to needy people. The total sum claimed was 241 pounds. Perhaps it was significant that when the Confederation met in Kilkenny, the tithes and other church income in the hands of the Anglican clergymen were given to the Catholic priests, a policy anticipated in Rathregan.[3]

Severe retribution was not long in coming to Kilcloon. By May 1642 Sir Charles Coote had sixty horse and officers at Naas which had been recovered from the rebels; Sir George Wentworth had the same number of horse and officers there also.[4] They set out with 350 horse and 150 foot to relieve Lady Offaly's castle in Kildare and Lady Jephson's castle in northeast Offaly. Having achieved those objectives, they wheeled north and took Trim, killing 60 rebels in taking it and executing the rest. Their policy in the countryside was a scorched earth one, burning and hanging as the opportunity arose. Coote, whose son was married to a sister of Wentworth's wife, soon acquired a reputation among the Irish for brutality and ruthlessness that was not altogether confined to the rebels. As one of his supporters, the Lord Justice, Parsons, put it delicately, "he was shot, it was thought, by one of his own troopers, whether by design or accident was never known, floods of English tears accompanying him to the grave."[5] His troops under a Colonel Stanford had killed upwards of 100 men, women, and children at Mulhussey, the home of Edward Hussey, where they were under protection (they were ordinary people who were allowed cultivate the land and were protected in so doing as long as they delivered a determined portion of the crops to the army), and one Conor Breslin was struck with a knife and bled to death. Over 100 labourers and women, "making their harvest", in the Spring of 1642, were reputedly killed by the garrison of Trim. In Kilbride, near Dunboyne, two women were reputed to have been hanged by the Trim troops together with two "old decrepit men who begged alms of them". Forty men, women, and children, in protection, "reaping their harvest in the autumn" in Bonestown near Dunshaughlin were killed by more troops from Trim, who had that day killed at Dunshaughlin a Mrs Alison Reid who was eighty years old.[6]

The policy was obviously to terrorise the ordinary people, tenants, yeomen, labourers and their wives, who naturally provided a sympathetic sea for the rebels to move in and made it possible for what would be called guerrilla war today, to thrive. Of course the experience of such tactics is more likely than not to stiffen resolve and resistance. At a time when supplies came from the immediate surrounding countryside for the armies, it caused shortages of food in any army present in one place, as the new garrison was to be for a prolonged period at Trim. In fact the presence of the garrison at Trim meant that the whole countryside between Trim and Dublin was effectively in the hands of the king's forces by May 1642.

On July 8th[7] Lieutenant Colonel Monk, marching west to meet the Marquis of Ormond's forces, observed a castle at Knock (Summerhill); "it was a great offence and annoyance to the garrison at Trim". He took it in two days, killed four score men and hanged the prisoners to boot. Rathcoffey and Clongowes Wood and Leixlip were taken and garrisoned a little earlier. The draconian methods of the royalist army were commended by the Lords Justices in a report on the 23rd September 1642. Athboy had been besieged by the rebels and 1500 troops were sent to Trim "to scatter them". The forces were led by a Lord D'Isle who made a circuit of Meath "burning, wasting, spoiling and destroyers of all the country around and of all the rebels, corn, hay and turf". He deprived the rebels of all cattle he could and when "he leaves, the rebels shall have neither house, hedge, nor food, nor fire" and so would starve.[8] In May 1642 an act was passed in the London parliament called The Adventurers' Act, encouraging London merchants and others with hard cash to contribute to the conquest of Ireland: this loan was to be repaid in the confiscated lands of those in rebellion in Ireland. It suited the Lords Justices to be severe enough to provoke as many of the Irish landowners as possible into rebellion. In the early months of 1642 many local rebel leaders were outlawed, among them Patrick Hussey, baron of Galtrim and his son Hugh, John and Marcus Hussey of Rodanstown (the latter appears in the depositions as one of those who sacked Maynooth in late 1641) Edward Hussey of Mulhussey, Valerian Wesley of Dangan, Walter Wesley of Blackhall, James Fitzgerald of Lackagh (and of Balfeighan); others were Thomas Geoghegan of Balfeighan, George King of Galtrim, Garret Plunkett and Patrick White of Rodanstown.[9]

In March 1642 Sir Philip Persivil submitted a list of places where cavalry and foot could be quartered, "bordering on Birmingham's country", on the border between west Kildare, Offaly and Meath.[10] His list makes an interesting comment on Kilcloon before the destruction heaped on it during the confederate wars. He described Mulhussey as a town and strong castle, able to receive 200 foot, Dooleystown (Dollanstown) as a vaulted castle able to receive 100, Calgath, another vaulted castle, fit to receive 50 foot, Balfeighan a town and castle fit to receive 100 men; nearby Garadice had a town and castle which could receive 200 men; Galley (Gallo) a town, castle and church fit for 200 men, Agherpallis, a town, castle and church fit for 200 men. Lynch's Knock at Summerhill could accommodate 40 foot and 20 cavalry.

By 1643 the king was in difficulties in a civil war with the parliament of England, and at home here the Kilkenny authorities, dominated by the Old English, sought to trade off their willingness to help their king for security of title in their lands and toleration for their Catholic religion. A truce was arranged in 1643, and prisoners were exchanged. It is recorded that George Foster was among them, "permitted for his corn at Kilgraigue".[11] In other words a change in official policy had been effected; the natives who lived in the English quarters, that is east of Trim, would be protected as long as they paid their levies to the state. The truce or cessation, as it was called, was renewed for another year in 1644.

The king was anxious to make peace with the confederates as soon as possible, so as to release rebel troops to serve him in England where, at Marsden Moor and at Naseby in 1645, he had been completely defeated by the army of the parliament of England. The Old English lords too wanted peace quickly, as they were all too aware of The Adventurers' Act of 1642 by which the English merchants had a claim on their land which were liable to be confiscated because of their rebellion. The Old English were prepared to settle for legal title to their lands, which would be confirmed by parliament, together with the tacit toleration of the practice of their Catholic faith. In 1646 such a peace, called after the chief representative of the king, the Marquis of Ormond, was signed, but within the confederate camp two distinct but related groups objected: the Ulster

Old Irish who happened to have the most talented soldier in Ireland in their ranks, Owen Roe O'Neill, wanted their plantation of 1609 modified or reversed. The other was the recently arrived (1645) papal nuncio, Archbishop Rinuccini and his supporters He was archbishop of Fermo in Italy and could not conceive of a Catholic state where Catholicism was not the established faith. He opposed the Old English who had agreed to accept what had been the status quo in matters of religion in the years before the rebellion, a tacit tolerance by the state of the private practice by Catholics of their faith. Part of the problem was, of course, that the tolerance of different religions which had been worked out in France, because of necessity in the beginning of the century, and was even then being worked out in Germany at the end of the Thirty Years War, was alien to an Italian prelate who lived and worked where Catholicism was the established and indeed the universal faith.

In any case, the nuncio and the Old Irish won out, but the ensuing bitterness was to weaken fatally the Confederation of Kilkenny. Something of this bitterness can be caught in a letter of 1643 written by Robert Hussey of Galtrim to a royalist commander called Cadogan, on the news that Owen Roe O'Neill and his army of Ulster were moving "already over the bridge of Balenecurre and intends, as Captain Thomas McGeoghegan (of Balfeighan, as we have seen) writes to his friends in Moynalvy, to have free quarters in these parts especially about Trim in revenge for injuries done to the Prince of Tircrohan" (Sir Lawrence Fitzgerald, whose daughter would soon marry Owen Roe O'Neill's son). They intend, he went on, (no doubt) a mischief no less than pillage and destruction of the English quarters. "God defend them and you from all your anti-Christian enemies, I mean the vultures of the North."[12] Owen Roe, was head of the Ulster army, and constant combat between his forces and those of the Scots under General Munroe had laid the province of Ulster waste; he now planned a move south into Meath to provision his army and harass the government forces there. He came as far east as Kells and Portlester near Athboy, leaving the east of the county and our parish still in the English quarters.[13]

The cessation of 1643 restored a little normal living in Kilcloon; at least the yeomen, tenants and farm labourers could go on with their work without fear of their lives from soldiers of the English army. People who had abandoned their property and were behind rebel lines were permitted to return and reside within the quarter designed for "His Majesty's Protestant subjects", together with their adherents, as long as they compounded for whatever they owed in taxes.[14] The proclamation was dated 21 November 1645 and among those addressed were Wesley of Dangan, Garret Lynch of the Knock, Robert Rochford (of Kilbride) and Jenico Rochford and Robert Hussey of Galtrim. By 1646, when the peace had been signed with Ormond on behalf of the king, a proclamation at Trim invited the rebels to come to English quarters and to be free to graze and plough lands in Deece, Ratoath, Navan, Lune, Dunboyne and Moyfenrath. In other words in this part of the country relatively normal life was being restored.[15]

In Kilkenny, negotiations were taking place between the king – who desperately needed confederate troops in his failing civil war against an increasingly puritan parliament – and the confederates who wanted security for their land titles, pardon for their being declared traitors in 1642, and tacit tolerance for their faith. The peace was signed in 1646, just before Owen Roe O'Neill's famous and conclusive victory over the Scots in Benburb. A party in Kilkenny led by the papal nuncio, Archbishop Rinuccini, objected to the peace for omitting from its terms open tolerance of the Catholic faith and confirmation to Catholic clerics of title to church property in Catholic hands since the beginning of the rebellion. The Ulster Irish had got no restitution of their lands planted forty years before, and when Owen Roe appeared with his army in Kilkenny, the peace collapsed, and the differences between the Ulster Irish and the Confederates widened. The situation was complicated by the victory of the parliament in England over the king, the defection of Lord Inchiquin to the parliament (he had been a royalist commander in Munster) and the handing over to Michael Jones, the parliamentary general, of Dublin, in 1647 by Ormond, before he went into exile. Effectively, Jones controlled the area about Kilcloon, especially since he had convincingly defeated a confederate army under Thomas Preston at Dungan's Hill, near Summerhill, in 1647. Incidentally, a description of the battle which took place in May 1647 reveals a countryside with mature grain waiting to be harvested, a fair reflection of reasonable conditions that had obtained since 1643 for those who tilled the lands of Kilcloon.[16] In 1647 Colonel Jones ordered the troops at Trim under penalty of death not to forage outside the walls of the town, to encourage the farmers to bring in supplies for sale in the town. His policy was more realistic than the scorched earth policy of Sir Charles Coote, Sir George Wentworth and Lord D'Isle, his predecessors, in 1642, which had been praised, as we have seen, by the Lords Justices.

There were complications of course. On March 6th 1648, Jones noted that inhabitants residing within the English quarter had divers friends who, adhering to the Irish, "do daily come into the quarters and do commit several murders, felonies and other outrages on the persons, goods and estate of the Protestants and their adherents within the said quarters, to their great terror and discountenance, which the said parties dost not attempt if they were not relieved, countenanced and supported in their evil courses by their said kindred and friends living under contribution and their tenants and followers." They had to make satisfaction to the aggrieved or bring in the bodies of malcontents, otherwise restitution was to be made out of those estates by their owners who "live under protection". In other words, the old landlords, even in areas controlled by parliament were back again at least in the persons of trusted agents, and guerrilla war was beginning again.

The deposition of one Patrick McGinnes of Meath, yeoman, on the 21st April 1648 perhaps reflects more precisely the conditions in the English quarters which included Kilcloon.[18] He had been sent by an English Major Cadigan (who back in 1643 had been in correspondence with Patrick Hussey of Galtrim) to Preston's camp where one Francis Nangle, priest of Galtrim, challenged him as a spy and only Robert Hussey of Galtrim saved him from being executed. There were many Tories around, he claimed, who robbed the English quarters, met and sold the spoil they had gathered. "William Walsh the Tory lives at his brother George's house where there were two cows of a prey Walsh and others took from about Kilcock". Eleven horses were stolen from the Lord Chief Baron. Brian McKegan who lived in Ratoath "knows well" the Tories who live about these parts and is a Tory himself. The deponent "lives at White's house at Ratoath and is able to discover much." In other words, the robberies were done by by those who had local support but were independent of any involvement with the confederate army, and their activities were symptomatic of a growth of mere lawlessness leading to anarchy.

On March 4th 1648 Jones had noticed that people were abandoning their houses, carrying their goods, leaving behind them only green corn for which they would return at harvest time.[19] He decreed that any farmer or inhabitant who had "gone over" since Christmas, and did not return within twenty days, should lose benefit of the corn which was to be sold for the benefit of the army. Jones wanted to make sure that the crops were harvested to the benefit of the army. Obviously the rebel or confederate quarters were considered substantially safer than the English ones, when the inhabitants left their homes and went there. With that proviso, it seems that though the landowners of Kilcloon, still adjudged traitors since 1642, probably kept away from their properties in the six parishes, the yeomen, tenants and labourers remained working in relatively normal circumstances paying a contribution in kind to keep the English army properly fed.

All this was to change in 1649 when Oliver Cromwell, who, having had the king executed in London in January, and being now master of England, brought an army of puritan zealots to Ireland. Their invasion was presented to them as a crusade to avenge the deaths of Protestants in 1641 – 42 at the hands of "barbarous wretches who had imbrued their hands in innocent blood".[20] In the next two years the pacification of Ireland was effected with brutal efficiency – first by Oliver Cromwell himself, and then when he had to return to England to crush the Scots and set up the Commonwealth of England, by his son-in-law, Henry Ireton. In the process starvation and famine stalked the island and the population of perhaps one million two hundred thousand in 1640 shrank to about eight hundred and fifty thousand in 1655, of whom perhaps one hundred and twenty thousand were Protestants, most of them newly come to the country as adventurers or soldiers. The stage was set for the confiscation of rebel properties, the paying off of the adventurers and soldiers and the settling of both as colonists in Ireland, to ensure that rebellions such as that of 1641 would never take place again. In the process, as was said of the Romans a millennium and a half beforehand, "they made a desert and they called it peace".

The Wentworths in Moyglare: 1638 to 1736

Thomas Wentworth from Yorkshire was a very ambitious young man; he came to the notice of King Charles I by strenuously opposing royal plans for taxation. But there was a meeting of minds, and a recognition of talent by the king, and soon Wentworth was one of the aides closest to Charles and was given a crucial position, president of the Council of the North. It was a position in which he was eminently successful. In 1633 he was sent to Ireland as lord deputy to assert the king's control of his Irish subjects. More importantly, he was to contribute, if possible, to the relief of the king's financial problems in England. The Irish wars of Elizabeth I had imposed such a drain on English finances that current revenues were not enough to cover current expenditure and interest on loans. Inevitably, requests for new taxes put Charles in conflict with his parliament, which alone could introduce them. (See illustration of Thomas Wentworth, Earl of Strafford, p xiv).

Wentworth in Ireland succeeded very well in asserting his position, raising the revenue and playing off the various factions there against one another to gain a freedom of manoeuvre none of his predecessors had enjoyed. But the success was only temporary. By 1640 because of the ripening hostility between the king and his parliament in England, and the coming together of the various mutually hostile groupings in Ireland, Old English, New English, and Old Irish in common hatred of Wentworth's so called "Rule of Thorough", Wentworth himself became a source of conflict between king and parliament. He was impeached largely on the evidence of his highhanded and illegal policies in Ireland. His king could not save him and he was beheaded in 1641 in London, lamenting that one should not put one's faith in princes.

In the seventeenth century, no less than in other centuries, public service was not seen as incompatible with personal gain and Wentworth was not an exception to other politicians of the time, whose actions in Ireland he curbed and condemned. Obviously he saw himself, even as late as 1640, as a fairly permanent feature in Irish affairs. He had begun what was to have been the biggest private residence in Ireland, at Jigginstown, outside Naas. Though a ruin now, and never finished, the proportions and even the quality of the brick used still give witness to his ambition. He amassed a large estate partly by plantation (as in Wicklow) and partly by purchase (as in Kildare around Naas).

To pay for such rapid expansion he took the farm of Irish customs (a procedure whereby a sum of money and at times a yearly rent was given to the state for the privilege of exacting the customary taxes on imports and exports) and when an ephemeral boom took place in Irish trade he made vast profits thereby. He held the tobacco monopoly, too, which by 1640 was promising to be as lucrative as the customs farm.[1]

In all these activities, official and private, Wentworth (created earl of Strafford and lord lieutenant of Ireland in 1640) had around him a number of gifted young men whom he had brought with him from Yorkshire and the Council of the North, his cousin Sir Christopher Wandesford, and his trouble-shooter in all businesses, public and private, Sir George Ratcliffe. His brother, George, also came to Ireland but his talents only flowered in the years after Strafford's death.

Ratcliffe was Wentworth's agent in the purchase of estates, which eventually consisted of thirty four thousand acres, plus twenty three thousand five hundred acres described as waste; these latter lands were mostly in O'Byrne country in Wicklow. In 1638 George Wentworth married a well-connected Irish heiress, Ann Rushe. Her brother, Thomas, owned the manor of Clones, County Monaghan, and besides other property in Fermanagh, land at Dunsink and Scribblestown in Dublin. He died in 1633 leaving three sisters as his heiresses. One had married Sir Charles Coote, another Sir Robert Loftus and the third was the wife of George Wentworth.[2] Obviously Wentworth was marrying into a key and influential extended family (Charles Moore, Viscount Mellifont, was Robert Loftus's brother in law) that would give him room to manoeuvre through the rough and shark-filled sea which Ireland was in confederacy and commonwealth times. Complicating his life was the way his brother had alienated many, including the Loftus connection, by dealing harshly with the peculation endemic in Irish government circles. An intricate law case which was referred at least twice to the House of Lords in London concerned Richard Loftus, Robert's father. He was sued by his daughter in law, Eleanor Rushe for a post-marriage settlement alleged to have been agreed verbally when she married his son in 1621. The Wentworth connection ensured that her suit succeeded; it formed part of the eighth article in the impeachment of Strafford for arbitrary abuse of power. The decision was reversed in 1642 and in 1662 and in 1678. The business involved some shadowy dealings of George Wentworth. Wentworth was judged in 1642 as liable to pay five thousand pounds to the Loftus estate, but when the case again surfaced in 1647 he had not done so.[3]

On the occasion of George Wentworth's marriage in 1638 his brother, soon to be viceroy and Earl of Strafford, wished to settle property on him which would yield five hundred pounds per annum. Hence negotiations for the purchase of Moyglare from Luke Delahyde which were conducted by George Ratcliffe. The property, carrying a mortgage in the name of the dowager countess of Kildare, changed hands for nine thousand pounds.[4] It was held in trust by George Ratcliffe for the next fourteen chaotic years, thereby avoiding the confiscation of Strafford properties consequent on his attainder and execution in 1641. Though most of Strafford's properties were returned to the second earl, William Wentworth, in 1642, Moyglare remained in Ratcliffe's hands, though, after his arrest in England in 1640, he never returned to Ireland. In 1652 the commonwealth authorities in London ordered Ratcliffe's estates to be sold and in 1652 Ratcliffe handed the manor over to the second earl, "already one year in residence". By 1654 George Wentworth was petitioning the commonwealth for the full estate, even though much of it was seized for use of the commonwealth "for and by reason of the delinquency of the several occupiers of the said land"; the lands included Butlerstown, Kilgraigue, Killeaney, Bannock and Porterstown. Wentworth called himself "knight of his highness, the lord protector, and farmer and debtor", and duly received most of the estate, and to ensure recognition of his ownership his name was entered, not that of Ratcliffe or of the second earl, as owner of the properties in the Civil Survey drawn up in 1654 to record the owners of the land of Ireland in 1641.[5] George Wentworth had been able to survive and even thrive in the very disturbed conditions of the decade 1640 – 1650. He was in the Irish council of state for the early years and in the time of fluid loyalties and shifting alliances he managed so to keep his head, both physically and metaphorically, that he was the obvious candidate to save, which he did, the manor of Moyglare for the Wentworths. He had withdrawn from active political life in 1647 when the king's deputy, the marquis of Ormond, handed Dublin over to the Cromwellian, Michael Jones. But a petition to the lord protector, Cromwell, in 1657, for pay owed to him in the confederate wars was favourably received.[6] George Wentworth, who had had a career in the army, found himself unemployed and remained so until 1661 when he had Moyglare confirmed to him under the Act of Settlement in the days of the new king, Charles II.

He was called to the Irish bar in 1663 and admitted to the king's council in the same year, and once again he enjoyed royal favour.. He had a letter from Charles II in 1663 to an unknown official in Dublin "remembering as you do the services and suffering with which he served his late majesty".[7] He was at the centre of things when, after the chaos of the recent wars and the consequent extreme fluidity and uncertainty in land titles, the pickings were good. Government positions were now available in the new dispensation, especially for those in the king's favour. On one occasion Wentworth wrote to a friend in government "I shall let you know when a place is vacant which you can get for me and shall rely on your kindness which I shall fully requite, at present I know nothing that is not already promised".[8]

His will, dated 1655, when he had two sons, William and Rushwee, and one daughter, Elizabeth, was proved in 1666.[9] Rushwee, who lived in Thanet in Kent, inherited Moyglare and he leased the estate to a single tenant who provided him with little trouble and a handsome income. In 1680 for example, the tenant was Richard Coote, son and heir of Richard, baron of Coloney, County Sligo, probably his second cousin.[10]

Not quite so useful was Roger Jones of nearby Dollanstown, who took Moyglare as a tenant of Mary Wentworth, heiress to her father, Rushwee, in 1705 on a lease of ninety years at a rent of five hundred and fifty pounds per annum (the same estate slightly encumbered with a mortgage in 1638 yielded five hundred pounds per annum).[11] By 1708 when Thomas, lord Howard, baron of Effingham had married Mary and had examined her estate he observed that Jones was substantially in arrears in his rent. Jones claimed he had spent substantial moneys on repairs.

Howard sent his bailiff out from England who decided that Jones could not pay up. Jones had in part succumbed to the temptation presented by vast quantities of land available at knock-down prices to a small group of Protestants. His brother in law, Thomas Connolly, parlied nothing into the greatest Irish estate of his day by successfully using one technique, (he bought land at knock-down prices and let it out on long leases at a substantial rent) but Jones used another, mortgage, in which he grossly overstretched himself leaving a shortage of cash for his Moyglare rent.

The steward allowed three hundred pounds for repairs out of the arrears and gave a warrant for payment of two thousand pounds of arrears within thirty days (the large sum due indicates that Jones took full advantage of Mary Wentworth's single status in England by paying little if any rent between 1705 and 1708).[12]

The bailiff on the estate, George Isodell, was instructed to order the undertenants to pay their rent to Jones up to Michaelmas 1708 (26th September) and after that to him. Jones's lease was cancelled and the steward took possession of the land and "mansion". The term used, mansion, seems to imply, interestingly, that at Moyglare there was an undefended, perhaps Tudor style mansion, which was in turn replaced by the Georgian mansion of 1785. On February 17th 1709, Jones changed his mind, forced some tenants at least to accept him as their lessor, entered the house and had Howard's bailiff Isodell put in prison. In his petition to the House of Lords in London, Howard complained that Jones "spoke very contemptuous and disrespectful words of your petitioner and of the peerage of Great Britain". Jones, obviously desperate, was leaning on his influence in the locality and in local government, but Howard, by successfully invoking his privilege as a member in the House of Lords, put him out.[13] By 1736 Howard was dead, and his two daughters, one married to George Venables Vernon of Sudbury and the other, Ann, married to William Younge, knight of the Bath and privy counsellor, were joint heiresses to Moyglare. They sold the estate to John Arabin of Dublin for twenty one thousand four hundred and fifty nine pounds, seventeen shillings and four pence, just over twice the amount paid by the Earl of Strafford in 1638.[14] If the rent agreed by Jones in 1705 of five hundred and fifty pounds indicates the real value of the estate, then the price paid in 1737 indicates that the price of land had doubled in thirty years and that there was a boom in Irish agriculture. Thus ended the Wentworth connection with Moyglare, which had lasted for almost a century.

Footnotes

Prelude to Oliver Cromwell: The Rebellion of 1641

1   c.f. The Government of Wentworth, 1632 to 40 and the breakdown of authority, 1640 to 1641, Aidan Clarke in A New History of Ireland, Vol.3, p243, ff.

2   History of Affairs in Ireland, Gilbert, Vol.1, p402.

3   The Depositions of 1641 in TCD library; there is an index there.

4   HMC, Ormond, Vol.2, p121. Contemporary London newspapers give a flavour of the news as reported; April 1642, "We have banished, hanged and killed all the Irish and papists in the town of Naas. There is a new sovereign with eight burgesses and fifty families of poor stripped English Protestants; Sir Charles Coote has given them all cattle, houses and land to relieve their presentments". May 17th 1642. "Admirable, Good, True and Joyful News from Ireland. Leixlip taken and garrison. From Naas to Cloncurry and Tircroghan to Castle Jordan...Seventeen priests taken and clapt into prison. Lord Moore with a troop of horse to Navan, killing and hanging near two fifty straggling rogues".

5   Borlase, History of the Irish Rebellion, p104.

6   A Collection of some of the massacres and murders committed on the Irish in Ireland since 23rd October 1641, cited in Cogan, Vol.1, p323.

7   HMC, Ormond, Vol.2, p160; Letters and papers relating to the Irish rebellion between 1642 and 1646, ed. Hogan, p69.

8   HMC, Ormond, Vol.2, p200, 204; History of Affairs in Ireland, Gilbert, Vol.3. p364, 366, 367, 370, 376, 384, 385, 386; Letters and papers relating to the Irish rebellion, ed. Hogan, p144,150.

9   Cal. Inq. Vol.I, Lagenia, Meath, Charles I, 22; The Outlaw Lists, 1641-1642 (The Oireachtas Library) Analecta XXIII.

10 The History of Affairs in Ireland, Gilbert, Vol.1, p49.

11 The History of Affairs in Ireland, Gilbert, Vol.1, p795.

12 HMC, Ormond, Vol.1, p54.

13 HMC, Ormond, Vol.2, p54.

14 HMC, Ormond, Vol.2, p29.

15 HMC, Ormond, Vol.1, p41.

16 History of Affairs in Ireland, Gilbert, Vol.1, p155.

17 HMC, Ormond, Vol.2, p74.

18 HMC, Ormond, Vol.2, p74.

19 HMC, Ormond, Vol.1, p72.

20 Abbott, Writings and Speeches of Oliver Cromwell, Vol.II, p127;Murphy, Cromwell in Ireland, p106.

The Wentworths in Moyglare: 1638 to 1736

1   c.f. Strafford in Ireland, Kearney. p171 ff

2   D.N.B. vol. XXXIV, Adam Loftus, 1st Viscount Loftus, p78.

3   HMC. MSS, Var. Vol.3, p185, 191, 226.

4   Office Book belonging to Paul Rycart, Rawlison 481, Analecta I, p105; Wentworth Papers NLI, Indenture between Sir George Radcliffe KT, and William, earl of Strafford, 1652. For Radcliffe's career c.f. The Dictionary of National Biography.

5   Wentworth Papers, Deeds 10560 ff, NLI.

6   C.S.P.I. 1647 to 1660, year 1657, p643; C.S.P.I. 1662, p142

7   C.S.P.I. 1660 to 1662, p350.

8   C.S.P.I. 1663-1666, p128, 306.

9   Genealogical Office, MS. 142.

10 Wentworth Papers, NLI, Indenture between Rushwee Wentworth and Richard Coote, 1680.

11 Ibid. d. 10560.

12 HMC. Lords Manuscript, 1708 to 10, p336.

13 Journal of the House of Lords, 9th December 1709, p23; House of Lords Manuscript, 2622.

14 Registry of Deeds, 85, 299, 60207.

Chapter 24

Kilcloon – 1650 to 1660

By 1652 the parliament of England had taken the last confederate cities, defeated the remnants of the royalist and confederate armies and was ready to elaborate, through an act of parliament, its vision for the future of Ireland. True, there was still unrest in Ireland. The authorities tried to keep it to a minimum by encouraging the emigration of former soldiers of the confederacy to Spain; the major figures in the confederation had gone to exile in France – or in the Low Countries. Many of the far-seeing attached themselves to the court in exile of the son of the executed king, now proclaimed as Charles II. The authorities also wished to crush the structures of the Catholic church by at first executing priests, as at Drogheda and Wexford in 1649, and then either by permitting them to go into exile or shipping them as indentured labourers to the sugar plantations of the Barbados. But the Tories, whom Jones had acted against in 1648, were still active, outlaws who, with some support from locals, lived on their wits and their knowledge of the countryside in which they had formerly lived.

In our area which had been controlled by the royalists or parliamentarians since 1642 relatively normal life went on, tempered among the landowners, and those with substantial leases or interest in property, by fear of what parliament's plans for them were. The Adventurers' Act of 1642 had haunted them in the previous eight years, as it threatened their title to property, and they must have been only too well aware of the thousands of parliamentary forces in the process of being disbanded who had not been paid their wages. Did parliament intend to go further and remove the whole race, and to where? That remained to be seen. In the meantime things were fairly normal in Kilcloon. No definite information survives, but one incident did find a place in the depositions or accounts of events, now in Trinity College, which throws some light on the scene.[1] It concerned the murder of Patrick Cusack of Blackhall in July 1651 by one John Elliott, former innkeeper of Mountain near Skryne. Elliott, who evidently had a dangerous temper, had killed one Philip McCusker of Skryne whom he had attacked with a sword while McCusker had his child in his arms. The reason Elliott gave for attacking McCusker was that he refused to identify himself when challenged by Elliott. In any case the witnesses to the killing of Patrick Cusack, who was with "protected and unarmed people", unanimously told how Elliott came up to them on horseback on the highway between "Islanduff and Danestown" near Skryne. They saluted him civilly and immediately Elliott turned his horse, and let off his pistol, which wounded Cusack, so that he only survived the incident by two days. The detailed accounts of witnesses reveal a society, peaceful, but on the edge. In his trial, Elliott said he needed his pistols for defence, that the incident was an accident, and that as he approached the group of people with Cusack he thought they were Tories, though he recognised them as he came near to them. His explanation for what had happened reveals the underlying tensions associated in every age with a military occupation. When the incident happened, Cusack's brother, who was living at Dangan since the beginning of the rebellion – the two were half brothers of Wesley of Dangan – went immediately to Trim, and informed the Cromwellian major and captain there of what had happened. They sent "Cornett Brian Hearne" with twelve horses to find Elliott. He had meanwhile fled north and was only taken on his return a year later. Obviously, the Cusacks were back on their properties, the Cromwellians were acceptable as guardians of the peace, and the events on the highway were exceptions to what could be expected in a relatively normal and peaceful society.

An account of another incident has survived however, concerning a family which had for centuries owned the manor of Balfeighan, the Fitzgeralds of Lackagh, County Kildare, which has echoes of how the Germans treated the Poles and the Russians during World War II. It happened in 1655 when the great transplantation to Connaught of the old landowners had begun and no one could be under any illusion about the plans of the authorities. There was an obvious increase in lawlessness. Tories and those who were from the old confederate army, or from families of old landowners, were raiding with the help of sympathetic locals, those who were claiming their lands under the government's plans.[2]

It was also a time when the Cromwellian government was worried that the whole enterprise might be threatened by the resistance of those who were displaced by it. In any case, in Lackagh, two Protestants who had been demobbed from the army and were obviously trying to claim the land given to them in lieu of pay, Dennis Brennan and Murtagh Turner, were murdered by some Tories in the locality. The reaction of the authorities was savage.

Four men, Conor Birne, Teige Moran, James Beacon and Tirlagh Dunn were convicted of the murder, sentenced to be hanged, drawn and quartered publicly, two of them in Lackagh and two of them in Dublin. The authorities went further; all the Irish inhabitants of the area, seventeen men and nineteen women "that are of the Popish religion" (are) to be sent under safeguard into Waterford, to the end that they may be speedily transported to the Barbados, or some other of the Plantation Islands belonging to his Highness and the Commonwealth, in America". There were four priests in the company, and Henry Fitzgerald, his wife, his son, daughter, daughter in law and widowed sister in law. He was the brother of James Fitzgerald, Lord of Lackagh in 1641, who had joined the rebels and had been outlawed. The property in Balfeighan was registered in the name of Eleanor Butler, mother of James and Henry. Henry, who seems not to have been involved in the rebellion, was expected to retain Lackagh for the family. The family asked that their goods and stock be returned to them. They were ordered to be sold and the proceeds used to pay for the food and sustenance of the family in the prisons and ships on their way to the Barbados, and to compensate the families of those who had been murdered. Special care was to be taken so that no goods or stock were concealed. It does seem that the sentence was carried out and that thirty nine presumably innocent people ended their days as indentured labourers, slaves in effect, in the Barbados, working on the sugar plantations. In contrast the outlawed head of the family, James Fitzgerald, eventually got back the Lackagh estate in the 1660s, shorn of all adjacent towns lands except the "town" of Lackagh itself, while the Balfeighan estate, in spite of the transfer of ownership to his mother, whether in the form of a dower allowance or as an insurance against an eventual confederate defeat, was lost forever.

Before the final pacification of Ireland in 1653, plans were already elaborated in parliament for the future government of the country, and the prologue to the Act of 1652 struck an ominous note when it stated that "a general extirpation of the race was not intended." The very strong anti-Catholic and anti-Irish influences in government insured that the act was one calculated to terrify the defeated inhabitants.[3]

The act specified people subject to the death penalty; those involved in the rebellion before 10th November 1641, one hundred and five named people, Jesuits or priests or persons in Roman orders who aided the war, those implicated in the death of anyone since 1st October 1641, and those in arms who did not lay them down before 12th August 1652. It is estimated that eighty thousand people were technically liable to be executed. Others were subject to confiscation of two thirds or one third of their property, the remaining portion to be assigned in areas decided by parliament. Included in this category were all who had not shown constant affection to the interests of the Commonwealth, in other words the vast majority of the landowners of Ireland. Others, presumably Protestants, who had not shown constant affection, were to lose one fifth of their property. All with real estate or property of less than ten pounds were pardoned. Obviously, the intention was to focus on landowners and to remove them. It seemed that all Irish Catholics not subject to death and confiscation were liable to be shifted from their lands and settled wherever parliament decided, and that transplantation was to be to Connaught. This was seen as a just punishment for rebellion and for the atrocities alleged in the depositions of 1641. In time the government policy was modified. The need to satisfy quickly the demands of two important groups took priority. The army in Ireland had not been paid and was becoming restless, and the adventurers of 1642 were impatiently demanding that their loans be converted into Irish land. The first plan was to divide Ireland into three: the area east of the Boyne and the Barrow was to be exclusively inhabited by English adventurers and soldiers, who could have English and Protestant tenants only, or at least tenants and labourers who were Protestant. The other area, excluding Connaught, was to have English and Protestant landowners with Irish tenants permitted; Connaught was for the Old English and the Old Irish Catholic landowners who were to be transplanted there.[4]

In other words, our parish was to have been, to use a modern term, completely and ethnically cleansed. In the years 1652 to 1654 when plans for settling Ireland were finalised, the inhabitants of Kilcloon must have been terrified seeing, as they must have, looming up before them, the end of their whole way of life, and indeed civilization, which had taken root and evolved after their ancestors came and settled in the parish five hundred years previously.

In time only land south of the Liffey and east of the Barrow were to be reserved for English settlers and Protestants. But when the time for action came the grand schemes for the complete resettlement of the country were seen as impracticable.[5] After 1655 the ruling junta in Ireland was gradually replaced by pragmatists with ideological and religious concerns pushed into the background. The logistics of implementing even the watered-down version of the original plan, which now envisaged the transplantation of Catholic landowners only, was a daunting operation. It was made even more complicated by the reluctance of those sentenced to be transported, to leave their lands, by the way those in charge of the operation naturally furthered their own interests, both in Connaught and in the rest of Ireland, and by the way knowledgeable and resourceful beneficiaries of the plantation skewed its operation to suit themselves. Lands were concealed by surveyors, and often the new owners colluded with the old owners who stayed on in their former properties as tenants. The entire undertaking was further complicated by the urgency of the operation.

The Civil Survey of 1654

There had been surveys of parts of Ireland before 1654, usually consequent on confiscations. As we have seen, the survey of confiscated Delahyde and Kildare lands in the 1540s reflects the then structure of landholding in the south of our parish. There had been surveys of parts of Ulster and Munster, necessary for distributing confiscated lands to the new arrivals. Also in 1636, to prepare for the questioning of land titles in Connaught which would have led to fines or plantation, a survey, called the Strafford Survey, after its inspirer, the Earl of Strafford, was made. But all these surveys were rough and ready ones; there was no standard measurement of land, and those whose lands were being surveyed were not very willing contributors to the accuracy of measurements. Besides, the surveyors were not exactly immune to the seventeenth century equivalent of today's brown paper envelopes. But when the confiscation of nearly all the land of Ireland was planned, a major and reliable survey was necessary. A survey called the Gross Survey was begun in 1654 but was soon judged inadequate. The Civil Survey, made all over the country in the years 1654 to 1656, was at least acceptable in its own day and has survived, to be published in our time, giving a very full picture of the land and its owners at the time it was made. It presents a full account of the landowners and the land of Ireland in 1641 before the rebellion broke out.

Ballymaglassan was owned by four people in 1641. Two of them, John Rochford of Kilbride and Valerian Wesley of Dangan, owned most of it. The first held Cookstown, Rowanstown, Waynestown, Staffordstown and Brownstown; the second had Brownrath, Lynaghtown, Blackhall, Ballymaglassan, Growtown and Polebane. Blackhall (big) was owned by Peter Hussey of Culmullen, and Culcoman by Fagan of Feltrim, Co Dublin. They were all Catholics. There does not seem to be consistency in describing buildings in the townsland; that, of course, was not the concern of the surveyors as their main purpose was to establish ownership of land to allow for its confiscation and regrant (each landowner was described either as Irish Papist or as Protestant). In some townslands there is no mention of houses. There are none mentioned in Cookstown, Rowanstown, Brownstown, Culcoman, Lismahon, in Ballymaglassan, though some of these are among the largest in the parish; cabins of the labourers and herds seem to have been generally omitted. We do know that Valerian Wesley's half brother, Patrick Cusack, was living at Blackhall in 1642 and in 1651, and all that is stated about that townsland is that it had a ruined old castle and three cottages. In Waynstown there were four farmhouses, two in Growtown, one with outhouses in Staffordstown, one with two cottages in Brownrath.

The land in Rathregan parish was owned by the Earl of Fingal, apart from Moyleggan owned by Barnwall of Lustown, a townsland in Dunboyne barony bordering on Moyleggan, and Creymore owned by Patrick Hussey, Baron of Galtrim. They were all Catholics. As in Ballymaglassan, the survey does not record many buildings in the parish. Some townslands, Moyleggan and Ribstown, have no account of any building, but Lismahon had "an old chappell", all traces of which have now vanished. There were also two cottages there. There was a farmhouse and three cottages in Woodland, one with three cottages in Creymore, one with "houses of office and two cottages" in Parsonstown, and a "thatch house" in Billiamstown (Belshamstown). These descriptions indicate that there was one major tenant in each townsland together with undertenants. That was a system of land tenure evident in the survey of Kildare and Delahyde lands in 1540, and will be seen in the organisation of the Moyglare estate in 1736 and in the rent rolls of the Fingal estates in the early eighteenth century. In Rathregan there was "a church, a mill, a stone house and outhouses and several farmhouses and cottages in ye towne and on the Hamlets". The stone house was probably that of Fingal's chief steward, perhaps a member of his own family. The number of houses and cottages indicates the presence of a village.

Rodanstown, like Rathregan, was owned entirely by Catholics whose names had been associated with the area since the early Middle Ages, Hussey of Rodanstown, Boyce of Calgath, Batterstown and Dollanstown. In Rodanstown was an old castle and church; in Dollanstown, a castle, a few houses and "ruinated mill"; in Calgath, a castle. Though nothing of these castles remains, they were probably tower houses of a fifteenth century date of which there were many in the barony of Deece, marking the home of small landowners who had upgraded themselves from being major tenants, like the Husseys of Mulhussey, sometime in the fifteenth century.

With the exception of Kilglyn, owned by one George Booth of Kilglin, a Protestant, who had acquired it early in the 1630s from Maurice Fitzgerald of Lackagh and Balfeighan, the rest of the parish of Balfeighan, Balfeighan itself, Piercetown and Padenstown, were owned by Eleanor Butler, a Catholic. She was the widow of Maurice Fitzgerald of Lackagh, who had died in 1637. Perhaps they were lands given for her support as widow, or perhaps her ownership was a device to ensure that when her son, the lord of Lackagh and Balfeighan, joined the Confederate Catholics in 1641 and was outlawed, the lands would still be preserved in the family. If that was the case, the effort was in vain. In Balfeighan was a "decayed castle"; it looks as if it was not in use in 1654 as an alternative dwelling to Lackagh, as it had been in the preceding centuries. In Kilglyn there was a stone house, which was probably Booth's own residence.

The townsland of Kilclone was owned by a Protestant army-man, Lieutenant Colonel Philip Ffernsley, who had been cultivating a presence in the area. It had been leased by Hussey of Rodanstown to Maurice Fitzgerald of Balfeighan for sixty one years. In turn he passed it to James Welsh of Shanganagh who leased it to Ffernsley. But most of the parish was owned by Edward Hussey of Mulhussey. Only in Mulhussey are buildings mentioned, "a castle, a house, a mill with seven cottages". The castle was of course the fifteenth century tower house of which the ruins still survive, which was built after the parish of Kilclone became the Manor of Mulhussey in 1406. Strangely, there is no mention of the church whose ruins still survive: perhaps this indicates the lack of interest shown by the surveyors in recording accurately anything beyond the owners, their religion, their acreages, and the land use, which alone were necessary for plantation purposes.

Moyglare was different from all the other parishes in that nearly all the townslands, Moyglare itself, Bryanstown, Barrocks, Kimmins, Harristown, Affolis, Owenstown, Killeaney, Bannocks, Moygaddy, (with the exception of fourteen acres belonging to the vicars choral of St. Patrick's Cathedral in Dublin, leased out to Andrew Forde of Dublin, a Protestant), Ballymagillin, Newtownmoyaghy and Croteshane (land mixed through Ballymagillin) was owned by Protestants; the last two by the Earl of Kildare and Andrew Forde, the rest by Sir George Wentworth, brother of the former Lord Deputy. Though held in trust for Wentworth by the Lord Deputy's fixer and land acquirer, Sir George Ratcliffe, it had been transferred to the second Earl of Strafford by Ratcliffe when he fell into serious disfavour with the commonwealth in 1651. The estate was then transferred fully to George Wentworth sometime afterwards; perhaps it was judged that he was most likely to preserve it in the plantation which was about to be transacted by the commonwealth government. In any case, he wrote to the council of state in 1654 looking for confirmation of his ownership, and setting out his fears that since several occupiers of land in Moyglare were liable to lose their properties this might adversely affect his rights on the estate. He need not have worried; by 1654 even royalist Protestants like himself, (he had been sacked from the army in 1647 by parliament) were safe. As the distinction between Catholic and Protestant in the survey indicates, the focus was on transplanting Catholics only. Two Catholics held land in Moyglare in 1641; one was George Foster of Kilgraigue, whose family had been there, perhaps, since the Norman conquest, and Robert Rochford of Kilbride, who held Butlerstown. Both owed minor feudal service to

Wentworth. The only buildings which appear in the Moyglare survey were "a large stone house, a mill, a pigeon house and farm houses" in Moyglare itself, a castle and six tenements in Moygaddy and "a farmhouse and seven or eight acres of timber wood" in Newtownmoyaghy. The castle in Moygaddy is still there, and it looks as if the "large stone house" at Moyglare is the mansion mentioned by Wentworth's heirs in 1709. Perhaps it was a Tudor mansion: we have evidence that it was burnt in 1643 and presumably was rebuilt soon afterwards.

The Civil Survey of 1654 reveals that the dimensions of the medieval manors or parishes set out after the twelfth century conquest still clearly defined the pattern of land owning in 1641.

Balfeighan was a Fitzgerald manor, as it had been since the fifteenth century, Rathregan was a Plunkett one, Moyglare had been sold as a unit in 1638, and Mulhussey was a Hussey manor, held directly from the king since 1406. Rodanstown with its two land owners reflects the hold of the Husseys, Barons of Galtrim, on that parish and the dominant presence of the Wesleys of Dangan and Rochfords of Kilbride in Ballymaglassan indicates that no real independent manor had ever evolved there at all. Apart from the court case involving the Cruices and the sheriff of Meath, Bacun, in 1289, and that only concerned a small part of the parish, no dominant family emerged there until the late Middle Ages, when the Wesleys and Rochfords appear as land-owners, owning by far the largest holdings in the parish.[2]

The survey gives much information on land use. The crop farming of the late Middle Ages had been modified by an increase in the cattle and sheep numbers all over the parish. In Moyglare twelve hundred and thirty one acres were arable, one hundred and thirty seven were in meadow and eight hundred and nineteen in pasture. In Rathregan there were eight hundred and twenty plantation acres arable, forty five in meadow and only seventy five in pasture. In Ballymaglassan the proportion of arable lands to meadow and pasture was more or less in line with that in Rathregan, 1024, 130, 262. The proportions in Kilclone, were as in Moyglare, 710, 40, 470; in Rodanstown, 400, 13 and 174; in Balfeighan, 360, 13, 280. Incidentally, there was one hundred acres of bog in the town-land of Mulhussey in Kilclone parish and various small amounts of so called "underwood" in the other parishes. Though the amounts may not be reliable, the proportions certainly were, with pasture accounting for a far bigger proportion of the land use in the four parishes in Deece barony than it did in Rathregan and Ballymaglassan, in the barony of Ratoath. Though the land measure used in the Civil Survey is different from our own, it is clear that more land in the four parishes in the barony of Deece was used for pasture in the 1650s than in the parishes of Rathregan and Ballymaglassan in Ratoath barony. It is also clear that if the situation in Moyglare in 1540 was typical of the whole parish, there had been a shift towards pasture everywhere.

Footnotes

1   Depositions in TCD Library.

2   The Fitzgeralds of Lackagh, by Walter Fitzgerald, Kildare Hist. Journal, Vol.1, p265.

3   Prendergast, Cromwellian Settlement of Ireland, 2nd ed., p93.

4   c.f. Introduction to the Books of Survey and Distribution, county Roscommon, ed. Simington; The Transplantation to Connaught, 1654-1658, introduction, ed. Simington. Prendergast, Cromwellian Settlement of Ireland, p245.

5   Ibid, p245.

The Civil Survey of 1654

1   The Civil Survey, Vol.5, Meath, p85, 87, 151, 153, 157.

Chapter 25

The Cromwellian Plantation

Because four of the parishes of Kilcloon are in the barony of Deece and two in the barony of Ratoath, most of the effects of the Cromwellion plantation can be seen in microcosm on the ground in Kilcloon. The barony of Deece had been assigned to the English merchants, mostly Londoners, who had ventured capital under the Adventurers' Act of 1642 to finance the re-conquest of rebel Ireland. They expected to be paid in the land confiscated from the rebel Irish. As we have seen, ambitious plans to exclude all Irish Catholics from most of Ireland were scaled down, though it was felt necessary to assert in the act of 1652 which was intended to begin the implementation of the Adventurers' Act, that "a total extirpation of the race was not intended". The eagerness of the adventurers for their reward was all the more pressing as for twelve years their investment appeared to have been at least as fraught as funds invested in Russian bonds in the days of the Tsar Nicholas II. The soldiers were all over the island and they too were seen as a danger to the stability of government as long as they were not paid and disbanded. They too were to be paid in Irish confiscated lands, conveniently enough for a parliament which was strapped for funds after twelve years of civil war. Part of the land laid aside for the soldiers was that of the barony of Ratoath in which two of the Kilcloon parishes, Rathregan and Ballymaglassan are situated. The ideological agenda was put to one side and financial considerations became paramount, especially after 1655 when the Lord Lieutenant, Henry Cromwell, Oliver's son, brought in a civilian government and replaced the puritanical army officers who had wielded substantial power in shaping government policy until then. In any case, the Grocer's Hall in London in late 1653 and early 1654 must have taken on some of the trappings of a carnival when a lottery was held to dispense Irish lands to the adventurers or their descendants who had banked on a successful conquest of Ireland twelve years previously.[1] It was like a lottery in which everyone won; there was something substantial for everyone in the house. A number of investors had deputed one of their number to attend and draw on their behalf. Thomas Briggs drew for himself, and for Thomas Hodges, Samuel Elliott, Robert Ellis and his brother Miles. With others, they drew the barony of Deece, and along with John Partridge, John Garth, Nathaniel Micklethwaite and Thomas Waterhouse were given grants in the south east of the barony, which included the four parishes in Kilcloon.

Thomas Brigg, a London merchant, had ventured two hundred pounds and could expect three hundred and thirty three plantation acres (of twenty one, as against sixteen and a half perches which was English measure); Miles, a London merchant tailor, had ventured fifty pounds and could expect two hundred and eight acres; Hodges, a London merchant, had ventured six hundred pounds and could expect one thousand acres; Samuel Elliott, also a London merchant, had ventured two hundred pounds and could expect three hundred and thirty three acres; Robert Ellis had ventured three hundred pounds in June 1642 to finance a naval assault on Cork, which was considered a "venture" under the Adventurers' Act and could expect one thousand acres. John Partridge seems to have been the heir to Alexander, a London merchant who had ventured eighty pounds in 1642; he or John had increased their stake to two hundred pounds by the time of the lottery and John got three hundred and thirty three acres. John Garth, a shoemaker, had ventured one hundred pounds and was to get one hundred and sixty six acres; Nathaniel Micklethwaite, a London fishmonger, had invested, at first, twenty five pounds and then topped his investment up to deserve one hundred acres, and Thomas Waterhouse, another fishmonger, had invested one hundred pounds and presumably would get one hundred and sixty six acres in south east Deece. William Lane from Sussex, who had ventured six hundred pounds and drew one thousand acres, and Sir Edward Turner of London who had ventured two hundred pounds and was assigned six hundred and sixty six acres, were due to get lands in the south west of the barony but in fact got substantial properties in Rodanstown. John Russell, an adventurer of two hundred pounds, a yeoman by profession, was granted four hundred and sixteen acres with Richard Barnard of London, an esquire, who had ventured two hundred pounds; both of these were to get land in the south west of the barony; Thomas and Richard Barnard, heirs presumably of Richard, the first adventurer, got land in Balfeighan, and John Russell with Richard Russell got grants in Kilclone. The prospect of going to Ireland where there was much disturbance, scarcity of food and labour and generally an uncertain future in an alien land did encourage some of the adventurers to sell their entitlements – presumably at a substantial discount. Certainly there was much trafficking in land and the whole arrangement that took the years after 1655 to organise and complete, was immensely complicated by the restoration to his father's throne of Charles II in 1660.

In the meantime, over in Rathregan and Ballymaglassan, the land was to be distributed among the soldiers as a way of disbanding them and paying their back wages. No record of their lottery and division survives, except in the records of the eventual Irish land settlement contained in the so-called "Books of Survey and Distribution"[2] of circa 1672. And that record accommodated the grants of King Charles II to his favourites after his restoration of 1661. Among them was his brother, James Duke of York, heir to the throne, who had a skillful agent employed in Ireland to sniff out likely properties where there were defects in the land title. He was granted the estates of the so-called regicides who had sat on the commission that sent Charles I to his execution, and other properties amounting together to one hundred thousand acres. There were also people high in government, like Lord Ranelagh and Lord Berkeley, who got land in Rathregan and Ballymaglassan. Some of the lands of the old landowners were restored in part or entirely to them. There were also sharp people who had been living a long time in Ireland and were now prepared to buy dubious rights in Irish land and, through knowledge of law and influence with the powerful, to make these rights absolute. Yet, even in 1672, some of the soldiers who were assigned land in Rathregan and Ballymaglassan in 1655 were still there. In Rathregan one Robert Shiels was allotted land; presumably he was the captain Robert Shiels who with others of his regiment had been granted land in the barony of Kilconway in Antrim, formerly the estate of the Marquis of Antrim, but had to be accommodated elsewhere when the Marquis had his vast estates restored by Charles II. The accommodation took place principally on the lands formerly owned by Robert Rochford of Kilbride; Shiels also got Moyleggan in Rathregan, formerly owned by Barnwall of Luston. Two smaller grants, one to John Sheely who got property formerly owned by the Baron of Galtrim at Cremore in Rathregan, and another to Robert Thornhill who got land at Cremore also and in Little Blackhall in Ballymaglassan parish, formerly owned by Peter Hussey of Culmullen, seemed to have been for soldiers also. But when the arrangements in the early 1660s took place, besides the restoration of much property of the old owners, there were various royal favours to be accommodated also, and William Petty who drew up the "Down Survey" maps, (see illustration of the Barony of Ratoath and the Barony of Deece, piii-iv) the foundation document on which the whole plantation depended, who had got bits and pieces of choice property all over Ireland, also got the townsland of Ballymaglassan.

As we have seen, a scheme that began as a politically inspired programme to clear the natives from the east of the country, including landowners, leaseholders and various kinds of tenants, gradually became a money-centred policy to pay off the adventurers and soldiers by replacing the old landlords, who were to be granted a proportion of their property in Connaught, when they were not subject to complete confiscation of land and loss of life.

Footnotes

1   C.S.P.I. 1642 to 1659, p5, 18, 50, 52, 54, 62, 65, 73, 82, 87, 90, 105, 119, 123, 125, 128, 133, 175, 179, 183, 311, 323, 343, (a list of those adventurers receiving land in the barony of Deece) 345, 545. The changing fortunes of each side in the English civil war between the king and parliament (it was parliament which passed the Adventurers' Act and the adventurers were predominantly supporters of parliament against the king) and its implications for Ireland can be traced in the fairly full records of those who adventured money in 1642 to finance the Irish wars or, in the next ten years, bought from them the rights conferred by the loans. Most adventurers were businessmen and women in a reasonably small way who were supporters of parliament in the civil war. Some were members of corporations, especially that of London. Some of these like Alderman Vincent of London, bought up rights to land in many Irish counties from those who had lost faith in the ultimate success of the venture. Many seemed to have sold their rights after they were awarded lots in the great lottery of 1654, preferring cash in hand to the uncertainties of settlement in Ireland. The presence of most of these adventurers in Ireland was temporary. In contrast many of the military officers who got Irish land and bought up the rights of the common soldiers of their regiments, put together large estates and eventually formed part of the Protestant ascendancy.

2   The Books of Survey Distribution, National Archives, manuscript.

Chapter 26

The Catholic Landowners in Kilcloon – 1650 to 1660

While officially all Catholic landowners were to have been transplanted to Connaught – only a relatively small proportion went there. The Dublin junta had encouraged over thirty thousand soldiers to go abroad to the armies of Spain and some of our landowners undoubtedly did so. Others, more farseeing, went to join the new king in France, proclaimed as Charles II when his father had been executed in 1649. Edward Hussey of Mulhussey was one of these, as was the new Lord Fingal (his father had died in a Dublin prison in 1649 and his mother, remarried to a Barnwall, got lands in Connaught) and Rochford of Kilbride. Garret Wesley, a minor, was given as a ward in 1652 to Henry Jones, some time scout master of Cromwell's army in Ireland, and after 1661, state bishop of Meath He was reared as a Protestant. But the other, smaller landlords, the Husseys of Rodanstown, Boyces of Calgath, Fosters of Kilgraigue, do not figure in the records; one can only assume that they remained as tenants in their former lands. Certainly the new owners, the adventurers, among whom the barony of Deece was subdivided, wanted knowledgeable people who knew the land, the way to till it most profitably and who would not give them any trouble. The minor landlords fitted this bill. In contrast, there was much confusion and complication in Connaught. In Connaught the old landlords in the area and the Catholic landlords from the rest of Ireland, who were receiving land there, were trying to find out precisely what properties were being granted to them by commissioners sitting at Loughrea and Athlone. Inroads were constantly being made in the amount of land available to the transplanted to accommodate the arrears of the disbanded soldiers. Only one Kilcloon landowner was indeed transplanted. Luke Delahyde of Moyglare was given seven hundred and seventy seven acres of land in the Baronies of Moycullen and Ballanahinch in County Galway. This creates a problem.[1] His address is given as Moyglare but he had already sold his Moyglare estate in

1638 to the Earl of Strafford which provided an endowment for the Earl's brother, George. However, if the measure of land in the Civil Survey, (a very rough and ready guide to the land involved in any case), was 16.5 perches to the acre and the measure used in the transplantation was 21 perches to the acre, then Delahyde's seven hundred and seventy seven acres in Connaught was roughly one third of the Moyglare estate and his grant the one third of an estate due in Connaught to an Irish Catholic who had not shown constant "affection" to the parliament. It seems likely that he had leased back Moyglare from the Wentworths in 1638 and as a leaseholder was transplanted to Connaught.

An interesting insight into government thinking and local apprehension is given in a letter of Sir George Wentworth "to the lord chief baron and his highness court of exchequer" on the 28th October 1654, just after the Civil Survey had been made in the barony of Deece.[2] It referred to four townslands in the parish of Moyglare from which as lord of the manor Wentworth derived a rent, Butlerstown held by Robert Rochford of Kilbride, Kilgraigue held by George Foster, Killeaney by Thomas Talbot of Dardistown and Bannocks by Sir Robert Talbot of Carton, Maynooth. They were then seized to the use of the commonwealth "for and by reason of the delinquency of the several occupiers of the said lands". Wentworth was obviously worried that when the lands were confiscated he would lose them completely, or perhaps he hoped to possess them completely and cut out the middlemen who were creaming off the income from the land. The Civil Survey was completed for the barony of Deece in March 1654 and the reference to these townslands is of interest. Though Foster is registered as owning Kilgraigue, Robert Rochford, Butlerstown, Robert Talbot, Bannocks, Wentworth himself is registered as being proprietor of great Killeaney. Perhaps Killeaney was given to Wentworth freely in compensation for the rents he lost in the other properties when they were confiscated. Certainly, in the Books of Survey and Distribution registering the state of land ownership in Moyglare about 1670, Kilgraigue was held by an adventurer or purchaser of an adventurer's land, Butlerstown was partly owned by the Rochfords and partly by the duke of York; Bannocks was partly owned by Sir Richard Talbot and partly by an adventurer. Killeaney was owned by Sir George Wentworth's heirs.[3] Obviously Sir George, though a royalist, who was dismissed from the army when the royalist cause collapsed on Ormond's surrender of Dublin to Michael Jones in 1647, still had useful connections with the new regime, and moreover, he was a Protestant.[4] This was to over ride the hostility he had shown to parliament in the 1640s and secure him his lands in the plantation.

It does seem, however, that the lands held as dower land by widows of landlords were also included in the confiscations. In our parish an example was the lands of Balfeighan, registered as belonging to Eleanor Butler, who was the widow of Sir Maurice Fitzgerald who died in 1637. In the Books of Survey and Distribution Luke Delahyde's name disappears from the County Galway. Many transplanters sold their rights at a very cheap rate to speculators, both Protestant and Catholic, and it could be that he was back, a leaseholder in Moyglare, in the 1660s. He is mentioned in Bishop Dopping's visitation of Meath in 1682 as patron of the parish of Moyglare, but, in the records, the Delahyde association with Moyglare seems to have ended at this time.

Footnotes

1   The Transplantation to Connaught, 1654 to 1658, ed. Simington, p78, 169.

2   Wentworth Deeds, N.L.I. d, 10560.

3   The Books of Survey and Distribution, Meath, Manuscript, N.A.

4   c.f. C.S.P.I. 1647 to 1660, p643, for a favourable reply from Oliver Cromwell, the Lord Protector, to Wentworth's petition in 1657 for back pay owed from the time he was a royalist commander before 1647.

Chapter 27

Religion in Kilcloon – 1650 to 1660

All the provisions of the 1652 Act were modified, save one, that subjecting "Jesuits and priests or persons in Roman orders who contrived, aided or abetted the war in Ireland," to confiscation of property and the penalty of death. This provision remained constantly in force, modified only slightly in that transportation to the Barbados or Continental Europe was gradually substituted for the death penalty.[1] Ironically the priests were not welcome in the Barbados as they provided a focus for the Irish who had been transplanted there. One thing we can be certain of is that whatever provisions for worship had been available in our parish in the 1640s when the royalists controlled the area between Dublin and Trim, and people like Coote and D'Isle were apt to execute priests taken with rebel forces, after 1652 there would have been no priests to make worship and the sacraments available to the people, at least until after 1657, when priests began to seep back into the country again. Their survival in service was problematical as were their conditions of living. In the early Cromwellian years many priests suffered death. When towns surrendered on terms, priests were specifically excluded from those provisions. And in 1653, the Statute of Elizabeth I of 1585, which had hitherto only applied in England, was extended to Ireland: under it Catholic clergy who served their people were guilty of treason and liable to the death penalty.[2] By 1654 the policy of the government changed slightly; the emphasis was on transportation of priests caught on active duty, and not on execution. In 1658 what can well be described as concentration camps were set up on the Aran Islands and Inisboffan for priests, where they remained until better times were heralded by the restoration of King Charles II in 1660.

Certainly, after 1642 there was no bishop active in Kilcloon, and the hostility to Catholic priests shown by Coote and D'Isle made it likely that there was little presence of Catholic worship or sacramental life in the area for nearly twenty years until the end of the 1650s. The east of Meath, which includes the six parishes of modern Kilcloon was under English control, royalist and parliamentarian, from 1642 onwards, and while that meant a reasonable stability in secular affairs – the people could at least sow and reap their crops – in matters religious there must have been little opportunity for the people to hear Mass, and receive the sacraments, especially that of Confirmation which required a bishop to confect it. No wonder Bishop McGeoghegan wrote of confirming ten thousand adults when he came to Meath in 1659, and of receiving heretics, as he called them, probably Catholics who slipped from their faith in Cromwellian times, but returned to their old faith when the pressures of persecution were lifted.

The main focus of the hostility of the Cromwellian regime, especially in its first five years, was on Catholic landowners and on Catholic priests. But the Church of Ireland was also the object of puritan disapproval. The Anglican liturgy was forbidden, the book of common prayer banned, and the income of the church in the parishes was sequestrated by the state to be paid to "godly ministers", "experimentally acquainted with the workings of the spirit of the Lord." The minister nearest to Kilcloon was Hugh Hannah, appointed to Knock, Summerhill, at a salary of sixty pounds a year.[3] In 1661, of course, the Established Church, having taken a severe knock in the Cromwellian years, was restored to its livings. But there had been no persecutions such as had attended the Catholic priests, who suffered execution and banishment. Any clergyman who had collaborated was given a living. In fact one, Henry Jones, who became bishop of Meath in 1661 and had been dean of Kilmore in 1641 took leave of absence from his vocation to become scout master of the Cromwellian army. His brother, Colonel Michael Jones, was a prominent Cromwellian: he had taken the Book of Kells into safekeeping when he took the town. It was the bishop who presented the book to Trinity College in Dublin where it is still on display. When he died in 1681, Anthony Dopping succeeded as bishop of the diocese.

The Poll Tax of 1659[1]

There is a record of population in the parish just at the end of the Cromwellian years. It is imperfect, though, as the four parishes in the barony of Deece are missing from it; only those in Ratoath, Rathregan and Ballymaglassan, are given.[1] There is also doubt as to what the figures present signify. The general modern consensus is that the figures represent those over fifteen years of age who were liable for tax. The overall population of adults is given, the number of Protestants and Catholics (called English and Irish) and the names of prominent people living there, called "titulados". The figures and facts are interesting, showing as they do, the two parishes just before the king was restored in England and just at the end of the Cromwellian plantation.

In the townsland of Rathregan there were thirty-two inhabitants over fifteen years of age and all of them were Catholic. That figure suggests a population of about seventy, if quarter of the figure given is of couples with children below fifteen years of age – at an average of five children per household. The figures given thus indicate that there was a village then in Rathregan, perhaps about the castle, where disturbed land surface today still indicates the presence of a number of houses which formed a village sometime in the past.

The absence of so called "English" or soldiers, who would by then have got their allotment there, is mysterious. Certainly, if soldiers did get land there, they must have been officers or of higher rank who got property elsewhere too and lived on the other property. In Belshamstown and Cremore there were fourteen and nineteen adults, of whom ten were Protestants in Belshamstown and four in Cremore. The names of two titulados are given, both English, William Robinson, gentleman, in Belshamstown and Jacob Peartree in Cremore. Their names are English and it seems likely that they were soldiers who had received their allotments in the 1650s. Robinson had gone by the mid 1660s when the Earl of Fingal got Belshamstown back. Peartree had also gone and was replaced by two other soldiers and by the heirs of the former owner, Hussey of Galtrim. Of the other townslands in the parish, Woodland had seventeen inhabitants, Ribstown four, Parsonstown twelve and Moyleggan five and all of them were Catholics.

Lismahon had two, both Protestants. There were two townlands which do not correspond to any in the Civil Survey or in modern times, Ramston and Poorestown; they had nine and five respectively, all Irish or Catholic, with one Michael Luttrell, otherwise unknown to history, as a titulado. It does seem as if the settlement of soldiers had not yet really taken place and that lands remained for distribution when the King was restored in 1661. Then other considerations besides settling soldiers' pay played their part in land distribution. The presence of two "English" in Lismahon and no "Irish" seems to indicate the presence of one soldier family settled there, but not found worthy of being termed titulado or a prominent landowner. Lismahon too went back to the Earl of Fingal in the 1660s. The total number of people given in the parish was 119, giving a rough and ready estimate of the entire population as less than, or about, 250.

The situation in Ballymaglassan was much like that in Rathregan. In Waynestown there were five Protestants over the age of fifteen, among whom was Robert Shiels Esq. and his brother, a gentleman. Shiels was an army man whose family remained in Waynestown until the nineteenth century. There were no Irish in Waynestown. In Brownstown, Brownrath, Little Blackhall, Growtown, Cookstown and Polebane there were respectively two, fourteen, sixteen, thirteen, six and fourteen people over fifteen years of age, all Catholic or Irish. In Big Blackhall there were twenty-three, of whom two were Protestant. Alexander Warren, gentleman, was a titulado and it seems reasonable to connect him with the Catholic Warren family of Warrenstown.

Again, as in Rathregan, there is very little evidence of planted soldiers if we leave out the two Shiels of Waynestown. It was relatively early in the next decade that the parish was given back to the old proprietors, like the Rochfords of Kilbride, Fagan of Feltrim and Wesley of Dangan, and to the king's ministers, Lords Fitzharding and Ranelagh and to the ubiquitous Sir William Petty. By 1672 Robert Shiels held part of Staffordstown, Rowanstown, and all of Growtown. Another soldier, Robert Thornhill, held land in Blackhall.

Unfortunately the census is missing for the barony of Deece and so it is not possible to compare the numbers and origin of poll tax payers in Kilclone, Balrodden, Moyglare and Balfeighan with those in the other two parishes. But if an estimate of 210 inhabitants for Ballymaglassan is acceptable, then the total population in the two parishes in Ratoath barony would have been about 450 people. By comparison, in 1901 there were only 104 people in Rathregan and 177 in Ballymaglassan, giving an overall population of 281.[3] But in 1841, just before the famine, there were 567 people in Ballymaglassan and 304 in Rathregan. Though the population in Ballymaglassan then was nearly three times larger than in 1659, Rathregan, with 304 in 1841, bears a reasonable relationship with the Rathregan of 1659 when there were 250 people there. Perhaps the existence of the village there was responsible for the high population of the parish. The 1841 figure represents a change from tillage to pasture in the use of land in the succeeding centuries. It also indicates a surprising normality of life in 1659 after the wars, plagues and plantations of the previous two decades. Perhaps the ongoing royal and parliamentary occupation of the six parishes from 1642 onwards, ensured that Kilcloon survived the wars, starvation, and the attendant plagues far better than the vast majority of the parishes of Ireland.

Footnotes

1   c.f. The Fitzgeralds of Lackagh by Walter Fitzgerald, Kildare Hist. Journal, Vol.I, p265.

2   c.f. Mercurius Politicus, "from Dublin January 15th (1653). This is a newspaper, a copy of which is in the British library.

3   History of the Diocese of Meath, Healy, Vol.1, p295, 300.

The Poll Tax of 1659

1   Census of Ireland, 1659, ed. Pender.

2   Census of 1901, Manuscript in N.A.

3   Census of Ireland, 1881, p694, 696.

Chapter 28

Land Ownership in Kilcloon – 1660 to 1672

When the king was restored in 1660 and appointed the Duke of Ormond as his deputy in Dublin, the dispossessed Irish Catholics expected to be restored to the lands they had recently lost in the plantation. But such matters are never as simple as that. Cromwellians had rallied to the king when they realised the way things were developing, and now with the other beneficiaries of the plantations, they formed a very strong lobby with connections even in the councils of their erstwhile Royalist enemies, led by the new lord deputy, the Duke of Ormond. All wished to preserve the greatly increased Protestant presence in Ireland. Charles II was well disposed to the old proprietors. After all they had made their peace with his representative, the then Marquis of Ormond, in 1649, which guaranteed the titles to their property and the tolerance of their religion (even guaranteeing to their clergy possession of income they had enjoyed in confederate times). But real politik or pragmatism prevailed. The commissioners adjudicating claims of Protestants and Catholics saw that even though there were seventy two clauses of instructions guiding them, eleven of which helped disqualify many former proprietors who were Catholics, far too many Catholics could prove innocence and successfully claim restitution of their lands.

These commissioners asked for and got an Act of Settlement, which would set up a court of claims to adjudicate innocence and a right to restitution. A sign of things to come was the naming of thirty-eight persons who were to be restored immediately. Among them was the Earl of Fingal, whose manor of Rathregan was taken from the soldiers who had acquired it and restored to him.[1] Strangely enough, the first to be adjudicated on were those who had not taken out decrees in Connaught. There were only seven months provided for the hearing of claims and when that time was up many of the proprietors still awaited judgement. It was of course a field day for lawyers and lobbyists and as is usual in such a fluid situation, special interests were successful in eating into the lands available. Merely to mention our own parish, in the final settlement reflected in the so-called Books of Survey and Distribution (dating from about 1672) the Duke of York, who had been granted a large establishment of one hundred thousand acres in 1661 and had a very effective agent sniffing out likely properties, got Butlerstown in Moyglare parish, and Batterstown and Warrenstown in the civil parish of Kilclone.[2]

Lord Ranelagh, a Dublin official in high favour, got land in Brownstown and Staffordstown, and part of Blackhall Little which had been granted to one Blackwood, one of those who had been implicated in the execution of Charles I. Lord Fitzharding, a high official in Dublin, was another favourite of the king and Charles bombarded Dublin with urgent requests to grant him land in many places. In Ballymaglassan he got another slice of Little Blackhall and Sir William Petty – who had successfully navigated a transfer of allegiance from the Commonwealth (he had been the author of the Down Survey maps on which most of the plantation had been based and so he knew good property from bad) got the townland of Ballymaglassan itself.

The old landowners fared worse in Kilclone, Rodanstown and Balfeighan than they did in Rathregan and Ballymaglassan, for there the adventurers, or those to whom they had disposed of their grants, remained. They did better in Moyglare and in the parishes of Ratoath barony, Ballymaglassan and Rathregan. In Kilclone parish, apart from the holding of eighty seven plantation acres collared by the Duke of York's agent for him, the lands taken from Edward Hussey, Collistown, Harristown, Mulhussey and Milltown, and those taken from Oliver Warren in Batterstown and Warrenstown, were retained by the adventurers who had got them in the great lottery of 1654 – John Russell, Richard Russell, Thomas Hodges and James Mortimer. One Roger Gregory had bought land there from the adventurers who got it in 1654. A Sir John Ffagg held Collistown and Harristown and though he may well have been an heir of one of the London adventurers, it is more likely that he purchased the lands from some adventurer who preferred cash in hand – little though it may have been – to his chances in a desolate, dangerous land with question marks hanging over many land titles. Certainly Ffagg's name does not appear in the list of adventurers drawn up in the 1650s.

Two properties owned by an army man and Protestant in 1641, Lieutenant Colonel Ffernsley, the townsland of Kilclone itself and part of Collistown, were probably disposed of by him to the Bishop of Ossory (Kilclone) and Roger Gregory (part of Collistown), both speculators in Irish land. Ffernesley had acquired on lease the lands of Moygaddy, fourteen acres and seven houses, owned in freehold by the vicars choral of St. Patrick's Cathedral in Dublin, from Andrew Ford, a Protestant who had them in 1641; Ffernesley sold his lease to Sir George Wentworth in 1664[3] and disposed of his Dublin properties in 1667. It seems likely that he disposed of his property in Kilclone and Collistown at the same time.

It is obvious that the holders of relatively small properties like the Boyces of Calgath, Fosters of Kilgraigue and Husseys of Rodanstown would fare badly. Boyce was declared innocent in 1661 but he was not restored to his ancestral acres; Foster was also declared innocent as he had taken no part in the war, at least after the cessation of 1643, but he did not get his lands back either.

In the parishes of Balfeighan and Rodanstown none of the old proprietors got their lands back. These parishes had been assigned to the adventurers. But as a sign of things to come, Pierstown and part of Paddenstown in Balfeighan were acquired from the adventurer who had won them in the lottery by one Roger Jones who had leased lands in the area in 1626. His family made their seat eventually at Dollanstown, leased Moyglare from the Wentworth heirs and held land in the parish until the nineteenth century. Thomas and Richard Barnard held Balfeighan, Thomas Gibson, Kilglyn (perhaps it was sold to him by George Booth). William Lane, an adventurer, held Rodanstown, Dollanstown, Butlerstown and part of Calgath; Sir Edward Turner, another adventurer held the rest of Calgath. Both evidently resisted attempts by a Colonel Tresswell and a Mr. Tempest to put them out, but both, by the end of the century, had been replaced as owners by the Speaker Connolly (see page 229).[4]

Moyglare of course remained in the hands of Sir George Wentworth, except for the Kildare lands still held by the Earl of Kildare in Newtownmoyaghy. The Foster property at Kilgraigue went to Sir John Ffagg. Land there owned in 1641 by Robert Rochford of Kilbride (Butlerstown and Affolis) were partly restored to his heir, Henry, and partly granted to the Duke of York and to Sir John Ffagg. Barrocks, formerly owned by Sir Robert Talbot, was partly restored to him and partly granted to Sir John Ffagg.

To sum up: the final settlement, in the four parishes of Kilcloon in the barony of Deece which had been granted in 1655 to the adventurers, showed that a number of adventurers still held their grants; a number had obviously sold them and the Protestant landowners, principally Sir George Wentworth and those to whom Colonel Ffernsley had sold them, were undisturbed. Major Catholic proprietors had got back portions of their confiscated lands, like Sir Henry Rochford and Sir Robert Talbot, but the smaller Catholic landowners, though declared innocent, got nothing.

The final land settlement of these parishes evolved in a very complicated way because of the conflicting claims of old proprietors, those of adventurers, speculators and regal grantees. Naturally, when titles were uncertain, land could be purchased at a few years' rent and claims of various kinds on grants, even regal ones, were dubious of effect. Claimants often bought out the claims of rivals to bolster up their own cases. Something of the complexity of the situation may be grasped in the case of Rodanstown parish.

In 1663 the state papers mention that Dollanstown, Butlerstown and Calgath had been owned in 1641 by Sir John Hussey of Rodanstown, gentleman, and by Christopher Boyce of Dollanstown, who were outlawed. Now the lands were in the possession of Simon Crane and Robert Hussey (John's son, who had been declared innocent in 1662) but the courts asked "Held by what title?"⁵ It seems to be more than a coincidence that one of the surveyors of the barony of Deece in the Civil Survey of 1654 was one Simon Crane. In 1664 a Colonel Daniel Treswell appealed, through his lawyer, to the Lord Deputy in Dublin. He had an order to possess custody of "Dollanstown, Batterstown, Roddenstown and Calgath" from the Lord Deputy. He had purchased these properties from Robert Hussey of Calgath, who had been decreed them in the court of claims. However, it appears that Colonel Treswell had found out that these lands, or part of them, were concealed as they did not figure in the official accounts of lands available at the time when surveys were rough and ready and presumably surveyors could be bribed. As a discoverer of the lands he had applied for a grant, paid off Robert Hussey – perhaps even by granting him a lease on the property on easy terms – and now discovered on his way to England that one Mr. Tempest also had an order of the Lord Deputy giving him custody of the said lands "to the great prejudice of the said Colonel, and excessive damage and disturbance of the several terre-tenants who have already paid their respective rents to the said Colonel". The good Colonel's lawyer emphasised that Treswell was the first discoverer of the lands and so was entitled to the grant of custody. Custody was duly granted, but evidently was not effective, as the adventurers, William Lane and Sir Edward Turner, held them in 1672. As late as 1688 there was a lawsuit whereby one Samuel Noysse objected to efforts by Robert Hussey to push him out of Calgath.⁶

The case of Edward Hussey illustrates another complexity of that most complex time. He had been far-seeing enough to join the king's court in exile and was one of the thirty eight to be restored by name to his substantial properties in the parishes of Kilcloon and other adjacent ones. He was declared innocent in consequence of the court of claims. A letter from the king came to the Lords Justices, 21st March 1661 appointing Edward Hussey, receiver general for the contributions of Meath where he lived; he had been commissioned to raise a troop of horse for "our services". He had been deprived by the late usurper of his lands but he took no lands in Connaught. The king commanded that he be restored.⁷ And yet he was not restored.

Some light is thrown on the mystery by a letter from a servant of Richard Talbot to Talbot's enemy, the Duke of Ormond in 1664. It had to do with pledges of money made to Talbot for his services in furthering the cases of "our poor gentry", among whom Lynch of the Knock and Edward Hussey are named. These had sold their estate for a "very inconsiderable consideration" and had besides, guaranteed title to the buyer, so that if the proposed Act of Explanation did not give the promised title, the sellers were due in law to compensate the buyers. Mentioned too is the fact that the Duke of Ormond was reputed by Talbot to provide for his own friends and relations in Munster and "here in the Pale", and that the rest (including Lynch and Hussey one presumes) were left to pursue their claims "on the general score".[8] Hussey never did get his estate back, but after the war of the three kings in 1692, one Meiler Hussey of Mulhussey was outlawed. Perhaps, as in so many other cases, the Husseys too were back in their own home and at least held part of the estate on lease from the new owners. Meiler's brother, Walter, lived at Donore in County Kildare. His son, Ignatius, conformed to the Established Church in 1718 and so became part of the Protestant ascendency; his son was the famous orator, Walter Hussey Burgh, who championed the Protestant Volunteers in the 1780s.[9]

Things turned out differently in Rathregan and Ballymaglassan, the two parishes of Kilcloon allocated to compensate the soldiers. In Ballymaglassan the substantial Wesley interest was completely restored. Garret Wesley had become a Protestant and so was granted most of the estates of his rebel Catholic grandfather, Valerian, in Dangan and in Ballymaglassan.

Henry Rochford, heir of Robert of Kilbride, another substantial landlord in Ballymaglassan, appealed to the king for his estates, spelling out how he had two brothers killed in the king's service, one at Worcester and the other in Ireland; he too had served abroad under the Duke of York and had suffered much. He had been dispossessed by the late usurper of his estate which was granted to one Blackwood, "one of the murderers" of the late king. Blackwood had got his "adventure" in Tipperary but contrary to the Adventurers' Act had applied for a change and got Rochford's former lands in Meath. Now Rochford (1662) was being kept from his land by a commissioner of claims, Lord Kingston, who had "bought the broken title since May last", that is Blackwood's title. This was contrary to the king's declaration that no commissioner for claims should meddle in land deals himself and Rochford asked to be restored. He died soon afterwards but a substantial proportion of the lands were given to his widow, as "her late husband served us loyally abroad".[10]

Fagan of Feltrim, who owned Culcoman in 1641, was completely restored. Royal favourites and high officials of the Dublin government, Lords

Ranelagh and Fitzharding, got slices of former Rochford lands in Staffordtown, Brownstown and Rowanstown; they got slices too of Little Blackhall, formerly owned by Peter Hussey of Culmullen, who was one of the few whose case for innocence was rejected in 1662. Mentioned already was the Wesley restoration to all his lands in the parish, with the exception of Ballymaglassan townsland itself, which choice morsel went to Sir William Petty. Of the rest who had land by the 1670s two were soldiers, Robert Shiel, who got part of Cookstown, Waynestown, Harlockstown, Staffordstown, Rowanstown and all of Grotown, and Robert Thornhill who got part of Little Blackhall where his family settled down at least until the 1690s.[11] The seat of the Shiels family was at Waynestown and it remained so until the nineteenth century.

In Rathregan, Thornhill got some land in Cremore, along with a John Sheely who seems to have been a soldier also. They shared it with the heirs of the Husseys, Barons of Galtrim, Hugh and James, who recovered part of their father's heritage. Robert Shiels got Moyleggan. In the rest of Rathregan, which had been set aside for soldiers in 1655, the Earl of Fingal was restored completely to the property he had owned in 1641, which included most of the whole manor.

To sum up the experience of these two parishes, both in the barony of Ratoath, which went to satisfy the soldiers of the Commonwealth; most land was restored, completely so to Fingal and Fagan of Feltrim, nearly so to Wesley of Dangan, and partially to the Rochfords of Kilbride and the Husseys of Galtrim. The Husseys of Culmullen, and Barnwall (who had Moyleggan) lost all, and the special provision for special cases which involved neither adventurers nor soldiers, ate up most of the rest of the lands available; by 1672, only three soldiers, at most, had any property there at all.

Footnotes

1   C.f. C.S.P.I. 1660-1662, p505. Where a payment to Lord Fingal of one hundred pounds per month to him was to be made until he was in possession of his estates. Naturally the payment was in arrears, but its existence certified by royal letter indicates that full repossession was only a matter of time.

2   National Archives, The Books of Survey and Distribution, Meath, Mss.

3   The History and Antiquities of the Collegiate and Cathedral Church of St. Patrick near Dublin, Mason, p96.

4   Gen. Office MS 141; The Books of Survey and Distribution (1672) Mss in N.A.

5   Inquis. Officum Rotulorum, Lagenia, Meath, 4 Charles II (1663).

6   HMC, Appendix IX, report, p143, ff. Perhaps it was not a coincidence that one of the surveyors of the baronies of Deece, Ratoath, and Dunboyne in 1654 was one Thomas Tresswell; The Boyce Papers in St. Patrick's College, Maynooth.

7   C.S.P.I. 1660 to 1662, p272.

8   HMC, Ormonde, Vol.3, p182 (28Oct.1664)

9   Irish Jacobites, Analecta XXII, p23.

10   C.S.P.I. 1660 to 1662, pp67,204; C.S.P.I. 1662 to 1665, p446, 461, 511.

11   John Thornhill of Blackhall was outlawed in 1689 for his opposition to James II.

Chapter 29

Religion in Kilcloon – 1660 to 1685

When Charles II was restored to the throne of his father in 1661, after thirteen years of exile, the Catholics of Ireland naturally expected that the peace, made between the confederates and the king's representative, the then Marquis of Ormond, in 1649, guaranteeing their land titles and the tolerance of their religion, would be honoured. But that did not happen.

Though some priests were still being arrested in the late 1650s and sent either to concentration camps in Inisboffan and Aran or to the Barbados, others had begun to return to Ireland in larger numbers than before. Persecution was still the norm; many Catholics abandoned their faith when priests could only rarely compromise their co-religionists by asking for shelter for themselves, and so were very scarce on the ground. Conditions were primitive. The Archbishop of Armagh, Edmund O'Reilly, in his first report to Rome in 1659 described the conditions in which the priests lived: "They (the priests) all live in much endurance and misery as to worldly things; they visit the sick by night; they celebrate Mass before and round about dawn, and that in hiding places and recesses, having appointed scouts to look around and with eyes and ears agog to keep watch lest the soldiers come by surprise."[1] If that reflects conditions at the end of the 1650s when change was in the air and the Cromwellian certainties were dinted by the possibility of the king's restoration and that of the old Church of Ireland, then what must have been the conditions in Kilcloon in matters of religion in the previous nine years when there was probably no Mass, no Sacraments and no Catholic burial? Archbishop O'Reilly went on to state that in the northern dioceses there were on average twenty two priests in each diocese. But things were better in Meath. Bishop Anthony McGeoghegan of Clonmacnoise was transferred to Meath in 1659. The last bishop, Thomas Dease, had died in 1652 in Galway, but because of the course of the confederate wars he was probably unable to visit the east of his diocese after the rebellion broke out in 1641. In his reports in 1661 and 1662 the Archbishop mentions Meath and Elphin as dioceses well stocked with priests. In Meath there were more than sixty. Today there are seventy-two parishes in the diocese and so a parish like ours would have at least the occasional presence of a priest to provide Mass and the Sacraments. In 1661 Bishop McGeoghegan reported that he had confirmed more than sixty thousand people, and as he put it, converted many heretics – presumably Catholics who for one reason or another had slipped from their faith in the Cromwellian persecutions.[2]

Because no bishop had been seen in Kilcloon since at least 1641, there must have been middle aged and older people queuing up to receive their Confirmation in those years 1659, 1660 and 1661. Bishop McGeoghegan in the same year had ordained thirteen priests, though only on condition that they went to Europe to "complete their studies". Persecution was to be the norm too for the first nine years of the king's reign. The Lord Deputy, the sometime Marquis, now Duke of Ormond, though he had been responsible for the peace in 1649 that bears his name, was anti-Catholic and tried to cause divisions among the clergy by encouraging a few friars to advocate a form of allegiance to the king which did not find favour with Rome. Secular priests were fairly well tolerated but local anti-Catholic judges could and did make life hard for ordinary lay Catholics. A "humble petition of the Catholique inhabitants of the baronys of Dunboyne and Ratoath", made in 1664, makes the point very well.[3] "That your distressed petitioners, above all others in the Province of Leinster of their condition, are prosecuted by capias and warrants from the Justices of Peace, or some of them, in the County of Meath, for theire appearance at the general sessions to be held for the said county, upon account of theire religion and are at present about one hundred and sixty of them, bound over to the next assizes for your poore petitioners, being all of them husbandmen and labourers, with fees and imprisonment will be utterly destroyed and altogether disabled either to save theire harvest or pay those subsidies and other inquisitions charged to them for the publique good, to the great disservice of his majestie and utter ruine of your petitioners, if not relieved by your lordship. They therefore humbly implore your lordship to be graciously pleased to graunt order to the judges and justices of peace sitting the next assizes for the said countie to suspend any prosecution against your poore petitioners on the said capias untill a further general course be taken with persons of theire conditions be better to enable them to inne theire harvest and pay theire publique dues. And they shall ever pray, etc..." An answer was given at Dublin castle, the 16th July 1664, "let the within petition be presented unto us at our next sitting at the council board, where the same should be taken into consideration and such further order given there upon as shall be thought fit. Signed: Ossory".

By 1669 Ormond was no longer Lord Lieutenant; his successor, Berkely, was tolerant of the Catholic church and allowed the new primate, Oliver Plunkett, to visitate his province and open schools to train young priests in Drogheda and elsewhere. Berkely, personally tolerant in religious matters, was concerned only to keep the lid on the Irish stew that had been bubbling up since the complicated solutions of the 1660s to the land question had been implemented only in part. Soon, Richard Talbot of Carton, representing many Catholics who had lost their land, was lobbying in London for change and his brother, Peter, now Catholic Archbishop of Dublin, was so high in royal favour that he seems to have been given a commission to regulate Catholic clerical affairs in Ireland. The time of tolerance did not last however; a new Viceroy was appointed in 1671 who, though cast in the Berkely mould, was moved to sporadic persecution of Catholics, especially of male religious like the Franciscans and Dominicans and those of the secular clergy who occupied high clerical office.[4]

The reasonable tolerance of Catholic worship especially as confected by secular clergy, continued until the famous and fictional plot of Titus Oates was elaborated in 1678. A mountebank and scoundrel, Titus Oates claimed that there was a Catholic plot to assassinate the king and replace him with his Catholic brother, James, Duke of York. The fictional plot happened to suit powerful politicians in England who wished to replace James as heir to the throne by the Duke of Monmouth, King Charles's Protestant but illegitimate son. No Catholic plot was complete without an Irish dimension, and in Ireland Peter Talbot, old and sick and recently returned to Ireland, was imprisoned (he died there in 1680). So was Oliver Plunkett, and despite efforts to save him by the old Duke of Ormond, he was transferred to England where the witnesses gathered to condemn him were presented as having a credibility that they had never enjoyed in Ireland. Oliver was condemned and executed.[5] This outrageous injustice helped defuse the effects and credibility of the plot and the king, dispensing with parliament, ruled until his death in 1685. In Ireland, a reasonable tolerance reigned, especially for secular clergy of whom there were three in the general area of our parish. They appear in the visitation of his diocese made by Anthony Dopping who had just become Church of Ireland bishop of Meath in 1682.

The Legendary Origin of the Little Chapel

One of the anomalies of parish organisation, which still demands an explanation, is the presence of the Little Chapel of the Assumption, a few yards from the Rye river which separates the parish of Kilcloon from the parish of Kilcock. The river also separates the diocese of Meath from that of Kildare and the ecclesiastical province of Armagh from that of Dublin. The little church is only a few hundred yards from the big church, as it is called, St. Coca's, the parish church of Kilcock. The little church has a very loyal following from people inside and outside the parish of Kilcloon.

A legend about its origins persists. Only twenty three years ago an old lady living in Kilcock insisted on going once a month to the sacraments in one of the Dublin parishes. Eventually, extreme old age made it difficult for her to continue so doing. The curate in Kilcock, Fr. Edward Moore, visited her to see if she wished to have communion regularly in her own home. Her reaction surprised him. She refused, she said, because he and his predecessors had deprived the people of Kilcock of Mass and the sacraments for over seven years of interdict. Soon afterwards, being a civil lady, she had second thoughts about her outburst. She sent for Fr. Moore, apologised, and received his ministrations until she died soon afterwards at the age of ninety-eight. People in Ireland have long memories, and the incident she referred to took place over three hundred years ago when Charles II was King of England. Naturally, it was the result of an ecclesiastical row in fluid times and the legendary side-effect of the events that took place was the foundation near the Rye river of what has become the Little Chapel.

Two elements shaped events in Kilcock in the early 1670s. The first was the fluid nature of Catholic life consequent on the recent destruction of church structures by Cromwell. It was a time of uncertainty for Catholic authorities, and uncertainty increases the likelihood of rows. The king, Charles II, was reasonably tolerant of Catholics. But the new landlords of the recent plantation were hostile and afraid. The New English of the pre 1641 variety were hostile too. On the statute books were laws imposing the death penalty for those exercising foreign juristiction in Ireland. This could be construed to include the activities of bishops appointed by the pope. Besides, the Dublin government was buffeted from all sides and internally divided; it proved difficult to keep a lid on religious quarrels and land quarrels which threatened the stability of the state.

The other element was the clash of strong personalities, especially in a situation where every priest and bishop had been more or less surviving on his own, working out his own strategy and answers to the complicated questions presented by his work and life among his persecuted parishioners. Men who had survived in raw circumstances, sometimes for twenty years, were finding it difficult to take orders from superiors who had for one reason or another spent those years in the comparative comfort of France, Spain or Italy. The two personalities that clashed in this incident were Peter Talbot, Archbishop of Dublin, and John Byrne, a Dominican friar. Both were talented, touchy people who had been involved in quarrels with their brethren since their training as priests began. Peter Talbot, a native of Carton, Maynooth, was high in the King's favour in London. He stated that he had a direct commission from the King to oversee the behaviour of the priests of Ireland. That hardly commended him to the new primate, Oliver Plunkett, to whom he refused to show his authorisation. Peter's brother, Colonel Richard Talbot, represented many dispossessed Catholic landowners lobbying for justice at the court of Charles II. His activities inevitably engendered an intense hatred for the family among the Protestant people who occupied and owned the planted lands. Archbishop Talbot tried to organise a collection of monies to support his brother in his mission in London and to grease the palms of powerful people there in favour of the dispossessed Catholic landowners of Ireland. Besides, an attempt was made by the Duke of Ormond in the years from 1661 onwards to split the Catholic clergy and bishops by supporting a statement of papal rights, which like the Gallican statements in contemporary France, were intended to limit the input of the papacy in each national church. This so called Remonstrance was rejected by the clergy of Ireland in 1666, though it had very strong supporters, especially among the Franciscans and Dominicans. Peter Talbot's family were enemies of the Duke of Ormond and all opposed the Remonstrance. It seemed that Talbot feared any public demonstration of Catholic rituals and practices which could be used by anti-Catholic parties in Ireland to put pressure on the government to intensify persecution and expel the clergy.

The other protagonist in the incident was the Dominican, John Byrne. Archbishop Plunkett, in one of his reports (1671) to Rome, defined Byrne in one sentence when describing the Dominican priory of Trim: they "have a convent at Trim of five friars; they have also a noviciate there. Among the friars is one named Fr. John Byrne, a great and learned preacher, but quarrelsome".[1] (See illustration of St. Oliver Plunkett's bust at Kilcloon, p xv). He had been a student in Salamanca in 1647, a professor at Prague in 1652, but caused dissension among the friars there and was sent to Lisbon in 1655 "pro pace Bohemie" (for the peace of Bohemia); he then went to Padua where he was refused permission to apply for a chair of philosophy, and was ordered back to Lisbon in 1660, but left secretly for Ireland before September 1661. Once in Ireland he was working on the side of the faction of Franciscans and Dominicans, sustained by Ormond, who worked to have the Remonstrance accepted by the Irish clergy. Byrne became prior of the Dominican house in Roscommon for a time soon after arriving in Ireland, and then prior of Trim, where he received "many of such good character to the order."[2] It seems that he either founded a priory at Kilcock or, more likely, moved the Trim priory there, it being "one of the greatest roads and markets of this kingdom". Perhaps he was encouraged to do so by opposition in Trim. A charismatic preacher, he was histrionic in presenting himself and his message, "who, not content to travel up and down the country in his monastic habit, ceases not to blow his horn to assemble the people in his chapel there to Mass and sermons."[3] This was the view of the vicars general of Kildare, John Wilson and Dominic Dempsey. Byrne, they said, had refused to modify his zeal to avoid giving neighbouring Protestants cause for complaint. They held that the government's moderation in not persecuting Catholic priests for exercising their functions should not be "abused by our indiscretion in being too public therein."[4] Fr. Byrne obviously would have none of that and he continued as before. Archbishop Talbot, a neighbour's son from Maynooth, and an enemy of all priests who favoured the Remonstrance as Byrne did, ignored the fact that Kilcock was in Kildare diocese – perhaps he felt justified in using the authority he claimed to have from the King to regulate the behaviour of the Irish clergy – and wrote to the parish priest of Kilcock to call on the parishioners to cease from frequenting Byrne's Masses. The people sided with Byrne and egged on no doubt by Archbishop Talbot, the two vicars general of Kildare forbade the saying of Mass and the conferring of the Sacraments in Kilcock. The parish priest of Kilcock would not allow the parishioners attend his Mass; he did baptise the children but forbade citizens of Kilcock to be their godparents. Byrne ignored this solemn interdict – as it was called – and thus in Talbot's eyes automatically incurred in canon law an excommunication laid down in such cases. This he proclaimed in Dublin at public Masses and going further he got Lord Dungan, a neighbour, and also his own nephew, from Castletown near Celbridge, to arrest Byrne and put him in jail.[5]

Byrne seems to have enjoyed adversarial encounters, and Sir Henry Ingoldesby, a Cromwellian planter and leader of the "Protestant interest" sniffed out political advantage. He visited Byrne in jail. Consequently he used the information acquired to stir up the House of Commons in London to oppose the Talbot interest, and this put pressure on the king to expel Colonel Richard from England and also Archbishop Peter with all regulars and bishops from Ireland. Byrne wrote to the Lord Lieutenant accusing Talbot of exercising foreign jurisdiction in Ireland, an activity which carried the penalty attached to high treason. He was accused too of claiming jurisdiction from the king over Catholic clergy, and of levying taxes on the clergy to finance Richard Talbot's activities in London. An array of Catholic bishops, including the primate, Oliver Plunkett, the bishop of Meath, Patrick Plunkett, the parish priest of Kilcock and various friars were called to give evidence at a tribunal, and the net result was that though the king tried for many months to resist it, a proclamation was issued in 1673, and in many cases enforced, expelling bishops, (Peter Talbot was expressly mentioned), and regular clergy and anyone exercising ecclesiastical jurisdiction, from the kingdom.[6]

Meanwhile, what about the poor Catholics of Kilcock with no Mass and no sacraments? All documentation about the interdict and excommunication of Fr. Byrne was sent to Bishop Patrick Plunkett of Meath for dissemination among his clergy. There are no documents on what follows, except legend, and the anomaly of the proximity of the Little Chapel to the big chapel at Kilcock. But both point to a conclusion, that the interdict, while on paper punishing the citizens of Kilcock, had its worst pain mitigated when the parish priest of the Meath parishes, just across the diocesan and parish border at Moyglare, perhaps using, as the story has it, the barn of a friendly householder on the Rye bridge, supplied Mass and the sacraments to the people of Kilcock. It was, it seems, a Meath solution to a complicated Kilcock problem which lasted for seven years. Who was the priest in Kilcloon who facilitated the solution? We really don't know for sure, but in 1669 a Garret Dease was ordained by Patrick Plunkett at a large ordination ceremony in Bealis, Co Meath and he appears in the documents working in Gallo in 1682, in Moyglare in 1690 and as parish priest of the six medieval parishes which form Kilcloon in 1704.[7]

There was in 1682 a priest named Plunkett, parish priest of Moyglare, and a Dr. James Plunkett appears in 1690 as parish priest of Rathregan and Rathbeggan, perhaps the same man; he was dead by 1704. Priests usually stayed in the one parish if they settled well there on good terms with Protestants and Catholics. Their local connection provided them with the only real protection against the persecution which sporadically broke out in the twenty five years of the effective reign of Charles II, 1661-1685. The legend is that some of the stubborn parishioners of Kilcock continued to frequent the chapel on the north side of the Rye water long after the interdict was lifted. And Miss Posy Stapleton, the old lady who reminded Fr. Moore of the omissions of his predecessors, showed just how strong the folk memory was. As for the two protagonists, Peter Talbot went into exile in spite of his great friendship with the king, as did his brother Richard. Peter came back home in 1676 but was thrown into prison when the witch-hunt associated with the Titus Oates plot began and died there in 1680. John Byrne was replaced as prior by Edward Quigley who was imprisoned in Mullingar jail in 1674, but survived to be once again prior of Trim in 1678.[9] The Dominican master general requested that Byrne leave Ireland in 1675 (he had meantime defended himself in a letter to the congregation of propaganda in Rome). He died in 1687.[10]

The Dopping Visitation[1]: 1682

One of the documents which best reveal the organisation and membership of the churches in our parish and diocese in the last quarter of the seventeenth century is the visitation that the Church of Ireland bishop, Anthony Dopping, made in 1682 when he became bishop, and again in 1693. Naturally the focus is on the structures and members of his own church, but he was careful to note also the presence of the parish priests and Catholic schoolmasters. It was made at a time of relative peace and tolerance. The persecution that had brought St Oliver Plunkett to the gallows was over; the king ruled without parliament, with the help of French subsidies and the influence and power of his brother and heir, James, Duke of York, a Catholic, was growing as the king's health began to deteriorate.

Dopping treated each medieval parish as a unit so each of our six parishes got separate treatment. In 1682 there were forty Protestant families in Moyglare, five in Kilclone, six in Balrodden (or Rodanstown) three in Balfeighan, six in Ballymaglassan and none in Rathregan. In many of the other parishes in the locality there were no Protestant families at all, Drumlargan, Culmullen, Rathbeggan, Knockmark and Kilbride; there were five in Dunboyne, three in Kilbrew, ten in Ratoath, four in Gallo, six in Galtrim, three in Kilmore. Moyglare then seems a great exception to the norm, which was one of a very small Church of Ireland population in the surrounding parishes. The significance of the phenomenon becomes clear when Dopping's report on other parishes in the diocese is taken into account. Naturally one would expect a substantial Protestant population in the towns, and it was so. In Mullingar there were "more Papists than Protestants"; Athboy had one hundred and fifty six Protestants; in Trim there were "many Protestants", in Clonard fifteen, in Kells fifty, but in Navan there were only seven families, in Delvin only five, in Duleek seven, twenty in St. Mary's Drogheda and twelve in Killucan. But in some rural areas like Moyglare, there was a substantial Protestant population and in some of these an explanation for the anomaly is given. In Rathmolyn there were thirty one families, in Lynally in Offaly, there were sixty Protestant families, thirty families in Ballyboy in County Offaly, and in Newtown Fertullagh a "hundred several Protestants come to church, but most of them Anabaptists placed by Major Lee." In Durrow there were thirty families in 1682, but only one in 1693. In Oldcastle, of the sixteen families there, most were Quakers. In Clonfad, County Westmeath, near Newtown

Fertullagh, there were twenty Protestant families but "some Anabaptists". The indications are that where there was an unusually large Protestant population a zealous landlord was responsible. Major Lee of Newtown Fertullagh favoured Anabaptists (those Protestants who rejected infant baptism and were firm supporters of Cromwell and his Puritans) and someone in Oldcastle (was it a Naper, whose father or grandfather, a colonel in the Cromwellian army, had got Loughcrew, in the Cromwellion plantation in liu of army pay?) favoured the Quakers. In Moyglare the Wentworths were absentee landlords by this time and had given over their Moyglare estates to the management of Richard Coote, their cousin, whose family was characterised by zealous anti-Catholicism. Strangely, Sir Luke Delahyde of Moyglare is given in 1682 as patron of the parish i.e. he could appoint a Protestant rector. If he were still alive in 1680 he must have been a very old man indeed, and was perhaps, some kind of tenant or leaseholder on a portion of the Moyglare estate. In any case, though the Protestant presence among tenants of Moyglare had begun in earlier times, the number of Protestant tenants who complained in the depositions of 1642/43 of being robbed and expelled by the confederates was very small. Their presence in relatively large numbers at Moyglare was a fairly brief one. Perhaps many of them did not survive the leasing of the estate to Roger Jones in the early eighteenth century. He seems to have been driven not by ideological considerations in exploiting land, but purely by mercenary ones. By 1733 the Protestant presence had shrunk to seventeen families of the established church and two dissenter families. In 1736, when the Wentworth heirs sold the estate, only the major leaseholders, those who held whole townslands, were Protestant.[2]

In all the parishes of Kilcloon it appears that in only one, Moyglare, was a priest present. Unfortunately, only his surname, Plunkett, is given, but in June 1690 the Catholic King James II nominated Catholic priests to over fifty parishes then vacant since many of the Protestant clerics had fled in 1688. To the combined parishes of Rathbeggan and Rathregan he nominated Dr. James Plunkett. Presumably since in 1690 the prospect for Catholics or James II were not too promising, the Plunkett connection with Rathregan was of some significance in the appointment, as was the appearance of one Plunkett as parish priest of Moyglare in 1682.[3]

Dr. James Plunkett was dead by 1704 when Garret Dease, nominated by King James in 1690 to Moyglare, was parish priest of the six medieval parishes which form the modern parish of Kilcloon. In 1681 he was mentioned in Dopping's visitation as priest of Gallo, the parish now in Summerhill but bordering on Balfeighan. He had been ordained in 1669 in Bealis, County Meath by Bishop Patrick Plunkett and after his ordination probably served as a priest in the area. It was customary and reasonable in uncertain times with sporadic persecutions, for a priest to remain in a parish where he had succeeded in settling and establishing good relations with Protestants and Catholics alike. That would have provided the best and only safeguard against official swings of policy against Catholic church personnel. In fact it seems likely that he or Dr. James Plunkett was the facilitator of the Meath solution to a Kildare problem which first established the predecessor of the Little Chapel near the Rye water over the bridge from Kilcock. There was, in 1682, a priest named Fitzsimons in Drumlargan, which is not far from our parish; he was dead probably by 1690, and certainly by 1704, when all serving priests were registered officially. It does seem that in 1682, apart from a Protestant school with a teacher called Perkins serving the forty Protestant families there, there were no schools noticed by Dr. Dopping in Kilclone, Balrodden, Balfeighan, Gallo, Ballymaglassan or Rathregan. The two centres of Church of Ireland worship in the parish were Moyglare and Balrodden. The impropriator of Moyglare who received the income from the tithes was Lord Duncan. The glebe land consisted of three acres attached to it. In 1682 the vicar of Moyglare, Thomas Mallory, lived at Maynooth. (By 1693 the vicar was Patrick Lindsay who "resides and preaches constantly"). Mallory and subsequently Lindsay were vicars there, but only the body of the church was repaired. The walls of the chancel were standing, but it is recorded as "ruined since 1641". However, as we have seen, it was ruined before 1622. The church had a clay floor, a roof with slates or shingles and the windows were glazed. Catechism was taught in Lent.

The other centre of Church of Ireland worship was at Rodanstown. The church was in good repair. There was no chancel. Henry Moneypenny was rector of Balrodden. He was also rector of Drumlargan, Kilclone, Balfeighan and Gallo, where churches and chancels were in ruins. These parishes, established as such in 1634, were united to Rodanstown in 1678. Every Sunday either Moneypenny or Mallory of Moyglare preached, and though there was a reading desk and pulpit, a "velvet pulpit cushion and a font at the west end," there were no utensils for communion, "a chalice had been taken away by Lord Chancellor Nugent". There was a bell, the windows were glazed, there was a clay floor and the roof was slated. It does seem that Moneypenny's ministry was a low church preaching one and that he lived in or near his parishes.

John Wilson, who had been rector of Rathregan since 1626 and was one of those who reported how he had been robbed in 1641, eventually returned as minister after the Cromwellian period and died in 1668. He was succeeded by Simon Digby, son of a bishop of Dromore; his stay in Rathregan, if indeed he ever stayed there, was brief. He was also appointed rector of Dunshaughlin in 1668. In 1670 he became also prebendary of Geashill and rector of Ballycommon in Kildare diocese, then dean of Kildare Cathedral and rector of St. Michan's, Dublin. Noah Webb succeeded him in Dunshaughlin in 1672, but Digby held on to Rathregan (or just its income) until he became bishop of Limerick in 1678. Noah Webb became rector of Rathregan in 1678, and it was joined in a perpetual union with Dunshaughlin in the same year. Though the rectory of the new union, consisting of a house, two out offices and twenty two acres of land, was still in Rathregan, Church of Ireland services took place only in Dunshaughlin. Presumably Noah Webb was one of those rectors who in 1688 fled to Dublin or to England, for Rathregan was one of the parishes to which Catholic priests were appointed in 1690 by James II. Webb's successor, Jerome Ryves, was appointed in 1696 when Webb, by then dean of the Cathedral of Leighlin, died, aged 58, and was buried in Dunshaughlin. Dr. Ryves was another absentee. In 1692 he was chancellor of Christ's Church which office he resigned to become dean of Killaloe, and was rector of Dunshaughlin and Tryvett from 1696 until 1699, when he became dean of St. Patrick's in Dublin as well.[4]

In 1682 the church and chancel of Rathregan were still standing but had been unroofed since 1641. The church of Dunshaughlin had a slated roof, glazed windows and a clay floor, like those of Moyglare and Balrodden.

Footnotes

1   Archbishop O'Reilly's Report was sent to Rome in 1660. C.f. Edmund O'Reilly, Thomas O'Fiaich, Fr. Luke Wadding, p203.

2   Millet, "Survival and Reorganisation", A History of Irish Catholocism, Vol.3, No.VII, p16, citing A.P.F. Fondo di Vienna, 15f, 86r; Prendergast, Cromwellian Settlement of Ireland , 2nd ed., p319.

3   H.M.C. IX report, appendix II, p128, 144.

4   Burke, Irish Priests in Penal Times, p38, 39, 40, 47; Moran, Oliver Plunkett, p79, 80, 85, 274, 279, for accounts of the persecutions.

5   Moran, Oliver Plunkett, p271 ff.

The Legendary Origin of the Little Chapel

1   The Letters of St. Oliver Plunkett, ed. Hanly, p189, 238, 368.

2   O'Heyne's, Irish Dominicans (1706) ed. Coleman OP, p259, 261. A very lauditary account of Byrne's life and activities are given. No one doubted his talents but in character he seems to have provoked intense opposition and intense support.

3   Burke, Irish Priests in the Penal Days, p33.

4   Burke, Irish Priests in the Penal Days, p30 ff.

5   The Letters of St. Oliver Plunkett,ed, Hanly, p368. In this letter sent 10th March 1673 Archbishop Plunkett called Byrne "very presumptious, just because he belongs to the ancient and noble family of Byrne, and is also puffed up by his learning."

6   Col. Hibernica, 22, p18 ff, 36 ff, 53 ff, documents from A.P.F. in Rome.; Burke, Penal Days, p30.

7   Dopping's Visitation, Ellison, Riocht na Midhe, Vol.5, 1972, p5; Cogan, Vol.1, p408; The Catholic Directory, 1838, p198.

8   Cogan, Vol.1, 408, Doppings Visitation, Riocht na Midhe, V, (1972), p5; he does not appear in the list of priests published in 1704.

9   Coleman's O'Heyne, p262.

10   Coleman's, O'Heyne, p262, also Archivium Generale Ord. Praed., Rome IV, 140, p175-6.

The Dopping Visitation: 1682

1   The Dopping Visitation, 1682, 1693, ed. Ellison, Riocht na Midhe, Vol.4, (1971) p28 ff, Vol.5, (1972) p3 ff.

2   Visitation of Meath, 1733, RC, 15-1/4; RC, 12-2, National Archives.; Registry of Deeds, 85-299-60207.

3   c.f. Cogan, Vol.1, p406, 408.

4   History of the Diocese of Meath, Healy, Vol.2, p304, 306.

Chapter 30

James II, 1685 to 1691
William III, 1691 to 1701

James II, a Catholic, succeeded his brother Charles in 1685. So began another decade like the 1640s which engendered great hope in Catholics for a time, and ended in despair. In Ireland the changes were marked by the appointment of a new Lord Lieutenant, the Earl of Clarendon, but the real power of making and implementing policy was in the hands of Colonel Richard Talbot from Carton, Maynooth, brother of the late Archbishop of Dublin, Peter Talbot – and former lobbyist at the court of Charles II. He was a Catholic, became in time Lord Lieutenant and eventually Duke of Tirconnell. He began to promote Catholic officers in the army and there was pressure to recall the Irish parliament to review the Acts of Settlement and Explanation whereby the Cromwellian plantation had been given permanence in 1662 and 1664. James obviously wished that his co-religionists in England and in Ireland should be tolerated in the practice of their faith, but he was not anxious to provoke unnecessary opposition in England by unduly favouring Catholics in Ireland.

Talbot did give Irish towns new charters, with Catholics once more as members of their corporations. The toleration that had succeeded the persecutions occasioned by the Titus Oates plot in 1678, as a result of which Oliver Plunkett had been executed, was now normalised. Clergy, including bishops, could wear their clerical garb publicly – some bishops even got small salaries from the state – and as parishes became vacant on the death or departure of the Church of Ireland occupants, they were not filled if the king was their patron. Catholic schools were opened and eventually a Catholic priest, Dr. Michael Moore, was appointed Provost of Trinity College Dublin.

But there was a crisis in England in 1688. James II's wife gave birth to a son, and to both Protestant and Catholic there and in Ireland, the prospect appeared of a line of Catholic kings in England. This would displace Mary, James's Protestant elder daughter, married to William of Orange, as heir to the throne. The result in England was the so-called "glorious revolution", whereby William and Mary were invited to take the English throne and James, his wife and son, fled to France.

Paradoxically, this in the short term encouraged the Irish Catholics, clergy and dispossessed landlords alike, because James was dependent on them to restore his fortunes and recover his lost throne. An Irish parliament was called in 1689, Protestant landowners and clerics fled to England, the Act of Settlement was reversed (and not to the approval of many prominent Catholics who had bought land since the 1660s from those Protestants who had acquired them under the plantations) and in our own area James appointed Catholic priests to fifty vacant parishes in the diocese of Meath, among them Moyglare (Garret Dease) and Rathregan with Rathbeggan (Dr. James Plunkett).[1] These appointments were announced on 4th June 1690 and the first of the two battles which sealed the fate of James II and indeed of the Irish Catholics who had put their faith in him, took place at the Boyne on July 1st 1690. The second, at Aughrim in County Galway, took place in July 1691 and with the surrender of Limerick and the signing of the treaty there, King William with his wife Mary became undisputed rulers of the British Isles.

There were two questions to be decided on William's victory. Many Protestants, fearful of the future, wanted wholesale confiscation of the lands remaining in Catholic hands in 1688. But the terms of the Treaty of Limerick which ended the war guaranteed security of title to those Catholics fighting at the time and living in rebel quarters.

The complicated procedures of interpretation of the terms of the treaty were debated in the Irish parliament, as were the precise date and implication of the outlawries proclaimed against James's supporters in general. Hussey of Galtrim was pardoned, as was Rochford of Kilbride and Hussey of Culmullen.[2] With the usual luck of his family, the Earl of Fingal was dead before being proclaimed an outlaw, and his son Peter, a minor, was then living with his mother in what is now Belgium and his estates were not touched.[3] Fagan of Feltrim was unfortunate in that congruence of a few adverse circumstances deprived him of his estates, including Culcommon in Ballymaglassan.[4] Meiler Hussey of Mulhussey was outlawed, but he was perhaps a tenant on the lands of his ancestors. Two others from our parish were declared outlaws, McEnally from Kilclone, perhaps a tenant or son of one and a Captain Richard Plunkett of Rathregan.[5] Plunkett was afterwards pardoned. Perhaps Lord Fingal had a junior member of his family chief steward of his manor of Rathregan living in the "stone house and outhouses" mentioned in the Civil Survey of 1654. By 1702 Matthew Corbally, a tenant, was living in the same place.

King William, personally a tolerant man, tried to implement the fairly generous terms agreed by his general, Ginkel, to end the war at the Treaty of Limerick, but he was forced to yield to his Protestant Irish parliament. It was fearful of a Catholic threat – it was a matter of numbers and of the political power conferred by land ownership – which in the next fifteen years put in place the laws known since as the Penal Laws. The first, in 1692, limited membership of parliament to Protestants (each member had to declare against the Catholic doctrine of the Eucharist). The next, in 1695, forbade Catholic education at home or abroad and prevented Catholics from carrying arms or owning a horse worth more than £5. In 1697 all members of religious orders, bishops or other dignitaries were banished the land. Quite a number went. In 1698 four hundred and twenty four went to France. By 1701 there were only four bishops in the country, and one was an invalid. In theory, the Catholic clergy, forbidden to study abroad, with no bishop at home to ordain them, would have died out in a generation. But these, like the best planned of outrageous and discriminatory laws, failed the test of public opinion and in 1704 the administration made a tacit admission of failure by passing an act of parliament whereby a priest could be registered to serve in each parish.

In the list of priests registered, there is for the first time a parish priest of Kilclone, Rathregan, Ballymaglassan, Rodanstown, Moyglare and Balfeighan, in other words of the modern parish of Kilcloon. He was Garret Dease, who at fifty seven years of age, had been identified by Dopping in 1682 as working in Gallo.[6] In other words, compared with the Cromwellian period, the structure of the church in the diocese of Meath remained intact, making available the parochial sacraments to the people, baptising their children and burying their dead. It is obvious, of course, that in the years of Charles II there must have been one or more chapels in the parish, perhaps a barn at the bridge over the Rye water in Kilcock, and a thatched hut somewhere in Kilcloon. We do know that long before 1733 there was such a Mass house in Batterstown or Rathregan, a wall of which could be identified at the beginning of the 20th century.[7] Perhaps the fortuitous survival of the Lords Fingal, as owners of most of Batterstown, helped. State laws are one thing, local influence and opinion are another, and in the Fingal rent rolls from the very beginning of the eighteenth century at least two parish priests appear, one in Slane and another in present-day Moynalvy, leasing small farms and ministering to their flocks. The priest in Slane was Edmund McKenna; Malachy Casey lived in Bolloghbane, now part of Moynalvy parish, near Kilcloon, in 1727 and was there at least until 1735.[8]

The allegiance of the vast majority of people, the persecutions endured, and the incipient nationalistic feelings stirred up by the wars of the preceding century, all, especially the first two, made it inevitable that even in the dark days of Queen Anne, 1702 – 1714, there was no doubt as to the religious allegiance of the vast majority of the inhabitants of what is now Kilcloon. The advantages of the established church were more apparent than real. The Church of Ireland was lumbered with the baggage of the medieval church, which left episcopal control minimal and relatively sanctionless; it was plagued with pluralism (one minister having many parishes, often many miles apart and sometimes indeed in England and in Ireland) and it was closely bound to the state. And the state appointed senior clergy with little regard to their spiritual vocation, but rather focused on their connections, their usefulness to the state and the part they were expected to play in government, like some of their medieval predecessors.

The Penal Laws against priests, bishops and religious were of course never applied universally, and were invoked only fitfully in some areas. A number of bishops appear in the 1704 list as parish priests. But the fear of the landowners whose title had been questioned and denied in the 1689 parliament ensured that the Penal Laws were focused on removing Catholics from land ownership, from professions like the law and education, and on preventing them for the forseeable future from being a political or social threat to what we now call the Protestant ascendancy. But one cannot keep people of talent down forever. The Catholics could still engage in trade, and with their continental connections, especially in France and Spain, they came to dominate foreign trade and through their resulting wealth helped eventually to bring about the relaxing and repealing of the Penal Laws.

Footnotes

1   COGAN, Vol.1, p406, 408.

2   Pardons, Irish Jacobites, Analecta XXII, p134.

3   BURKE, Irish Family Records, 1853, p396.

4   c.f. Annesley, MSS, XX, 95. Note in The Williamite Confiscations in Ireland 1690 to 1707, Simm, p35, 36.

5   Irish Jacobites, Analecta XXII, p23, 23, 25.

6   Dopping Visitation, ed. Ellison, Riocht na Midhe, Vol.5, 1972, p5.

7   History of the Diocese of Meath, 1690 to 1993, Curran, p529 (Vol.2).

8   In the Fingal Papers. Surveyed by Peter Lacy, 1702.

Chapter 31

The use and ownership of land in Kilcloon about 1700

Of the two manors, Moyglare and Rathregan, which survived intact into the eighteenth century, enough records survive to tell us how they were administered and how the land was used.

In 1736 the Moyglare estate was sold by the Wentworth heirs to a Huguenot consortium led by one John Arabin.[1] Moyglare itself, the townsland, was then possessed by Edward McAuley and his undertenants, Moygaddy and Ladymeadow by Henry Ingolsby (an ex army officer and perhaps Fr.John Byrne's friend), "Kimmins and Barracks" by Henry Shiels and undertenants, Affolis and Crotashane by Richard Fitzsimons and undertenants, Harristown by William Archer and undertenants, Old Graigue by Michael Franks and undertenants, Bryanstown, Ballymagillin and Raheen Kill by William Fitzsimons, the great and little Killeaney by John Nix and undertenants. There were two annual fairs at Moyglare and a weekly market on Tuesdays. Many of the names of the main tenants who leased out one or more townslands seem to have been Protestant, while the rest of the forty Protestant families there when Dopping's visitation was made in 1682 seem to have left. There were only seventeen Protestant families and two families of dissenters (probably Presbyterians) there in 1733. The Fitzsimons holdings were held by the widow of William Fitzsimons before 1762; for these and other holdings in Garadice, Moynalvey and Newtown Rathgormley, she and her daughter, a minor, received eleven hundred pounds one shilling and eleven pence rent, of which two hundred and sixty two pounds, eighteen shillings and two pence was profit. It is obvious that the head landlord and the major leaseholders derived a substantial living from the labours of the undertenants.

The way land was used is revealed in the rent rolls of the Fingal or Plunkett estate at Rathregan.[2] The main Plunkett tenant in 1697 was Richard

Corballis, esquire, of Rathregan and Batterstown, who had a lease for twenty-one years from 1698 and paid rent of one hundred and twenty pounds per annum. His Rathregan holding was one of six hundred and eighteen English acres. In addition he bound himself "to do suit at the manor court, grind at the mill of Rathregan", enclose the premises within the first seven years with "a good quick sett ditch on both sides of the road" and to keep repaired "the castle and other buildings and improvements" on the premises. Corballis had obviously replaced Colonel Richard Plunkett of Rathregan, as chief tenant. Plunkett had been outlawed in 1688 for supporting King James in the wars and was pardoned afterwards in 1691. The Corballis, or Corbally family were to have land in Rathregan until the nineteenth century and there are family monuments in Rathregan cemetery and in Batterstown church.

In 1702, an agent for Lord Fingal surveyed the parish lands. Rathregan itself, he reported, had "a kindly soil for ploughing but inconvenient for a tenant, being narrow and long." Some part of the farm "is very poor ground but it is all well husbanded by the said tenant who lives upon it". Woodland was held by Daniel Loo and Corballis. It was "poor ground by being too much ploughed and is basely husbanded". It was one hundred and ninety seven English acres in extent and on it were two cabins. Portane, taken by Daniel and Edmund Loo, was a townsland of two hundred and fifty acres. It was all ploughed and was very good land: there were some cabins on it. Belshamstown, of one hundred and ninety nine acres, was leased to the widow Usher, whose late husband had been Marcus Usher, a Protestant minister. She let out one half of the land to John Toole, an ale house keeper, and farmed the rest herself. Parsonstown, of two hundred and sixty seven acres, was leased for forty pounds to Christy Corballis and Thomas Lewis. "It is poor, cold and spongy ground". The tenants "lie upon it". Lismahon was leased to Michael Shiels for thirty pounds (199 acres). It was poor, cold ground and "Mr. Shiels lost a great many sheep upon it, for it is not proper for a flock". Nicholas Kealy leased Ribstown, (one hundred and eighty four acres) for twenty-five pounds. The survey, which extended to all Lord Fingal's estates in the rest of Meath and Cavan, was thorough, and the same pattern as in Moyglare, of whole townslands being set to tenants can be discerned. A substantial part of the land was ploughed and needed undertenants to work it.

In short, as the eighteenth century began, we can observe, on the basis of two major estates, one in the south of the parish of Kilcloon and one in the north of it, one in Deece and one in Ratoath, that the pattern of landholding had not changed since the Norman conquest – except in those manors disrupted by the Cromwellian plantations, Mulhussey (Kilclone),

Balfeighen and Rodanstown. Ballymaglassan was soon a reasonably compact unit again, substantially owned by the Wesleys of Dangan.

The other three, split among adventurers and some of the old inhabitants, were put together in the initial accumulation of lands in 1691, which would eventually form part of the greatest estate in Ireland. William Connolly was the son of an innkeeper in Ballyshannon who had become a Protestant, and was outlawed in the patriot parliament of James II in 1689. William became a lawyer and specialised in acquiring estates all over the country, by fair means and foul. (See illustration of William Connolly, known as the Speaker, 1662–1729, p xv).

He married Catherine Conyngham, daughter of a Williamite general and sister of Henry Conyngham of Mount Charles in Donegal. Her marriage portion was 2,300 pounds with which he bought his first estate, buying out varied interests, with different and flawed titles to the same property. The lands he bought were Rodanstown, Dollanstown, Batterstown and Calgath – the townlands that make up the parish of Rodanstown – and Pagestown, Hardrestown, Mulhussey and Milltown, which made up most of the old manor of Mulhussey or Kilclone. He bought three townlands in Moyglare, Little Killeaney, Butlerstown, Bannocks, and one, Porterstown, in Rathbeggan. Richard Jones of Dollanstown married Connolly's sister-in-law, Mary Cunningham. He too was ambitious to create a large estate but was not quite as successful as Connolly.[4] The years 1690 to 1703 were golden years for unscrupulous and clever lawyers, and the prince of them all was William Connolly. A paragraph from a contemporary pamphlet may sum up the opinions held by many of his contemporaries about his activities and the mysterious and rather questionable sources of his wealth.

The pamphlet was written about 1702.

"He (William Connolly) *is one whom fortune in a frolicsome mood has raised from the lowest of the people to make him equal in estate with the peers of the realm. When his majesty obtained his glorious victory at the Boyne, this man could not reckon so many pounds of his own as he does thousands now. His yearly expenses had from that time exceeded his visible acquisitions; his manner of living so profuse that he got followers and was called Prince Connolly – the discreet and upright gazed at this glittering meteor and admired from what undiscovered mine he had raised so much riches. But now the mystic knot is untied; the commissioners for enquiry into the forfeitures opened the scene and the trustees set him in a true light".*[5]

Though there were dark clouds over his motives and methods, there was no doubting his abilities. He went on to become speaker of the House of Commons, Prime Minister in effect, who could deliver majorities to the government in power in Dublin even in difficult and unpromising circumstances. After 1691 he made his country home in Rodanstown, and it seems likely that the early eighteenth century house, now occupied by the Faulkner family, was built by him. The only church built in Kilcloon since the Middle Ages was that at Rodanstown. (See illustration of Rodanstown, p viii). Its ruins reflect the architectural taste of the early eighteenth century and was probably inspired by him. He went on to build the largest Georgian mansion in Ireland at Castletown in Celbridge, but died in 1729 before he had an opportunity to live in it.

The extent of his holdings in the parish reflects his capacity to acquire lands with doubtful titles at knockdown prices at a time when only Protestants could acquire them by sale. Vast land holdings were up for sale and only those with access to cash or credit could buy them. Connolly's technique was to buy property cheaply, say at £1 an acre and let it out on long lease for 50p per acre per annum, thus quickly realising capital for more acquisitions. So the pattern for leasing lands in the Connolly estate, which included Balfeighan, Rodanstown and Kilclone, was as we have found it in the older manors of Rathregan and Moyglare.

Footnotes

1   Registry of Deeds, 85 299 60207.

2   N.L.I, Uncatalogued Fingal Papers; surveyed by Peter Lacy, 1702.

3   The Connollys of Castletown, Lena Boylan, Quarterly Bulletin of the Irish Georgian Society, Vol.11, No.4 (1968), p1, ff.

4   Irish Genealogist, Vol.1, No.XII, October 1942.

5   The Williamite Confiscation in Ireland, 1690 to 1703, J.G.Simm, p126, cites this paragraph entitled "Account of Prince Connolly" from "A letter from a soldier to the Commons of England occasioned by an address now carrying on by Protestants in Ireland in order to take away the fund appropriated for the payment of the arrears of the army."

Acknowledgments

The Great Jubilee in Kilcloon

In the Spring of 1999 a meeting was held in the Parish Centre to consider the various ways the Jubilee and Millennium in the year 2000 could be fittingly celebrated in the parish of Kilcloon.

A project to renew Batterstown and its environment had been ongoing for some time and was very successful on the ground in drawing community response and in attracting funds from various agencies, national and local, concerned with the rural development. The project in Batterstown was both an encouragement and a pointer to what could be accomplished in the parish of Kilcloon generally.

As time went by a number of projects were initiated and concluded successfully. A liturgy group planned the ceremony for the 31st December 1999; which consisted of a church ecumenical service which was very well attended as was a wine and canapé reception for all afterwards in the Parish Centre. An ecumenical service was planned for the renewed Batterstown church during Church Unity Week in January. From the liturgy group also came a project for a plinth for a statue of the Blessed Virgin Mary in the church. It was made by a local cabinetmaker of American burr oak and maple wood, and was presented by him on the occasion of the Jubilee. An apostolic work group set up in the parish in 1999 saw 25 ladies crocheting a banner for the church on the theme of the Our Father. Another parishioner undertook to produce three Jubilee banners, one for each of the parish churches to be hung there in perpetual reminder of the Jubilee. Perpetual eucharistic devotion was introduced on Tuesdays and Thursdays in the parish church and on Thursdays in the Little Chapel and at Batterstown.

The success of the New Year's Eve celebration was enhanced by the opening of an exhibition of the history of the parish in fourteen maps prepared by Michael O'Donnell of Maynooth Post Primary School and fifteen of his pupils. It was decided as a consequence to have a free parish barbecue at Midsummer 2000 at which another project undertaken – the turning of waste ground, left after Ballynare Crossroads had been staggered, into a Jubilee Garden – would be opened. In time, through the good offices of Brian Fitzgerald, chairman of the Meath County Council, one of the sculptures commissioned by the Meath County Council for the Millennium became a highlight of the garden. It was a head in bronze of St. Oliver Plunkett by Betty Newman Maguire, and was unveiled at the barbecue on Sunday, June 18th, at 6 p.m.

Yet another project complimenting the history of the parish in maps – was an effort by the children of the primary schools of the parish to do as their predecessors had done in the 30s, take a questionnaire to the older people of the parish and ask them about the customs, legends, and unusual features of the countryside. The same thing happened in the national schools all over Ireland in the 1930s, and made Ireland and Estonia the possessors of the richest folklore collection in the world. The project was completed in the Autumn of 1999, was put on display after the service on December 31st and will be preserved for posterity.

Another project was proposed and completed in the Jubilee year itself: the long awaited parish radio. By August 2000, twenty receivers had been distributed and the service was poised to go beyond the normal broadcasts of morning Masses, week-end Masses, weddings and funerals in the parish church to music, children's programmes and news and sport.

Another project initiated in the late 1990s but completed in the Jubilee year is the history of Norman Kilcloon. So much information, surprisingly, surfaced in researching the project, that it was decided to split the history of the parish into two, the first part dealing with the six hundred years of Norman Kilcloon – 1171 – 1700, and the second with Kilcloon from 1700 to the present day. Fittingly, at the centre of the parish is the bust of Oliver Plunkett, perhaps the finest product of the Norman race which colonised, controlled and inhabited Kilcloon for nearly six hundred years. (See illustration of St. Oliver Plunkett, p xv).

Yet another project, this time for the Little Chapel area of the parish, was begun: the renewal of St. Brigid's Well at Bridestream – which had, over the years, fallen into neglect. Through the generous co-operation of the landowner and an enthusiastic committee, it is hoped to complete the refurbishment in the Spring of 2001. Also in that area, projects were initiated involving the statues, formerly in the Little Chapel itself, and a possible grotto in the church yard. Plans as of August 2000 remained to be elaborated.

The structure of the various related groups and committees perhaps present a model for future developments. The central committee, made up of representatives from each group, concerned itself with presenting the cases for funding the various projects to agencies – local (like Meath Leader Group) and national (the Millennium Committee) – to draw down funds. The groups which sponsored the various projects concentrated on what was to be done and presented their cases for finance to the Central Committee Group.

In a way, this model is one which perhaps is a viable one for financing and encouraging local initiatives which make an essential contribution to the cohesion and wellbeing of the community yet are not commercially viable. Perhaps the focus of FAS will shift from combating unemployment through local development to local development itself, using in the process older people, even retired people, who have no future in the jobs market.

Be that as it may, the Jubilee – Millennium events in Kilcloon (there was also a parish pilgrimage to Lough Derg, and to the cathedral in Mullingar for vespers, and, of course, involvement in the diocesan pilgrimage to Slane where fifteen thousand celebrated the coming of Christianity to the area of our diocese) in a variety of ways reflected and enhanced the familial dimension of the community which makes up the parish of Kilcloon.

The lessons of what can be achieved by communal involvement in enhancing the community itself, will not be lost on future generations.

Jubilee Year – 2000

Jubilee Committee for the Parish of Kilcloon – 8th March 1999.

Pat Lynch – *Chairman*
Michael Crowley – *Secretary*
Elizabeth Jennings, Michael Fahy, Marguerite Frawley, Michael O'Carroll, Pat Ward, Breda Barker, Adrien Conway, Donal McCarthy, Philip McCormack, Irving Ferris, Mary Mangan, Fr. G. Rice, Fr. J. Brogan.

Jubilee Garden Committee

Breda Barker, Patsy Burke, Pat Ward, Christy McNulty, Michael O'Carroll, Fergal Dillon, Irene Corcoran, Rosemary McCarthy, Mary McCarthy, Dessie O'Brien, Tommy Reilly, Liam Reilly.

Parish Radio

Irving Ferris, Fergal Dillon, Ivan Kiely, Aedemar Corcoran

Liturgy Committee

Elizabeth Jennings – *Chairperson*

Members:

Sheila Crampton, Mary Barry, Margaret Clarke, Peter Garret, Maura Goldrick, Billy Strickland, Fr.O.Skelly, Breda Lucas, Ben Porter, Catherine Hodge, Margery Kelly, Nancy O'Halloran, Fr. G.Rice

Little Chapel Jubilee Committee

Brendan Burke, Benny O'Keeffe, Michael Reilly, Ann Ryan, Peter Mallon, PJ Walsh, Nancy Cahalin, Nancy O'Halloran, Margery Kelly, Maura McGinley, Mary Mangan, Cathleen Flynn, Tony Prunty

Jim Birchell, owner of the land at St. Brigid's Well, facilitated the committee and made possible the renewal of the holy well itself.

Jubilee Banners

Helen Hanifin

Plinth for Our Lady's statue

John Lee

Group which crocheted the Our Father for the church.

Helen Hannifin, Frances Dwyer, Mary Barry, Marge Doolin, Jacqueline Connealy, Julia Strickland, Rosanna Byrne, Brigie Pigeon, Mary Flaherty, Aileen Garrad, Mary Ferris, Breda Lucas, Ann Gleeson, May O'Brien, Mary Martin, Veronica Madden, Teresa O'Neill, Ann Malone, Catherine Ward, Irene Coyne, Carmen O'Neill, Vera Ward, Mary Burke, Breda Fahy, Helen Hanifin.

Batterstown Organising Committee

Philip McCormack, John Clancy, John Mark Clancy, Ann Tynan, Marguerite Frawley, Seamus Gaughan, Benny Coldrick, Kevin McGowan, Bernard Corbett, Martin Kearney

Barbeque Committee

Michael McNamee, Mary McCarthy, Pauline Hughes, Noleen Moore, Mary McNamee, Ann Powell, Gerry O'Brien, Dessie O'Brien, Donal McCarthy, Liam Moore, Ivan McNamee, Fergal Dillon, Ivan Kiely, Jimmy Leddy, Joe Breen, Teresa McNamee, Pamela Flinter, Catherine Corrigan, Michael Fahy, Jason Reilly

Kilcloon 2000 Map

The teacher in charge was Michael O'Donnell and the pupils were from Post Primary Maynooth. John Corrigan, Liam Rattigan, Craig Savage,

Rebecca Ryan, Sarah O'Donnell, Tracey Leonard, Emma Houlihan, John McCarthy, David Nelson, Jonathan Kerins, Pamela Fahy, Sinead Glynn, Niamh O'Doherty, Emer Lynch, Emer Ryan.

Groups from the three schools who completed the folklore project:
Kilcloon National School

Orla Ni Odhrain – *Teacher*

Pupils: Stephen Carty, Sheena Cassidy, Laura Conway, Sarah Corcoran, Laura Creevey, Matthew Crehan, Liam Fagan, Brian Farrell, Declan Gallagher, Una Healy, Dara Larkin, Damien Lucas, John McCabe, Thomas McCann, Eanna McDermott, Siobhan Mulligan, Darren Murphy, Sarah Murphy, Lisa O'Hanlon, Doireann O'Neill, Joseph O'Riordan, Jonathan Reilly.

Mulhussey National School

Joan Kelly – *Teacher*

Pupils: Joseph Fahy, Aedeana Conneely, Patrick Duffy, Declan Dalton, Ciarán Weldon, Claire McGuinness, Claire Burke, Yvonne Kelly, Mary Louise Martin.

Rathregan National School:

Mary Costello – *Teacher*

Pupils: Joanna McCabe, Dara Keogh, Thomas Delany, Linda Delany, Aoife Hughes, Mike Gralton, Ann Marie Gralton, Rebecca Smith, and Jane Dolan.

Contributors

Baker, Barry & Miriam
Old Post Office, Kilcloon,
Co. Meath

Barcoe, James & Nora
Blackhall, Kilcloon,
Co. Meath

Behan, Peter & Mary
Blackhall Little, Kilcloon,
Co. Meath

Beirne, Mel
6 Kilcloon Lawns, Kilcloon,
Co. Meath

Bermingham Family
Brownstown, Kilcloon,
Co. Meath

Brady, Chris & Mitsy
Penn Springs, Brownstown,
Kilcloon, Co. Meath

Brady, Michael
The Willows, Harristown,
Kilcloon, Co. Meath

Breen, Jerry
Harristown, Kilcloon,
Co. Meath

Brennan, Tom
Collistown, Kilcloon,
Co. Meath

Bright, Kevin & Judy
Goodwins Hill,
Batterstown, Co. Meath

Brophy, Marion
Kilgraigue, Kilcloon,
Co. Meath

Brosnan, Eileen
Red Road, Batterstown,
Co. Meath

Burke, James & Esther
Pagestown, Kilcloon,
Co. Meath

Burke, Patsy & Mary
Moygaddy, Maynooth,
Co.Kildare

Byrne, Noel & Kitty
Killeaney, Maynooth,
Co. Kildare

Buckley, Jean & Gerard
Skelligs, Kilgraigue,
Maynooth, Co. Kildare

Callanan, Rose
Brownstown, Kilcloon,
Co. Meath

Carey, Paul & Siobhan
Coolcommon, Batterstown,
Co. Meath

Carr Family
Moyleggan, Batterstown,
Co. Meath

Carr, Sonny
Moyleggan, Batterstown,
Co. Meath

Cassidy, Noel
Brownstown, Kilcloon,
Co. Meath

Cassidy, Oliver & Nuala
Collistown, Kilcloon,
Co. Meath

Cawley, Michelle & Edward
Ballymaglassan House,
Dunboyne, Co. Meath

Clarke, M & T
Ballynare, Kilcloon,
Co. Meath

Coffey, Brian
Dogwood, Harristown,
Kilcloon, Co. Meath

Colgan Family
Ribstown, Batterstown,
Dunboyne, Co. Meath

Collins, Barney & Rose
Kilgraigue, Kilcloon,
Co. Meath

Condon Family
School Road, Mulhussey,
Kilcock, Co. Meath

Connell, Julia
Pagestown, Kilcloon,
Co. Meath

Conroy, Pat
Brownstown, Kilcloon,
Co. Meath

Corcoran, Paul
Kilcloon, Co. Meath

Corrigan, Catriona
Ballynare, Kilcloon,
Co. Meath

Corrigan, Celia
Collistown, Kilcloon,
Co. Meath

Corrigan, John & Maura
Ballynare, Kilcloon,
Co. Meath

Creevy Family
8 Kilcloon Lawns, Kilcloon,
Co. Meath

Crowley, Michael
Emoclew, Batterstown,
Co. Meath

Cullen, Deirdre & Michael
Brownstown, Kilcloon,
Co. Meath

Cunningham, N.
Kilcloon, Co. Meath

Cummins, Kevin
Killeaney, Maynooth,
Co. Kildare

Cummins, Noleen
Killeaney, Maynooth,
Co. Kildare

Cuthbert, Felicity & Peter
Brownstown, Kilcloon,
Co. Meath

Daly, Philip
Green Grove, Batterstown,
Co. Meath

Dean, Thomas & Mary
Moyglare, Maynooth,
Co. Kildare

Delany, G
Ribstown, Batterstown,
Co. Meath

Devaney, Sean
Brownstown, Kilcloon,
Co. Meath

Dillon, Maura
Blackhall, Kilcloon,
Co. Meath

Dolan, Vincent
Kilgraigue, Kilcloon,
Co. Meath

Dolan, Martin &
Marguerite, Tudor Lodge,
Batterstown, Co. Meath

Doolin, Paddy
Killeaney, Maynooth,
Co. Kildare

Dowd, Michael & Sheila
Kilgraigue, Kilcloon,
Co. Meath

Doyle, Pat & Kay
Blackhall, Kilcloon,
Co. Meath

Dunbar Family
Brownstown, Kilcloon,
Co. Meath

Dunne, James
Pagestown, Kilcloon,
Co. Meath

Dunne, Una
Pagestown, Kilcloon,
Co. Meath

Farrelly, Noel
Blackhall, Kilcloon,
Co. Meath

Farrelly, Lena
Killeaney, Maynooth,
Co. Kildare

Fitzgerald, Des
Pagestown, Kilcloon,
Co. Meath

Fitzpatrick, Michael &
Bridie, Killeaney,
Maynooth, Co. Kildare

Flaherty, Michael & Mary
Kilgraigue, Maynooth,
Co.Kildare

Flynn, Mossie
Kilgraigue, Maynooth,
Co. Kildare

Gallagher, Cathal
Moyleggan, Maynooth,
Co. Kildare

Gannon, Martin &
Josephine, Quarryland,
Batterstown, Co. Meath

Gannon, Margaret &
Patrick, Quarryland,
Batterstown, Co. Meath

Glynn, John
Killeaney, Maynooth,
Co. Kildare

Goggins, Seamus & Louise
Killeaney, Maynooth,
Co. Kildare

Graham Family
Kilgraigue, Kilcloon,
Co. Meath

Griffin, Maura & Kathleen
Kilgraigue, Kilcloon,
Co. Meath

The Guckian Family
Brownstown, Kilcloon,
Co. Meath

Hannifin, Madeleine &
Timmy, Knock Na Gore,
Pagestown, Kilcloon,
Co. Meath

Hatch, Adrienne
4 Brownstown, Kilcloon,
Co. Meath

Heaney, Michael & Betty,
9 Brownstown, Kilcloon,
Co. Meath

Heanue, John
Pagestown, Kilcloon,
Co. Meath

Heanue, Peggy
Pagestown, Kilcloon,
Co. Meath

Hodge, Declan & Catherine
Ballynare, Kilcloon,
Co. Meath

Hora, Peggy & Brendan
Red Road, Batterstown,
Co. Meath

Houlihan, Justin & Emma
Harristown, Kilcloon,
Co. Meath

Hughes, Joe & Margaret
Piper Hill, Batterstown,
Co. Meath

Hughes, John
Belchamstown,
Batterstown, Co. Meath

Hughes, Tom & Pauline
Killeaney, Maynooth,
Co. Kildare

Jennings, Eddie, Edel &
Dermot, The Glebe,
Batterstown, Co. Meath

Jennings, Tom & Elizabeth
The Robe, Harristown,
Kilcloon, Co. Meath

Jennings, Rita
Mulhussey, Kilcock,
Co. Meath

Joyce, Michael & Carmel
Kilcloon, Co. Meath

Keely, Fiona & Dermot
Portane, Batterstown,
Co. Meath

Keane, John & Jane
Rathregan, Batterstown,
Co. Meath

Keogh, Gerry & Deirdre
Lismahon, Batterstown,
Co. Meath

Kerins, Frank
Mulhussey, Kilcock,
Co. Meath

Kiely, Michael & Ann
Inis Fennell, Brownstown,
Kilcloon, Co. Meath

Leddy, Jimmy
Kilgraigue, Kilcloon,
Co. Meath

Ledwith, J. V.
Rathregan, Batterstown,
Co. Meath

Lillis, Michael & Marie
8 Brownstown, Kilcloon,
Co. Meath

Lohan, Patrick
Blackhall Little, Kilcloon,
Co. Meath

Lucas, Paul & Breda
Kilgraigue, Kilcloon,
Co. Meath

Lynch, Elizabeth
Killeaney, Maynooth,
Co. Kildare

Lynch, Nicholas
Batterstown, Kilcloon,
Co. Meath

Pat Lynch & Family
Batterstown, Co. Meath

Malone, Pat & Ann
Lismahon, Batterstown,
Co. Meath

McCabe, John & Rita
Brownstown, Kilcloon,
Co. Meath

McCarthy, Donal & Mary
Killeaney, Maynooth,
Co. Kildare

**McCarthy, Michael &
Mary**
Killeaney, Maynooth,
Co. Kildare

**McCarthy, Michael &
Rosemary,** Moygaddy,
Maynooth, Co. Kildare

McCarthy, Sean & Mary
Blackhall, Kilcloon,
Co. Meath

McGovern, J.
The Red Road,
Batterstown, Co. Meath

McElligott, Kathleen
Colistown, Kilcloon,
Co. Meath

McEvoy, Teresa
Moyleggan, Batterstown,
Co. Meath

**McGowan, Jim &
Catherine**
Belchamstown,
Batterstown, Co. Meath

McKeith, Niall & Dervilla
Brownstown, Kilcloon,
Co. Meath

McNamee Family
Brownstown, Kilcloon,
Co. Meath

Monaghan, Alan
Colistown, Kilcloon,
Co. Meath

Moore, Liam & Noleen
Killeaney, Maynooth,
Co. Kildare

Mullally Family
Brownstown, Kilcloon,
Co. Meath

Mulligan, Richard
Brownstown, Kilcloon,
Co. Meath

Mulligan, Oliver
Killeaney, Maynooth,
Co. Kildare

Mulreid, Tom & Jennifer
Brownstown, Kilcloon,
Co. Meath

**Murphy, Kieran &
Elizabeth**
Colistown, Kilcloon,
Co. Meath

Murphy, Martin
Kilgraigue, Kilcloon,
Co. Meath

Murphy, Kathleen
Little Blackhall, Kilcloon,
Co. Meath

Murphy, Patricia
Pagestown, Kilcloon,
Co. Meath

Murphy, Willie
Colistown, Kilcloon,
Co. Meath

Murray, Margaret
Colistown, Kilcloon,
Co. Meath

Nelson, David
Killeaney, Maynooth,
Co. Kildare

Nolan, Matthew & Ann
Growtown, Batterstown,
Co. Meath

Nolan, Tom & Patricia
Blackhall Little, Kilcloon,
Co. Meath

Nolan, Christy
Kilcloon, Co. Meath

Nolan, Patrick
Belchamstown, Drumree,
Co. Meath

Nolan, Thomas & Rosaleen
Belchamstown, Drumree,
Co. Meath

Neville, Ann
Mulhussey, Kilcock,
Co. Meath

O'Brien, Ambrose
Kilgraigue, Kilcloon,
Co. Meath

O'Brien, Maureen
Rathregan, Batterstown,
Co. Meath

O'Brien, Mrs. Nora
Harristown, Kilcloon,
Co. Meath

O'Carroll Family
Brownstown, Kilcloon,
Co. Meath

O'Connor Family
Kilcloon, Dunboyne,
Co. Meath

O'Donnell, Fionnula &
Maeve, Kilgraigue,
Kilcloon, Co. Meath

O'Dowd Family
Brownstown, Kilcloon,
Co. Meath

O'Dwyer Family
Colistown, Kilcloon,
Co. Meath

O'Hora, Ann
Kilgraigue, Kilcloon,
Co. Meath

O'Leary, Catherine,
Willie, Peter,
Ribstown, Batterstown

O'Meara, John
Blackhall, Kilcloon,
Co. Meath

O'Reilly, Christopher
Kilgraigue, Kilcloon,
Co. Meath

O'Reilly, E & E
Killeaney, Maynooth,
Co. Kildare

O'Reilly, Jackie & Joan
Kilgraigue, Kilcloon,
Co. Meath

O'Reilly, Tommy & Mary
Kilgraigue, Kilcloon,
Co. Meath

Pender, John
Rathregan, Batterstown,
Co. Meath

Plunkett, Kevin
Rathregan, Batterstown,
Co. Meath

Plunkett, T & C
Portane, Batterstown,
Co. Meath

Powell, Liam
Harristown, Kilcloon,
Co. Meath

Quigley, J, I & J
Rathregan, Batterstown,
Co. Meath

Rattigan, Willie & Dolores
Brownstown, Kilcloon,
Co. Meath

Renehan, John
Blackhall, Kilcloon,
Co. Meath

Ryan, CA & KM
Rathregan Court,
Batterstown, Co. Meath

Roberts, Fiona & Jason
Rathregan, Batterstown,
Co. Meath

Sheeran, Florence
Colistown, Kilcloon,
Co. Meath

Smith, Dessie
Batterstown, Co. Meath

Strickland, Ann
Moyleggan, Batterstown,
Co. Meath

Strickland, Julia & Billy
Moyleggan, Batterstown,
Co. Meath

Sweeney, Kevin & Celia
3 Brownstown, Kilcloon,
Co. Meath

Taffe, Tom & Miriam
Red Road, Batterstown,
Co. Meath

Tobin, D & C
Kilgraigue, Kilcloon,
Co. Meath

Toomey, Kevin
Rathregan, Batterstown,
Co. Meath

Tupp, Zara
Batterstown, Kilcloon,
Co. Meath

Ward Pat & Valerie
Kilcloon, Co. Meath

Ward, Raymond & Vera
Kilcloon, Co. Meath

Ward, Marie
Kilcloon, Co. Meath

Weafer, John
Pagestown, Kilcloon,
Co. Meath

Weldon, Kathleen
Mulhussey, Kilcock,
Co. Meath

Whelan, Breda & John
Pagestown, Kilcloon,
Co. Meath

Whelan, Tony & Eileen
Killeaney, Maynooth,
Co. Kildare

Whitty, Patricia
Belchamstown, Drumree,
Co. Meath

Woods, Eamonn
Harristown, Kilcloon,
Co. Meath

Woodpark Stud
Dunboyne, Co. Meath

Index

Note on placenames and personal names: placenames and personal names vary a little over the centuries; unless otherwise indicated, placenames listed are in Co. Meath; early Norman names "De Lacy" etc. are listed under "De".

235

Published by Kilcloon Jubliee Committee
© Gerard Rice 2001
Design: Carton LeVert, Dublin
Printing: Wood Printcraft, Dubiln